Integrated Series in Information Systems

For other titles published in this series, go to
http://www.springer.com/series/6157

INFECTIOUS DISEASE INFORMATICS

Syndromic Surveillance for Public Health and BioDefense

Hsinchun Chen
Daniel Zeng
Ping Yan

Springer

Hsinchun Chen
Department of Management
Information Systems
Eller College of Management
University of Arizona
1130 E. Helen Street
Tucson, AZ 85721
USA
hchen@eller.arizona.edu

Daniel Zeng
Department of Management
Information Systems
Eller College of Management
University of Arizona
Tucson, AZ 85721
USA
and
Chinese Academy of Sciences
zeng@email.arizona.edu

Ping Yan
Department of Management
Information Systems
Eller College of Management
University of Arizona
Tucson, AZ 85721
USA
pyan@email.arizona.edu

ISSN 1571-0270
ISBN 978-1-4614-2539-7 e-ISBN 978-1-4419-1278-7
DOI 10.1007/978-1-4419-1278-7
Springer New York Dordrecht Heidelberg London

Printed on acid-free paper

Springer is part of Springer Science+Business Media (www.springer.com)

TABLE OF CONTENTS

PART II: SYNDROMIC SURVEILLANCE SYSTEM CASE STUDIES

PREFACE

Introduction

Preparation for, early detection of, and timely response to emerging infectious diseases and epidemic outbreaks are a key public health priority and are driving an emerging field of multidisciplinary research, infectious disease informatics. As a critical component of this effort, public health surveillance has been practiced for decades and continues to be an indispensable approach for detecting emerging disease outbreaks and epidemics. Although traditional disease surveillance often relies on time-consuming laboratory diagnosis and the reporting of notifiable diseases is often slow and incomplete, a new breed of public health surveillance systems has the potential to significantly speed up detection of disease outbreaks. These new, computer-based surveillance systems offer valuable and timely information to hospitals as well as to state, local, and federal health officials. They are capable of real-time or near real-time detection of serious illnesses and potential bioterrorism agent exposures, allowing for a rapid public health response. This public health surveillance approach is generally called syndromic surveillance, which is defined as "an ongoing, systematic collection, analysis, and interpretation of 'syndrome'-specific data for early detection of public health aberrations."

In recent years, a number of syndromic surveillance approaches have been proposed. According to a recent study conducted by the US Centers for Disease Control and Prevention (CDC), roughly 100 sites throughout the country have implemented and deployed syndromic surveillance systems. These systems, although sharing similar objectives, vary in system architecture, information processing and management techniques, and algorithms for anomaly detection, and have different geographic coverage and disease focuses.

We see a critical need for an in-depth monograph that analyzes and evaluates these existing syndromic surveillance systems and related outbreak modeling and detection work under a unified framework. In particular, the monograph aims to meet the following critical and timely needs.

1. As the body of the syndromic surveillance literature grows rapidly, we see a critical need to provide an integrated and synthesized treatment of the current state of the art, identify challenges and opportunities for future work, and promote fruitful interdisciplinary research. In particular, most existing books on syndromic surveillance (and more generally, biosurveillance) focus primarily on statistical modeling and analytical work. They largely ignore informatics-driven perspectives

(e.g., information system design, data standards, computational aspects of biosurveillance algorithms, information visualization, and system evaluation). This monograph, with a strong Information Technology orientation, will help fill in this important gap and will provide an accessible review of the field for researchers from a wide range of backgrounds who are working or have an interest in public health surveillance.

2. Because of its practical significance, syndromic surveillance is starting to attract students at all levels from a variety of backgrounds ranging from public health, computer science, information systems, software engineering, public administration and policies, and geographical information systems, among others. These students need an approachable textbook that introduces the key concepts behind syndromic surveillance, the related research framework, the critical research questions and methodologies, systems challenges and the state of the art of syndromic surveillance implementation, and case studies, providing contexts to discuss related technological, analytical, and policy considerations in an integrated manner. The book will present such materials from a multidisciplinary perspective to encourage and promote cross-area training, and to accommodate the variety of the backgrounds of the interested students.
3. The monograph will also provide a much-needed comparative study for public health practitioners and offer concrete insights that could help future syndromic surveillance system development and implementation. Because of the recent rapid developments, it is difficult for public health policy makers, and practitioners from both government agencies and the private sector, to follow up with the body of syndromic surveillance research. This book is intended to serve the purpose of communicating to the policy makers and practitioners recent research findings, related policy and implementation considerations, and case studies containing discussions of concrete application scenarios.

Scope and Organization

The monograph aims to present its chapters in a manner understandable and useful to students, researchers, and professionals. The main coverage of the fifteen chapters is listed below:

- Chapter 1 will discuss the motivation behind syndromic surveillance and offer a high-level overview of the field from research, systems, and implementation perspectives. It will also summarize the major challenges hindering syndromic surveillance system development and adoption.

- Chapter 2 will present a conceptual framework used throughout the book to analyze various kinds of syndromic surveillance systems and their components. In addition, a comprehensive summary of all the systems surveyed in our study will be presented in this chapter.

- Chapter 3 will be primarily focused on sources of data for syndromic surveillance and related data standards and messaging protocols. It will present how various types of public health-related data have been used for surveillance purposes and how effective they are. It will also survey technical work to facilitate data collection, sharing, and transmission from the point of view of knowledge representation and protocols.

- Chapter 4 will present an introductory summary to data analysis and exploration techniques that have been applied to public health syndromic surveillance. The focus will be on various outbreak detection methods, including those monitoring for unusual patterns, indicative of possible outbreaks worth further investigation, in temporal, spatial, and spatial-temporal domains.

- Chapter 5 will discuss data visualization and information dissemination issues in the context of syndromic surveillance. Visualization is an important informatics tool to help public health analysts explore and analyze typically voluminous surveillance datasets, preferably in an interactive manner. Information dissemination also plays an important role in syndromic surveillance as mandated and voluntary data sharing and reporting need to take place within and across public health departments and partnering agencies such as homeland security and public safety.

- Chapter 6 will focus on system assessment and other policy issues. These issues have been traditionally under-studied or under-appreciated. This chapter will attempt to address such issues through a principled and theory-grounded evaluation and assessment framework based on the Information Systems literature.

- Chapters 7–14 will report several real-world case studies, summarizing and comparing eight syndromic surveillance systems, including those that have been adopted by many public health agencies (e.g., RODS and BioSense).

- Chapter 15 will conclude the monograph by discussing critical issues and challenges to syndromic surveillance research and system development, and future directions.

Audience

The primary audience for the monograph includes the following:

- Upper-level undergraduates and graduate-level students from a variety of disciplines including but not limited to public health, biostatistics, information systems, computer science, and public administration and policy will benefit from learning the concepts, techniques, and practices of syndromic surveillance.

- Researchers in public health and IT are expected to find this book to be an excellent and comprehensive source of current and comprehensible reviews of the recent advances in the field and benefit from its multi-disciplinary angle. It will also help promote community development across disciplines and between academia and practitioners.

- Government public health officials (e.g., epidemiologists at all levels of government) and private-sector practitioners (in both healthcare and IT industries) will be interested in this book as it provides an up-to-date review of current syndromic surveillance research and practice, critical evaluation of current technologies and approaches, and discussion of real-world case studies.

AUTHOR BIOGRAPHIES

Dr. Hsinchun Chen is McClelland Professor of Management Information Systems at the University of Arizona. He received a B.S. degree from the National Chiao-Tung University in Taiwan, an MBA degree from SUNY Buffalo, and the Ph.D. degree in Information Systems from the New York University. Dr. Chen has served as a Scientific Counselor/Advisor of the National Library of Medicine (USA), Academia Sinica (Taiwan), and National Library of China (China). Dr. Chen is a Fellow of IEEE and AAAS. He received the IEEE Computer Society 2006 Technical Achievement Award and the INFORMS Design Science Award in 2008. He is author/editor of 20 books, 25 book chapters, 180 SCI journal articles, and 120 refereed conference articles covering Web computing, search engines, digital library, intelligence analysis, biomedical informatics, data/text/Web mining, and knowledge management. His recent books include: *Mapping Nanotechnology Knowledge and Innovation (2008*), *Digital Government: E-Government Research, Case Studies, and Implementation (2007); Intelligence and Security Informatics for International Security: Information Sharing and Data Mining (2006)*; and *Medical Informatics: Knowledge Management and Data Mining in Biomedicine (2005),* all published by Springer. Dr. Chen was ranked #8 in publication productivity in Information Systems (CAIS, 2005) and #1 in Digital Library research (IP&M, 2005) in two bibliometric studies. He serves on ten editorial boards including: *ACM Transactions on Information Systems, IEEE Intelligent Systems, IEEE Transactions on Systems, Man, and Cybernetics, Journal of the American Society for Information Science and Technology, Decision Support Systems,* and *International Journal on Digital Library*. He has been an advisor for major NSF, DOJ, NLM, DOD, DHS, and other international research programs in digital library, digital government, medical informatics, and national security research. Dr. Chen is the founding director of the Artificial Intelligence Lab and Hoffman E-Commerce Lab. The UA Artificial Intelligence Lab, which houses 30+ researchers, has received more than $25M in research funding from NSF, NIH, NLM, DOD, DOJ, CIA, DHS, and other agencies. The Hoffman E-Commerce Lab, which has been funded mostly by major IT industry partners, features one of the most advanced e-commerce hardware and software environments in the College of Management and helps contribute to the quality and ranking of the UA MIS Department (ranked as a top-5 program by *U.S. News & World Report* since 1989). Dr. Chen was conference co-chair of the ACM/IEEE Joint Conference on Digital Libraries (JCDL) 2004 and has served as the conference/program co-chair for the past eight International

Conferences of Asian Digital Libraries (ICADL), the premiere digital library meeting in Asia that he helped develop. Dr. Chen is also (founding) conference co-chair of the IEEE International Conferences on Intelligence and Security Informatics (ISI) 2003–2009. The ISI conference, which has been sponsored by NSF, CIA, DHS, and NIJ, has become the premiere meeting for international and homeland security IT research. Dr. Chen's COPLINK system, which has been quoted as a national model for public safety information sharing and analysis, has been adopted in more than 1,600 law enforcement and intelligence agencies. The COPLINK research had been featured in the *New York Times, Newsweek, Los Angeles Times, Washington Post, Boston Globe,* and *ABC News*, among others. The COPLINK project was selected as a finalist by the prestigious International Association of Chiefs of Police (IACP)/Motorola 2003 Weaver Seavey Award for Quality in Law Enforcement in 2003. COPLINK research has also been expanded to border protection (BorderSafe), disease and bioagent surveillance (BioPortal), and terrorism informatics research (Dark Web), funded by NSF, CIA, and DHS. In collaboration with selected international terrorism research centers and intelligence agencies, the Dark Web project has generated one of the largest databases in the world about extremist/terrorist-generated Internet contents (Web sites, forums, blogs, and multimedia documents). Dark Web research supports link analysis, content analysis, Web metrics analysis, multimedia analysis, sentiment analysis, and authorship analysis of international terrorism contents. The project has received significant international press coverage, including: *Associated Press, USA Today, NSF Press, Washington Post, Fox News, BBC, PBS, Business Week, Discover magazine, WIRED magazine, Government Computing Week, Second German TV (ZDF), Toronto Star,* and *Arizona Daily Star*, among others. Dr. Chen is the founder of the Knowledge Computing Corporation, a university spin-off software company, and a market leader in law enforcement and intelligence information sharing and data mining. He has also received numerous awards in information technology and knowledge management education and research including: AT&T Foundation Award, SAP Award, the Andersen Consulting Professor of the Year Award, the University of Arizona Technology Innovation Award, and the National Chiao-Tung University Distinguished Alumnus Award. He was also named Distinguished Alumnus by SUNY Buffalo. Dr. Chen has served as a keynote speaker at major international security informatics, medical informatics, information systems, knowledge management, and digital library conferences. He is a Distinguished/Honorary Professor of several major universities in Taiwan and China (including Chinese Academy of Sciences and Shanghai Jiao Tong University) and was recently named the Distinguished University Chair Professor of the National Taiwan University. Dr. Chen serves as the Program co-chair of the

International Conference on Information Systems (ICIS) 2009, to be held in Phoenix, Arizona.

Dr. Daniel Dajun Zeng received M.S. and Ph.D. degrees in industrial administration from Carnegie Mellon University, Pittsburgh, PA, and the B.S. degree in economics and operations research from the University of Science and Technology of China, Hefei, China. Currently, he is an Associate Professor and Honeywell Fellow in the Department of Management Information Systems at the University of Arizona, Tucson, Arizona, USA. He is also a Research Professor at the Institute of Automation in the Chinese Academy of Sciences. Dr. Zeng's research interests include software agents and their applications, social computing, spatio-temporal data analysis, and security informatics. He has coedited 15 books and published more than 140 peer-reviewed articles in Information Systems and Computer Science journals, edited books, and conference proceedings. He has received multiple best conference paper awards and teaching awards. His research has been mainly funded by the US NSF, US DHS, MOST, and NNSFC. He is currently serving on the editorial boards of 15 Information Technology-related journals including the IEEE Intelligent Systems. He has also played a key role in starting the IEEE International Conferences series on Intelligence and Security Informatics, and the NSF Biosurveillance and Biosecurity Workshop Series. He served as co-chair or Program co-chair of 25 international conferences or workshops in the areas of security informatics, biosurveillance, social computing, and e-business. He is currently serving as the Chair of the INFORMS College on Artificial Intelligence, the VP for Technical Activities of the IEEE Intelligent Transportation Systems Society, and the President-Elect of the Chinese Association for Science and Technology, USA.

Ms. Ping Yan is a Ph.D. candidate in the Department of Management Information Systems at the University of Arizona. She received her B.S. in computer science from the University of Science and Technology of China, Hefei, China, and her M.S. in computer science from the Chinese University of Hong Kong, Hong Kong, China. She has been working on spatial-temporal data analysis and its application in public health informatics and marketing.

ACKNOWLEDGMENTS

We thank our research partners and collaborators who have contributed to the reported research efforts. In particular, we thank the members of the NSF-funded National Center of Excellence for Infectious Disease Informatics (BioPortal), Dr. Cecil Lynch from Ontoreason, Dr. Michael Ascher from UC Davis, Dr. Millicent Eidson and Dr. Ivan Gotham from the New York State Department of Health, Mr. Ken Komatsu from the Arizona State Department of Health Services, Dr. James Kvach formerly with the Armed Forces Medical Intelligence Center, Dr. Quanyi Wang from the Beijing CDC, Dr. Chwan-Chuen King from the National Taiwan University, for insightful discussions and project collaborations, and Mr. Jian Ma, Mr. Hsin-min Lu, Mr. Chunju Tseng, Mr. Chang Wei, and Mr. Luke Huston, for their research contributions and system implementation efforts.

We acknowledge support from the following US National Science Foundation grants: NSF Information Technology Research Grant IIS-0428241, "ITR-(NHS)-(DMC): A National Center of Excellence for Infectious Disease Informatics;" NSF Grant IIS-0839990, "Transnational Public Health Informatics Research: US-China Collaboration;" NSF SBIR Grant IIP-0638203, "SBIR Phase I: BioPortal – An Informatics Infrastructure for Infectious Disease and Biosecurity Information Sharing, Analysis, and Visualization," and NSF IIS Grant IIS-0748308, "US/China Digital Government Collaboration: US-China Infectious Disease Informatics and BioSurveillance Workshop." We also thank support from the US Department of Homeland Security through DHS Center of Excellence in Border Security and Immigration (2008-ST-061-BS0002)

The second author is an affiliated professor at the Institute of Automation, the Chinese Academy of Sciences, and wishes to acknowledge support from an international collaboration grant (2F05N01 and 2F08N03) and a Research Talent grant (2F07C01) from the Chinese Academy of Sciences, a National Basic Research Program of China (973) grant (2006CB705500) from the Ministry of Science and Technology, a 863 grant (2006AA010106), a Research grant from the Ministry of health (2009ZX 10004-315), and an Innovative Research Group grant (60621001) and an Emergency Response Research grant (90924302) from the National Natural Science Foundation of China.

LIST OF FIGURES

LIST OF TABLES

Part I

SYNDROMIC SURVEILLANCE SYSTEMS

Chapters 1–6 are dedicated to detailed discussions of syndromic surveillance systems from the perspectives of system and algorithmic design. Chapter 1 summarizes the primary concepts and major objectives of syndromic surveillance. Challenges hindering syndromic surveillance system development and adoption are discussed. Chapter 2 presents a conceptual framework used to survey existing syndromic surveillance systems and analyze these systems' components. These system components include Data Sources and Collection Strategies, Data Analysis and Outbreak Detection, Data Visualization, Information Dissemination and Alerting. Each component is presented in depth in Chapters 3–5 respectively. Chapter 6 focuses on system assessment and other policy issues attempting to address such issues through a principled and theory-grounded evaluation and assessment framework based on the Information Systems literature.

Chapter 1

INFECTIOUS DISEASE INFORMATICS: AN INTRODUCTION AND AN ANALYSIS FRAMEWORK

Syndromic surveillance is concerned with continuous monitoring of public health-related information sources and early detection of adverse disease events. In practice, syndromic surveillance systems are being increasingly adopted to meet the critical needs of effective prevention, detection, and management of infectious disease outbreaks, either naturally-occurring or caused by bioterrorism attacks. From an academic standpoint, syndromic surveillance research is by nature multidisciplinary and has been attracting significant attention in recent years. This monograph presents a comprehensive review of the state of the art of syndromic surveillance research and system development efforts from the perspective of information science and logies. On the basis of a detailed analysis of more than 50 local, state, national, and international syndromic surveillance systems and a review of about 200 academic publications, in this monograph we discuss the technical challenges, applicable approaches or solutions, and the current state of system implementation and adoption for key components of syndromic surveillance systems ranging from system architecture, data collection and sharing, data analysis, and data access and visualization. In addition, we present several case studies to compare several state-of-the-art syndromic surveillance systems. The purpose of these case studies is to illustrate the information technology-driven technical discussions in an integrated, real-world context. We also briefly touch upon critical nontechnical issues including data sharing policies, and system evaluation and adoption.

This introductory chapter briefly discusses the importance of syndromic surveillance and what we believe to be/is a unique niche this book intends to fill.

H. Chen et al., *Infectious Disease Informatics: Syndromic Surveillance for Public Health and BioDefense*, Integrated Series in Information Systems 21, DOI 10.1007/978-1-4419-1278-7_1,

In this time of increasing concern over the deadly and costly threats of infectious diseases caused by natural disasters or bioterrorism attacks, preparation for, early detection of, and timely response to emerging infectious diseases and epidemic outbreaks are a key public health priority and are driving an emerging field of multidisciplinary research. A few recent disastrous events that threatened the public health of large populations around the world include the Severe Acute Respiratory Syndrome epidemics (SARS) originated in Asia (Li et al., 2004), the outbreak of Avian flu in East Asian countries (NBII, 2006; USDA, 2006), and the ever pending threats of bioterrorism since the anthrax attacks in October 2001 (Buehler et al., 2003; Cronin, 2005; Siegrist, 1999).

Public health surveillance has been practiced for decades and continues to be an indispensable approach for detecting emerging disease outbreaks and epidemics. Early knowledge of a disease outbreak plays an important role in improving response effectiveness (Pinner et al., 2003). Although traditional disease surveillance often relies on time-consuming laboratory diagnosis and the reporting of notifiable diseases is often slow and incomplete, a new breed of public health surveillance systems has the potential to significantly speed up detection of disease outbreaks. These new, computer-based surveillance systems offer valuable and timely information to hospitals as well as to state, local, and federal health officials (Dembek et al., 2005; Pavlin, 2003). These systems are capable of real-time or near real-time detection of serious illnesses and potential bioterrorism agent exposures, allowing for a rapid public health response. This public health surveillance approach is generally called *syndromic surveillance*, which is defined as an ongoing, systematic collection, analysis, and interpretation of "syndrome"-specific data for early detection of public health aberrations.

The rationale behind syndromic surveillance lies in the fact that specific diseases of interest can be monitored by syndromic presentations that can be shown in a timely manner such as nurse calls, medication purchases, and school or work absenteeism. In addition to early detection and reporting of monitored diseases, syndromic surveillance also provides a rich data repository and highly active communication system for situation awareness and event characterization. Multiple participants provide interconnectivity among disparate and geographically separated sources of information to facilitate a clear understanding of the evolving situation. This is of significant importance for event reporting, strategic response planning, and disaster victim tracking. Information gained from syndromic surveillance data can also guide the planning, implementation, and evaluation of long-term programs to prevent and control diseases, including distribution of medication, vaccination plans, and allocation of resources (Mostashari and Hartman, 2003).

In recent years, a number of syndromic surveillance approaches have been proposed. According to a study conducted by the Centers for Disease Control and Prevention (CDC) in 2003 (Buehler et al., 2003), roughly 100 sites throughout the country have implemented and deployed syndromic surveillance systems. These systems, although sharing similar objectives, vary in system architecture, information processing and management techniques, and algorithms for anomaly detection, and have different geographic coverage and disease focuses. We see a critical need for an in-depth review that analyzes and evaluates these existing systems and related outbreak modeling and detection work under a unified framework. Such a study presented in an easily accessible manner will be useful for researchers who are working or have an interest in public health surveillance as a review of the state-of-the-art syndromic surveillance research and practice. It will also provide a much-needed comparative study for public health practitioners and offer concrete insights that could help future syndromic surveillance system development and implementation.

This monograph serves to investigate the surveillance capacity and effectiveness of existing syndromic surveillance systems so as to present a synthesized review of the state of the art in syndromic surveillance research and practice and provide insights and guidelines for future research and system implementation. In comparison with several review articles that were published in this area (Bravata et al., 2004; Lober et al., 2002; Mandl et al., 2004; Yan et al., 2006), this monograph, a significantly extended version of a recent review that we completed and published in a journal article format (Yan et al., 2008), focuses on an in-depth description of technical components of syndromic surveillance systems and frames the related research questions from an IT and informatics perspective.

More specifically, this monograph serves the following purposes: (1) to provide an updated review of existing system development efforts and emerging syndromic surveillance techniques; (2) to identify the emerging needs and challenges; (3) to present in a synthesized manner the research and development efforts of public health agencies, research institutions, and the industry from an IT perspective; and (4) to serve as a tutorial for IT researchers interested in the emerging field of syndromic surveillance and infectious disease informatics. This survey aims to help answer the following questions:

- Is syndromic surveillance an effective approach to the public health surveillance problem? To what extent are existing systems already serving the purpose of early event detection, situation awareness, and response facilitation? How can their usability and effectiveness be validated?

- What information sharing, outbreak detection and information access and visualization techniques have been implemented and how do these techniques perform? Are there any technical barriers to the design and implementation of these approaches in public health?
- What is the deployment status of existing syndromic surveillance systems in the United States and other parts of the world? Are there any legal or administrative challenges hindering their wide adoption?

This book investigates a number of public health syndromic surveillance systems and related outbreak modeling and detection research, with the specific emphasis on the most promising practices in applying advanced information technologies to public health surveillance. It is mainly focused on major efforts from the public health agencies, research institutions, and the industry in the United States. Some other countries with major syndromic surveillance practices, including Canada, the UK, Australia, Japan, and Korea, are also included in the survey.

To prepare this book, we have reviewed about 250 publications from 1997 to 2008. To identify related work, we searched archival journals including but not limited to *Journal of Biomedical Informatics*, *Journal of American Medical Informatics Association*, *Journal of Advances in Disease Surveillance*, *Journal of Urban Health*, *Artificial Intelligence in Medicine*, and *Annual Review of Information Science and Technology*. These journal articles were mainly retrieved from online bibliographical databases including *PubMed Medline*, *ScienceDirect*, and *SpringerLink*. Our literature search used both general keywords such as "syndromic surveillance" and "biosurveillance," and keywords pertaining to various technical aspects of syndromic surveillance such as "outbreak detection," "spatial surveillance", and "bioterrorism preparedness." In addition, we investigated other research outlets, including proceedings and presentation material from various workshops (e.g., Arizona BioSurveillance Workshops 2006, 2007, and 2008, and Rutgers DIMACS Working Group on BioSurveillance Data Monitoring and Information Exchange). User manuals and system brochures that are available electronically (e.g., from state/national health department Web sites) were also studied.

Our work reported in this book aims to be comprehensive and is based on a systematic study of over fifty syndromic surveillance systems. (Our review does not count implementations of one system in multiple sites.) We believe these surveyed systems represent most of the known syndromic surveillance systems for which technical descriptions in varying degrees of detail are available from public sources. Technical approaches or solutions from each system are carefully catalogued and analyzed based on their purpose, input assumed, and output produced. The similarities and differences between these approaches are identified and their relative strengths and weaknesses summarized. In addition, an attempt has been made to perform a "post analysis," cutting across all these systems with the objective of assessing the extent to which a particular technical approach has been used to meet a specific functional requirement of syndromic surveillance.

Our discussion of public health syndromic surveillance systems is based on a conceptual framework (Figure 1-1) that views syndromic surveillance as composed of three main functional areas: data sources and collection strategies; data analysis and outbreak detection; and data visualization, information dissemination, and reporting. Most modern syndromic surveillance systems can be conceptualized following this framework.

The first area is primarily concerned with where and how to collect data. The related issues include data entry approaches, data sharing protocols, and transmission techniques. The second area involves modeling, analysis, and data mining approaches to monitor for data anomalies and to discover whether the aberrant data condition is caused by a real change in disease occurrence. The syndrome classification process, a critical step that occurs between data collection and anomaly detection, focuses on classifying the raw, observational data into syndrome groups to provide a meaningful representation with the appropriate level of abstraction and granularity to detect aberrations in any monitored illness. The third area involves data visualization, user interface, and information dissemination functionalities. Public health officials, epidemiologists, and when appropriate, emergency response and homeland security personnel, interact with the syndromic surveillance systems through these components to access detailed information for further investigation, gain situational awareness, make decisions about alert generation and dissemination, and collect information needed for response planning and event management.

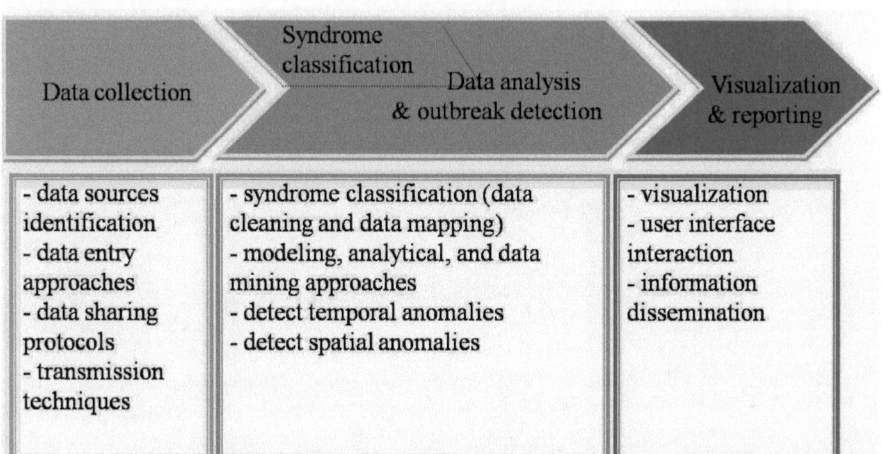

Figure 1-1. Conceptual syndromic surveillance system architecture.

This monograph consists of two main groups of chapters. The first group, Chapters 2–6, follows the above framework, discussing various components of syndromic surveillance systems and approaches. The second group, Chapters 7–14, presents integrative case studies based on representative systems and typical application scenarios.

We conclude this introductory chapter by summarizing the key features of each ensuing chapter. In Chapter 2, a summary of syndromic surveillance systems surveyed in our study, most of which have been adopted in real-world applications, is presented. Chapters 3–5 discuss technical material related to data collection, data analysis and outbreak detection, and data visualization and information dissemination, respectively. System assessment and other policy considerations are reviewed in Chapter 6.

From Chapter 7 to Chapter 14, in each chapter, we report a case study with a particular syndromic surveillance system, covering BioSense, RODS, BioPortal, ESSENCE, NYC SS, EARS, Argus, and HealthMap. Chapter 15 concludes this book by discussing critical issues and challenges to syndromic surveillance research and system development, and proposing some future directions.

Chapter 2

PUBLIC HEALTH SYNDROMIC SURVEILLANCE SYSTEMS

In this chapter, we summarize the key local, state, national, and international syndromic surveillance systems and related ongoing research programs of interest covered in our study. This summary provides the needed background information and application contexts. It also offers a current snapshot of syndromic surveillance practice in general. Note that as our primary focus is on public health surveillance, closely-related issues such as response planning and resource allocations strategies after an event is confirmed (e.g., Carley et al., 2003) are beyond the scope of this study.

For each system surveyed, we list its main contributors and stakeholders. We also include an overall system/project description, relevant data sources, syndromes monitored, data analysis and outbreak detection methods implemented, frequency of data collection and analysis, whether a GIS component is used, and its deployment strategy and status.

Although our review is intended to be detailed and comprehensive, our effort has been hampered by the unavailability of the technical details of many syndromic surveillance systems from either the published literature or the publicly available sources such as project Web sites. Furthermore, despite our best effort, our literature review is unlikely to be exhaustive. As such, we may have missed some interesting and emerging local and/or international syndromic surveillance system implementations. Nonetheless, our review should provide the readers with a fairly detailed and up-to-date snapshot of the state-of-the-art research and successful implementations of syndromic surveillance systems for public health and biodefense.

H. Chen et al., *Infectious Disease Informatics: Syndromic Surveillance for Public Health and BioDefense*, Integrated Series in Information Systems 21, DOI 10.1007/978-1-4419-1278-7_2,

1. SUMMARY OF NATIONWIDE SYNDROMIC SURVEILLANCE SYSTEMS

Thirteen nationwide syndromic surveillance systems plus two open source global public health status monitoring systems have been identified in our study. Table 2-1 presents a summary of these systems. Below we provide additional information for each of these systems.

CDC's BioSense system is a national initiative to support early outbreak detection by providing technologies for timely data acquisition, near real-time reporting, automated outbreak identification, and related analytics (Bradley et al., 2005; Ma et al., 2005; Sokolow et al., 2005). BioSense collects ambulatory care data, emergency room diagnostic and procedural information from military and veteran medical facilities, and clinical laboratory test orders and results from LabCorp. BioSense also monitors over-the-counter (OTC) drug sales, and laboratory test results for environmental samples collected through the BioWatch effort. In its most recent implementation, BioSense aims to monitor 11 syndrome categories including fever, respiratory, gastrointestinal illness (GI), hemorrhagic illness, localized cutaneous lesion, lymphadenitis, neurologic, rash, severe illness and death, specific infection, and botulism-like/botulism.

The Real-time Outbreak Detection System (RODS) is grounded in public health practice and focuses on collecting surveillance data for algorithm validation and investigating different types of novel data for outbreak detection (Espino et al., 2004; Tsui et al., 2003). It has been connected to 500+ hospitals' emergency departments nationwide for syndromic surveillance purposes. RODS collects chief complaints from emergency rooms, admission records from hospitals, and OTC drug sales data in real-time. Syndrome categories including respiratory, GI, botulinic, constitutional, neurologic, rash, hemorrhagic, and others are monitored with a collection of data analysis methods.

In 1999, the Walter Reed Army Institute of Research (WRAIR) created the Electronic Surveillance System for the Early Notification of Community-based Epidemics (ESSENCE) (Lombardo et al., 2004). ESSENCE has been used to monitor the health status of military healthcare beneficiaries worldwide, relying on outpatient ICD-9 diagnostic codes for outbreak detection (Burkom et al., 2004; Lombardo et al., 2003, 2004). Military and civilian ambulatory visits, civilian emergency department chief-complaint records, school-absenteeism data, OTC and prescription medication sales, veterinary health records, and requests for influenza testing are used by ESSENCE to evaluate health status with a focus on cases of death, GI, neurological, rash, respiratory, sepsis, unspecified infection, and others. ESSENCE has been deployed in the

National Capital Area, and 300 military clinics worldwide by 2003 (Lombardo et al., 2003).

The Rapid Syndrome Validation Project (RSVP) is an Internet-based population health surveillance tool designed to facilitate rapid communications between epidemiologists and healthcare providers (Zelicoff, 2002; Zelicoff et al., 2001). Through RSVP, patient encounters labeled with syndrome categories (including flu-like illness, fever with skin findings, fever with altered mental status, acute bloody diarrhea, acute hepatitis, and acute respiratory distress) and clinicians' judgment regarding the severity of illness are reported to facilitate timely geographic and temporal analysis (Zelicoff, 2002).

The Early Aberration Reporting System (EARS) is used to monitor bioterrorism activities during large-scale events. Its evolution to a standard surveillance tool began in the New York City and the national capitol region following the terrorist attacks of September 11, 2001 (CDC, 2006a; Hutwagner et al., 2003). Emergent department visits, 911 calls, physician office data, school and work absenteeism, and OTC drug sales are monitored for 42 syndrome categories (Hutwagner et al., 2003). EARS has been implemented in emergency departments in the state of New Mexico. It was also used for syndromic surveillance purposes at the 2000 Democratic National Convention, the 2001 Super Bowl, and the 2001 World Series.

The National Bioterrorism Syndromic Surveillance Demonstration Program covers a population of more than 20 million people. This program monitors and analyzes disease cases for neurologic, upper/lower GI, upper/lower respiratory, dermatologic, sepsis/fever, bioterrorism category A agents (anthrax, botulism, plague, smallpox, tularemia, and hemorrhagic fever), and influenza-like illness (ILI). These data utilized are derived from electronic patient-encounter records from participating healthcare organizations including ambulatory-care encounters and urgent-care encounters (Lazarus et al., 2001, 2002; Platt et al., 2003; Yih et al., 2004). This project provides a testbed for analyzing various outbreak detection algorithms and implements a model-adjusted SaTScan approach and the SMART algorithm (Kleinman et al., 2004).

The Bio-event Advanced Leading Indicator Recognition Technology (BioALIRT) program examines the use of spatial and other covariate information from disparate sources to improve the timeliness of outbreak detection in reaction to possible bioterrorism attacks (Buckeridge et al., 2005a; Siegrist et al., 2004). In a number of regions including Norfolk, Virginia; Pensacola, Florida; Charleston, South Carolina; Seattle, Washington; and Louisville, Kentucky, the BioALIRT system monitors military and civilian outpatient-visit records with ICD-9 codes, and military outpatient prescription records for unusual ILI and GI occurrences.

BioDefend is another program that aims to develop an effective and practical approach for rapid detection of outbreaks (2006b; Uhde et al., 2005). Patient encounter information is collected automatically or manually from clinics, emergency departments, and first aid stations at the first point of patient contact. Syndrome categories monitored include respiratory tract infection with fever, botulism-like, ILI, death with fever, GI, encephalitis/meningitis-like illness, febrile, rash with fever, fever of unknown origin, sepsis, contact dermatitis, and nontraumatic shock.

Biological Spatio-Temporal Outbreak Reasoning Module (BioStorm) aims to integrate disparate data sources and deploys various analytic problem solvers to support public health surveillance. The framework is ontology-based and consists of a data broker, a data mapper, a control structure and a library of statistical and spatial problem solvers (Buckeridge et al., 2002; Crubézy et al., 2005). It monitors and analyzes data such as 911 emergency calls collected from San Francisco, emergency department dispatch data from the Palo Alto Veterans Administration Medical Center, and emergency department respiratory records from hospitals in Norfolk, Virginia. On the basis of a customized knowledge base, BioStorm has implemented a library of statistical methods analyzing data as single or multiple time series and knowledge-based methods that relate detected abnormalities to knowledge about reportable diseases.

BioPortal is another biosurveillance system that provides a flexible and scalable infectious disease information sharing (across species and jurisdictions), alerting, analysis, and visualization platform (Chen and Xu, 2006; Zeng et al., 2005b). The system supports interactive, dynamic spatial-temporal analysis of epidemiological, textual and sequence data (Chen and Xu, 2006; Thurmond, 2006; Zeng et al., 2005a). BioPortal makes available a sophisticated spatial-temporal visualization environment to help visualize public health case reports and analysis results. Similar to EARS, BioPortal uses customized syndrome categories, which were developed by the State of Arizona Department of Health Services and hospitals in Taiwan (Lu et al., 2008). A number of retrospective and prospective spatial-temporal clustering (hotspot analysis) approaches are developed and implemented in BioPortal for outbreak detection purposes. They are Risk-adjusted Support Vector Clustering (RSVC) (Zeng et al., 2004a), Prospective Support Vector Clustering (Chang et al., 2005, 2008), and space-time correlation analysis (Ma et al., 2006).

Bio-Surveillance Analysis, Feedback, Evaluation and Response (B-SAFER) is a Web-based infectious disease monitoring system that is part of the open source OpenEMed project (http://openemed.org/) for use in urgent care settings (Umland et al., 2003). It collects chief complaints, discharge diagnoses and disposition data for detection analysis concerning a group of syndromes including respiratory, GI, undifferentiated infection, lymphatic, skin, neurological, and other. The collected data are analyzed daily by a first-order model that uses regression to fit trends, seasonal effects, and day-of-week effects (Brillman et al., 2005).

INtegrated Forecasts and EaRly eNteric Outbreak (INFERNO) incorporates infectious disease epidemiology into adaptive forecasting and uses the concept of an outbreak signature as a composite of disease epidemic curves (Naumova et al., 2005). The system has been tested with a dataset of emergency department records associated with a substantial waterborne outbreak of cryptosporidiosis that occurred in Milwaukee, Wisconsin, in 1993.

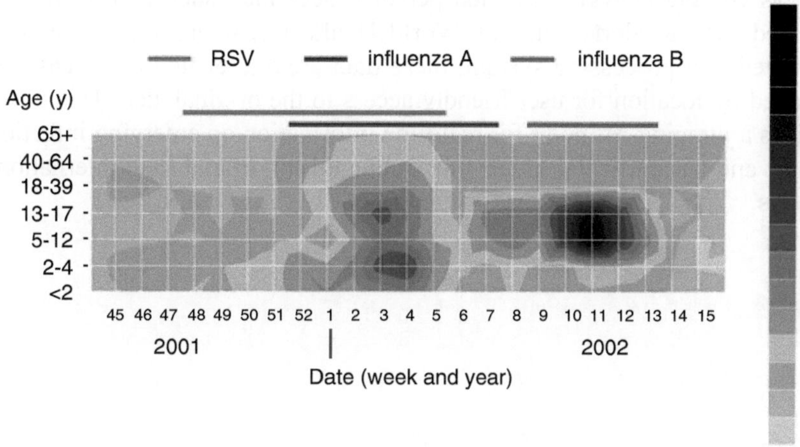

Figure 2-1. Surface-plot of scaled ED visits by age, with predominant RSV and influenza A and B periods indicated (Olson et al. 2007).

The DiSTRIBuTE project is a proof-of-concept, distributed, influenza surveillance system. DiSTRIBuTE uses aggregate, influenza-like illness (ILI), emergency department data from existing syndromic surveillance systems developed by state and local public health departments. Data are aggregated by age group and three-digit zip code. The DiSTRIBuTE project complements traditional influenza morbidity surveillance by providing a consistent, timely, year-round, high volume, regional, age-group-specific indication of febrile illness in the community (Figure 2-1).

Two other global scale real-time disease event detection and tracking systems are taking a different approach from the systems discussed above. The Argus and HealthMap projects monitor online media from global sources, instead of disease cases reported by hospitals, clinics, and other health facilities. The two systems are built on top of open sources, exemplifying an idea of open development for public health informatics applications. Argus, developed at Georgetown University, relies on Internet technologies as "harvesting engines" to capture information relevant to the definitional criteria for biological-outbreak severity metrics. The system automatically collects official disease reports from WHO or unofficial international health status reports from ProMED as indicators of possible biological events, and relies on its team of multilingual analysts to evaluate the associations between the online media and existence of adverse health events.

HealthMap brings together disparate data sources to achieve a unified and comprehensive view of the current global state of infectious diseases and their effect on human and animal health. This freely available Web site integrates outbreak data of varying reliability, ranging from news sources (such as Google News) to curated personal accounts (such as ProMED) to validated official alerts (such as World Health Organization). Through an automated text processing system, these data are aggregated by disease and displayed by location for user friendly access to the original alert. HealthMap provides a jumping-off point for real-time information on emerging infectious diseases and has particular interest for public health officials and international travelers.

Table 2-1. Thirteen nationwide syndromic surveillance systems and two global online disease intelligence projects.

System	Stakeholders	Monitored datasets	Syndrome categories	Data analysis methods	Frequency	GIS
BioSense	CDC	Multiple	11	CUSUM,[1] EWMA,[2] and SMART[6]	Daily	Y
RODS	U. of Pittsburgh and Carnegie Mellon U.	Multiple	8	Autoregressive modeling, CUSUM, scan statistics, WSARE,[3] PANDA[4] and others	Every 8 h	Y
ESSENCE	DoD-GEIS[5] and Johns Hopkins U	Multiple	8	CUSUM, EWMA, WSARE, SMART, and scan statistics	Daily	Y
RSVP	Sandia National Lab and State of NM Dept. of Health and clinicians, Los Alamos National Lab (LANL), U. of NM	Multiple	6	CUSUM, EWMA and wavelet algorithms	Daily	Y
EARS	CDC	Multiple	About 42	Shewhart chart, moving average, and variations of CUSUM (C1-MILD, C2-MEDIUM, and C3-ULTRA)	Daily	N
National Bioterrorism Syndromic Surveillance Demonstration Program	Harvard Medical School's Channing Lab	Multiple	12	Model-adjusted SaTScan™ approach and SMART	Daily	N
BioALIRT	DARPA, Johns Hopkins U., Walter Reed Army Institute of Research, U. of Pittsburgh and Carnegie Mellon U., etc.	Multiple	ILI, GI	Algorithms developed by RODS, CDC, ESSENCE, and IBM	Daily	N
BioDefend	U. of South Florida's Center for Biological Defense and Datasphere, LLC	Multiple	12	Time series pattern deviation detection, based on a 30-day rolling mean as threshold	Daily	N

System	Stakeholders	Monitored datasets	Syndrome categories	Data analysis methods	Frequency	GIS
BioStorm	Stanford U.	Multiple	Customized	A library of statistical methods and knowledge-based methods	N/A	N
BioPortal	U. of Arizona, U. of California, Davis, Kansas State U., National Taiwan U., Arizona/California Dept. of Public Health Services, New York State Dept. of Health	Multiple	40+	RSVC, Prospective SVC, and correlation analysis	N/A	Y
B-SAFER	DoD's National Biodefense Initiative and Dept. of Energy, in collaboration with the Los Alamos National Lab, U. of New Mexico Health Sciences Center, and the New Mexico Dept. of Health	Multiple	7	First-order model	Daily	N
INFERNO	Sponsored by National Institutes of Health	Multiple	GI	Retrospective daily time series	N/A	N
DiSTRIBuTE	International Society for Disease Surveillance (ISDS)	Multiple	ILI	Group aggregates by age and jurisdictional area	Daily	N
Argus	Argus Research Operations Center (AROC), ISIS Center, Georgetown University Medical Center	Multiple	N/A	Web Scanning, online media processing, epidemics caused social disruption detection, evaluation and tracking, Wilson – Collmann Scale heuristic staging model	N/A	N
HealthMap	Harvard Medical School and the Children's Hospital Boston Informatics Program	Multiple	N/A	Google Maps, xajax PHP AJAX library, Open Source Web Design (Blue Sky template by Jonas John), Fisher-Robinson Bayesian filtering	N/A	N (Google Maps)

[1]CUSUM: Cumulative Sums

[2]EWMA: Exponentially Weighted Moving Average

[3]WSARE: What is Strange About Recent Event

[4]PANDA: Population-Wide Anomaly Detection and Assessment

[5]DoD-GEIS: DoD-Global Emerging Infections Surveillance and Response System

[6]SMART: Small Area Regression and Testing

2. SUMMARY OF SYNDROMIC SURVEILLANCE SYSTEMS AT THE LOCAL, COUNTY, AND STATE LEVELS

Twenty syndromic surveillance systems implemented at the local, county, and state levels have been identified in our study. Table 2-2 presents a summary of these systems. Note that technical information about these systems is often much more difficult to locate (in many cases unavailable publicly) when compared with nationwide systems.

The syndromic surveillance system implemented in New York City uses ETL (extract, transform, and load) middleware technology from iWay Software over secure, Web-based reporting channels to receive and process a high volume of daily reports at a central data repository. A custom analytical application based on spatial data analysis software SaTScan and ArcView desktop GIS and mapping software from ESRI is used to perform statistical analysis and related visualization functions (Heffernan et al., 2004a, 2004b).

Syndromic Surveillance Information Collection (SSIC) is a complex, heterogeneous database system intended to facilitate the early detection of possible bioterrorism attacks (with such agents as anthrax, brucellosis, plague, Q-fever, tularemia, smallpox, viralencephalitides, hemorrhagic fever, botulism toxins, staphylococcal enterotoxin-B, among others) as well as naturally occurring disease outbreaks including large foodborne disease outbreaks, emerging infections, and pandemic influenza (Karras, 2005).

The Automated Epidemiological Geotemporal Integrated Surveillance (AEGIS) system is a surveillance effort initiated by the Children's Hospital Informatics Program at the Harvard-MIT Division of Health Sciences and Technology since 2000 at the state of Massachusetts. The system adopted a modular design to address the challenges of scalability, robustness, and data security issues due to an emerging demand of integrating real-time public health surveillance systems into regional and national surveillance initiatives (Reis et al., 2007) (Figure 2-2). The system consists of modeling modules, detection modules, and client modules.

Table 2-2: 20 syndromic surveillance system implementations at local or state levels

System	Stakeholders	System description
Syndromic Surveillance Project in New York City	New York City Dept. of Health and Mental Hygiene (NYCDOHMH)	Central data repository, ETL data processing, and analytical tools based on SaTScan and ArcView desktop GIS
SSIC	U. Washington	Focus on early detection of possible bioterrorism attacks
Automated Epidemiological Geotemporal Integrated Surveillance (AEGIS)	Children's Hospital Informatics Program at the Harvard-MIT Division of Health Sciences and Technology	A modular design to facilitate multiple health surveillance systems integration
Syndromal Surveillance Tally Sheet	EDs of Santa Clara County, California	A manual system relying on triage nurses' counts of the numbers of patients presenting the syndromes of interest
Syndromic Surveillance Using Automated Medical Records	Greater Boston	Outbreak detection with health plan data in the Greater Boston area
New Hampshire (NH) Syndromic Surveillance System	Division of Public Health Services, NH Dept. of Health and Human Services (NH DHHS)	A system collecting syndromic data from multiple sites including EDs, schools, workplaces, as well as other electronic health surveillance systems such as BioSense
Connecticut Hospital Admissions Syndromic Surveillance	Connecticut Dept. of Public Health (CDPH)	The system monitors hospital admission data

Catalis Health System for syndromic surveillance in a rural outpatient clinic in Texas	Texas Dept. of State Health Services (DSHS)	In 2003, the Texas Regional Health Dept. piloted the Catalis software system monitoring three types of syndromes: Rash Fever illness, meningoencephalitis and ILI. The system proved to be 100 percent sensitive in reporting syndromes to the state
NC DETECT http://www.ncdetect.org/	North Carolina Division of Public Health (NCDPH)	NC DETECT provides statewide early event detection by monitoring data from EDs, the Carolinas Poison Center, and the Pre-hospital Medical Information System
SENDSS https://sendss.state.ga.us/sendss/login.screen	Georgia Division of Public Health	SendSS is a reporting and tracking tool of notifiable diseases deployed in Georgia. It is a web-based application allows case report, analysis and messaging among other functionalities
Syndromic surveillance system in Miami-Dade County	Office of Epidemiology & Disease Control, Miami-Dade County Health Dept.	The system monitors chief complaints data on a daily basis. The analysis system is coupled with ESNENCE. Public health status alerts are reviewed by an analyst each day
Early Event Detection in San Diego	San Diego County	The system monitors ER visits, paramedic transports, 911 calls, school absenteeism, and OTC sales for early event detection
Communicable Disease Reporting and Surveillance System https://cdrs.doh.state.nj.us/cdrss/login/login.jsp	New Jersey Dept. of Health and Senior Services (NJDHSS)	Since 2001, NJDHSS implemented the surveillance system to characterize ED visits/admissions trends, detect aberrations and generate daily reports (via e-mail or facsimile) of the number of ED visits and admissions from all 84 acute care hospitals with EDs statewide

System	Stakeholders	System description
EED in South Carolina	South Carolina Dept. of Health and Environmental Control	Major capability of the system includes surveillance with BioSense, OTC sales, and Palmetto Poison Center
Indiana's pilot program for syndromic surveillance	Indiana State Dept. of Health	Include a variety of sources: coroners' reports, calls to the Indiana Poison Control Center, school absenteeism counts, lab test orders, veterinary lab results, and reports from day-care centers
National Capitol Region's ED syndromic surveillance system	Maryland, the District of Columbia, and Virginia	The system uses chief complaints for syndromic assignment
Michigan Disease Surveillance System Syndromic Surveillance Project	Michigan Dept. of Community Health (MDCH)	The Michigan system uses RODS developed at the University of Pittsburg for outbreak detection. By 2007, 65 facilities from across Michigan have participated the project
HESS and HASS	Missouri Dept. of Health and Senior Services	The state-wide syndromic surveillance uses ESSENCE and BioSense to analyze and visualize the syndromic data that are electronically reported by 85 hospitals across Missouri
North Dakota Department of Health Syndromic Surveillance Program	North Dakota Dept. of Health	Chief complaint data from nurse advice call center and EDs are analyzed for syndromic surveillance utilizing a commercial software RedBat®
Syndrome Reporting Information System (SYRIS)	Lubbock Health Dept.	The status of the health of the community can be instantaneously communicated among doctors, public health officials, or government officials via time series or GIS analysis and visualization

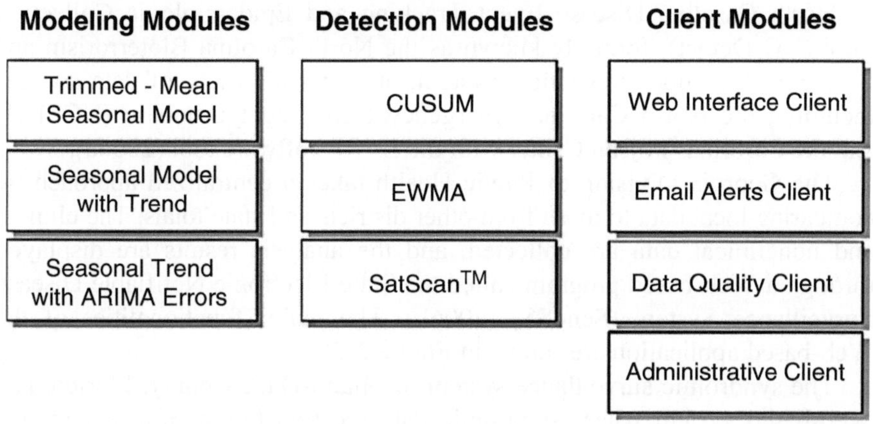

Figure 2-2. Modeling, detection, and client modules implemented in the current AEGIS system (Reis et al., 2007).

The Syndromal Surveillance Tally Sheet program is based on the triage nurses' counts of the numbers of patients presenting the syndromes of interest collected from emergency departments of Santa Clara County, California (Bravata et al., 2002). (This manual system was proved to be staff and resource intensive and was replaced by an ESSENCE implementation in 2005).

The system used in the greater Boston area is for rapid identification of illness syndromes using automated records from 1996 through 1999 of approximately 250,000 health plan members in the area (Lazarus et al., 2001).

New Hampshire Syndromic Surveillance System collects information from multiple sites in New Hampshire including emergency departments, 23 city schools, 5 workplaces, participating pharmacies, as well as military and veteran medical facilities, and LabCorp through the BioSense program. Data are either key punched or electronically transferred into the Syndromic Tracking Encounter Management System (STEMS) for analysis and geocoding (Miller et al., 2003).

In the state of Connecticut, a Hospital Admissions Syndromic Surveillance system is implemented by the Connecticut Department of Public Health. This system monitors hospital admissions from the previous day rather than outpatient visits as most other syndromic systems do (Dembek et al., 2004, 2005).

Catalis Health System for syndromic surveillance in Texas interfaces with available clinic practice management systems to produce a standardized dataset via a point-of-care electronic medical record (EMR). This system supports data flows directly from clinic providers to the health department for syndromic surveillance. Rural counties with limited epidemiological resources have benefited from this approach (Nekomoto et al., 2003).

North Carolina Disease Event Tracking and Epidemiologic Collection Tool (NC Detect), formerly known as the North Carolina Bioterrorism and Emerging Infection Prevention System, analyzes a variety of data sources including the North Carolina Emergency Department Database (NCEDD) and the Carolinas Poison Center with the EARS software tool (2006d).

The Georgia Division of Public Health takes a centralized approach by comparing local data to those from other districts and state totals. The clinical and nonclinical data are collected, and the analysis results are displayed through a Web-based program called the State Electronic Notifiable Disease Surveillance System (SendSS) (2006k). The major functionalities of the Web-based application are shown in Figure 2-3.

The syndromic surveillance system in Miami-Dade County, Florida, is a Web-based system where syndromic data are transferred from emergency departments to an ESSENCE server for data analysis and anomaly detection (2006m). On a daily basis, 14 county hospitals automatically transmit deidentified chief complaint data to the surveillance system. Each chief complaint is then placed into one of 10 syndrome categories including respiratory, gastrointestinal, hemorrhagic, influenza-like, shock/coma, neurologic, fever, febrile, rash, botulism-like, and other. ESSENCE performs automatic data analysis, establishing a baseline with a 28-day average. Daily case data are then analyzed against this baseline to identify statistically significant increases. An MDCHD analyst evaluates all alerts and develops a summary report on each day (Zhang et al., 2007).

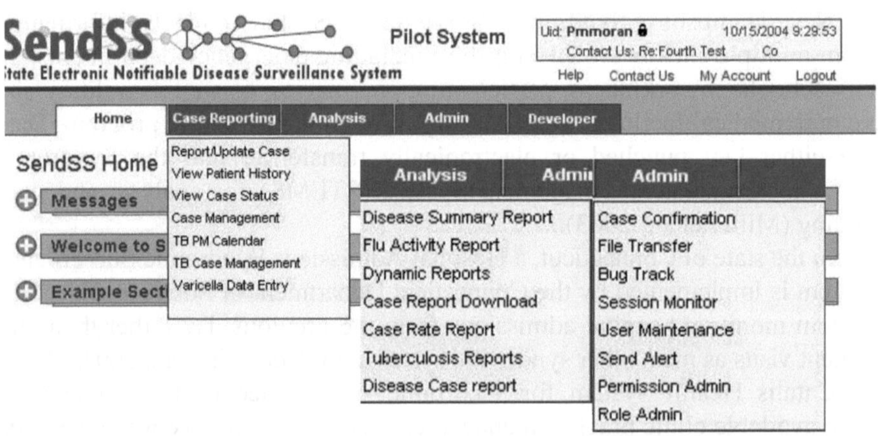

Figure 2-3. Homepage and menu navigation of SendSS Web application (2006k).

The Early Event Detection system in San Diego constantly monitors emergency room visits, paramedic transports, 911 calls, school absenteeism data, and OTC sales for early event detection. It supports interoperability with local SAS/Minitab installations, ESSENCE, and BioSense (Johnson, 2006).

The New Jersey syndromic system includes four components: emergency department-based surveillance using visit and admission data from participating hospitals statewide and a modified CUSUM method to detect aberrations, OTC pharmacy sales surveillance from RODS, an ILI surveillance module, and a Web-based Communicable Disease Reporting System (CDRS) for real time data transmission and reporting (Hamby, 2006).

The Early Event Detection (EED) system in South Carolina provides syndromic surveillance capabilities at the state/local level, using data from BioSense, OTC sales, and Palmetto Poison Center (Drociuk et al., 2004). The EED system is among a number of disease surveillance systems in South Carolina, including ESSENCE, BioSense, and sentinel providers network with ILI reporting. As of February 2006, there were 536 distinct sources providing OTC drug sales data.

Indiana's pilot program for syndromic surveillance is currently taking in data from 17 hospitals, most of them in Indianapolis. Indiana's system is expected to include a variety of sources: coroners' reports, calls to the Indiana Poison Control Center, school absenteeism counts, lab test orders, veterinary lab results, and reports from day care centers (Lober et al., 2002).

National Capitol Region's Emergency Department syndromic surveillance system is a cooperative effort between Maryland, the District of Columbia, and Virginia that uses chief complaints for syndromic assignment. Using a syndrome assignment matrix (Begier et al., 2003), the emergency department visits are coded into one of eight mutually exclusive syndromes: "death," "sepsis," "rash," "respiratory" illness, "gastrointestinal" illness, "unspecified infection," "neurologic" illness, and "other."

The Michigan Syndromic Surveillance Project tracks emergent care registrations per day (primarily ED, some urgent care) and Poison Control Call Center data using RODS. MDCH and participants exchange data in real-time using virtual private networks (VPNs) to secure the data and HL-7 as the messaging format. Detection algorithms run every hour and send email alerts to public health officials when deviations are found. State and regional epidemiologists are provided with Web access to the charts and maps of the data analytical results (2006g).

The Hospital Electronic Syndromic Surveillance (HESS) and hospital admission syndromic surveillance (HASS) systems, implemented in the State of Missouri, are designed to provide an early warning system of public health emergencies including bioterrorism events, and offer outbreak detection and epidemiologic monitoring functions. HESS collects data electronically from existing electronic systems and requires all hospitals to participate, whereas HASS receives data on a paper form from selected sentinel hospitals (2006f). They use ESSENCE and BioSense to analyze, visualize, and report electronically ED data collected through HESS Reporting Rule. By 2007, electronic feeds were being collected automatically from 85 hospitals across the state. Figure 2-4 shows statewide syndromic surveillance coverage in Missouri.

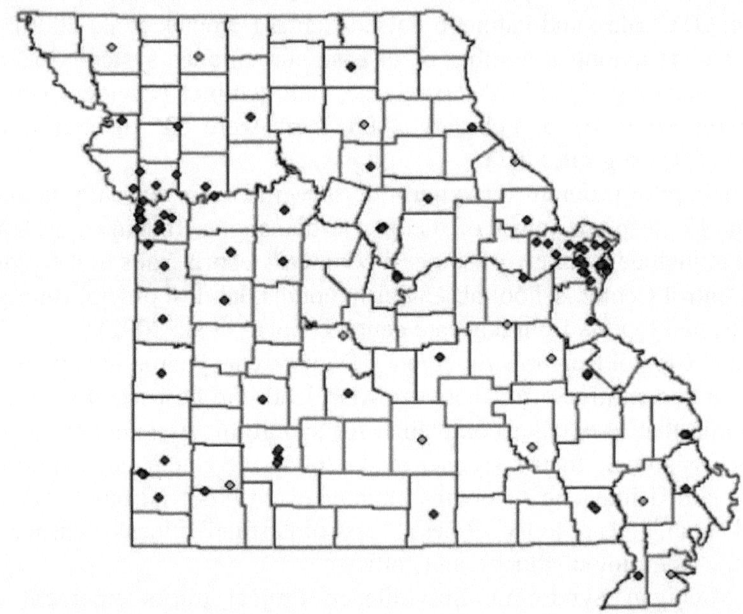

Figure 2-4. Missouri syndromic surveillance coverage; *lighter dots* are HASS, and *darker* are HESS hospitals (Resch et al., 2007).

The North Dakota Department of Health Syndromic Surveillance Program is based on chief complaint data received electronically from seven large hospital emergency departments located in North Dakota's four largest cities. In addition, data from a call center in North Dakota's largest city are received and reviewed daily. They use the natural language translation tool SympTran® to translate free text chief complaints into symptoms and then group those into six syndrome groups (Goplin et al., 2007). Data analysis functions are provided by the commercial software called RedBat. The RedBat system will be briefly introduced in the next section. Over 50% of the state's population is currently involved in this program (2006h). They have also developed the North Dakota Electronic Animal Health Surveillance System for animal disease surveillance. The data analysis capability is provided by the CDC EARS.

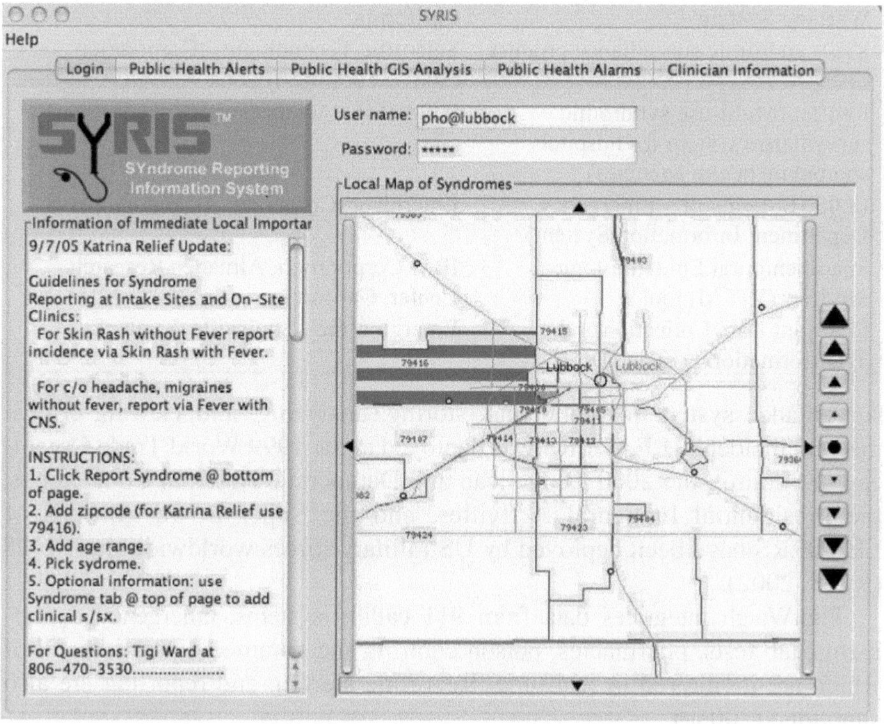

Figure 2-5. Screenshot of SYRIS system.

Syndrome Reporting Information System (SYRIS) is a Web-based, real-time, clinician-driven syndromic surveillance system implemented in Lubbock, Texas (Figure 2-5). It provides two-way communication between clinicians and public health officials for high specificity, high signal-to-noise ratio outbreak detection in both human and wildlife species diseases.

3. SUMMARY OF INDUSTRIAL SOLUTIONS FOR SYNDROMIC SURVEILLANCE

We now discuss seven representative industrial solutions for syndromic surveillance, as summarized in Table 2-3.

The Lightweight Epidemiology Advanced Detection and Emergency Response System (LEADERS) is an Internet-based integrated medical

Table 2-3. Seven industrial solutions for syndromic surveillance.

System	Company
LEADERS	Idaho Technology, Inc., Salt Lake City, Utah
FirstWatch Real-Time Early Warning System	Stout Solutions, LLC., Encinitas, California
STC syndromic surveillance product	Scientific Technologies' Corporation (STC), Tucson, Arizona
RedBat (Multi-use syndromic surveillance system for hospitals and public health agencies)	ICPA, Inc., Austin, Texas
EDIS (Emergisoft's Emergency Department Information System)	Emergisoft Corporate, Arlington, Texas
Spatiotemporal Epidemiological Modeler (STEM) tool	IBM Corporation, Almaden Research Center, California
Emergint Data Collection and Transformation System (DCTS)	Emergint, Inc., Louisville, Kentucky

surveillance system for collecting, storing, analyzing, and viewing critical medical incidents. LEADERS was deployed at the 1999 World Trade Organization Summit, the 2000 Republican and Democratic National Conventions, the Presidential Inaugural Activities, and the Super Bowl. Portions of LEADERS have been deployed by US military forces worldwide since 1998 (Ritter, 2002).

FirstWatch integrates data from 911 calling systems, emergency departments, lab tests, pharmacies, poison controls and paramedic practices, all of which are monitored in real-time. Real-time alerting and reporting are also supported (2006e).

The Web-based STC syndromic surveillance product is compatible with the CDC NEDSS Logical Data Module (LDM). Its current clients include public health departments in Connecticut, Louisiana, New York City, and Washington, DC. The analysis and alerting algorithms implemented in the system such as CUSUM, 3rd Sigma, and STC's Zhang Methodology are applied to a variety of data sources that include OTC sales, school nurse visits, and emergency rooms (2006l).

RedBat automatically imports existing data from hospitals and public health agencies. Besides outbreak detection, it is also capable of tracking injuries, reportable diseases, asthma, and disaster victims (2006i).

Emergisoft is a software solution for syndromic surveillance that has been employed in the 1996 Olympics in Atlanta and in the metropolitan areas of New York City and Los Angeles (Emergisoft, 2006).

A Spatiotemporal Epidemiological Modeler (STEM) tool, developed at the IBM Almaden Research Center, can be used to develop spatial and temporal models of emerging infectious diseases. These models can involve multiple populations/species and interactions between diseases. GIS data for every county in US have been integrated into the STEM application (Ford et al., 2005).

Emergint provides a syndromic surveillance system for data collection and processing. It can interface with care providers, laboratories, research organizations, and federal and state health departments. Emergint also provides data aggregation analysis as well as visualization functions (2004a).

4. SUMMARY OF INTERNATIONAL SYNDROMIC SURVEILLANCE PROJECTS

The National Health Service (NHS) in the UK operates a NHS Direct Syndromic Surveillance system that monitors the nurse-led telephone helpline data collected electronically by the Health Protection Agency from all 23 NHS Direct sites in England and Wales (Doroshenko et al., 2005). Syndromes monitored include cold/influenza, cough, diarrhea, difficulty breathing, double vision, eye problems, lumps, fever, rash, and vomiting. Data streams are analyzed every 2 hours by statistical methods such as confidence intervals and control chart methods (Cooper et al., 2004).

In Southeast Asia, the Association of Southeast Asian Nations (ASEAN) has developed the Early Warning Outbreak Recognition System (EWORS) for disease surveillance. EWORS collects data from a network of hospitals and provides technical approaches to distinguish epidemic from endemic diseases (EWORS, 2006). Free-text or ICD-9 coded symptom reports can be collected through EWORS to monitor a number of infectious diseases, including malaria and hemorrhagic fever due to Hantaan virus infection. Statistical analysis methods are used for daily data analysis and visualization. The system is currently implemented by public health departments of Indonesia, Cambodia, Vietnam, and Laos.

In some high-income countries, syndromic surveillance has been a very effective approach to supporting real-time public health monitoring. However, in developing countries, where public health is more in hazard, while the information communication infrastructure is more fragile, syndromic surveillance systems are more critically needed but difficult to implement. Chretien identified such difficulties, and discussed some of the successful syndromic surveillance implementation cases in a recent work. Availability of technologies for health data capture and transmission in these underdeveloped areas and countries are investigated. Operational experiences of systems such as EWORS are presented (Chretien et al., 2008).

Table 2-4. Ten international syndromic surveillance systems.

System	Agency
National Health Service (NHS) Direct Syndromic Surveillance	Operated by the National Health Service of UK
Early Warning Outbreak Recognition System (EWORS)	Association of South East Asian Nations
Alternative Surveillance Alert Program (ASAP)	Health Canada
Military syndromic surveillance for dengue fever outbreak	French Guiana in South America
Emergency Department Information System in Korea	Korea
Experimental Three Syndromic Surveillances in Japan	National Institute of Infectious Diseases, Japan
Australian Sentinel Practice Research Network (ASPREN)	The Royal Australian College of General Practitioners; the Dept. of General Practice, U. of Adelaide; Australian Dept. of Health and Ageing
New South Wales ED surveillance system	New South Wales, Australia
ILI surveillance in France	France
UMR S 707 ("Epidemiology, Information Systems, Modeling" project)	France

The Alternative Surveillance Alert Program (ASAP), initiated by Health Canada, currently monitors gastrointestinal disease trends by analyzing OTC antidiarrheal and anti-nausea sales data, and calls to Telehealth lines (Edge et al., 2003). The system is planned to be deployed at the community, provincial, and national levels.

A syndromic surveillance system called 2SE FAG system (Surveillance Spatiale des Epidémies au sein des Forces Armées en Guyane) was established to serve the military forces in French Guiana, a French overseas department in South America in 2004. The statistical analysis of military syndromic surveillance data with 2SE FAG is performed with Current Past Experienced Graph (CPEG) and the Exponential Weighted Moving Average (EWMA) method (Meynard et al., 2008). They showed that the system detected the dengue fever outbreak, which occurred in 2006 several weeks before traditional clinical surveillance, allowing quick and effective outbreak surveillance within the armed forces (Meynard et al., 2008).

In Korea, 120 emergency departments from 16 provinces and cities are now connected to the Korea Emergency Department Information System for daily analysis of acute respiratory syndrome. The system was initially developed for the 2002 Korea-Japan FIFA World Cup Games (Cho et al., 2003).

Japan's National Institute of Infectious Diseases (NIID) has developed a syndromic surveillance system based on EARS syndrome categories and

EARS software to analyze OTC sales data, outpatient visits, and ambulance transfer data in Tokyo (Ohkusa et al., 2005a, b). Approximately 5,000 sites nationwide in Japan are now connected to this system. The system was used for the 2000 G8 Summit and 2002 FIFA World Cup Games.

The Australian Sentinel Practice Research Network (ASPREN) is a national network of general practitioners who collect and report data on selected conditions such as ILI for weekly statistical analysis (Clothier et al., 2006). It is now being used by about 50 general practitioners nationwide in Australia.

The New South Wales ED surveillance system routinely collects computerized ED patient information from 30 EDs in New South Wales (Hope et al., 2008). The ED provisional diagnoses are classified into 37 syndromes, including gastrointestinal, influenza, pneumonia, other/unspecified respiratory infections, all injury and mental health presentations. Statistical control charts are used to automatically detect increases in syndrome activity, using Poisson z-scores of observed vs. expected day-of-week. Surveillance reports are updated four times per day (Muscatello et al., 2005).

Influenza-Like illness (ILI) surveillance is practiced in 11,000 pharmacies throughout France (about 50% of all pharmacies in France) in 21 regions. This ILI surveillance system is a Web-based system that collects medication sales and weekly office visit data to provide forecasts of influenza outbreaks using a Poisson regression model (Vergu et al., 2006).

The French "Epidemiology, Information Systems, Modeling," group headed by Guy Thomas has been developing a Web-based application for online epidemiological time series analysis. The application allows estimating the periodic baseline level and associated upper forecast limit. The latter defines a threshold for epidemic detection. The burden of an epidemic is defined as the cumulated signal in excess of the baseline estimate (Pelat et al., 2007).

5. SYNDROMIC SURVEILLANCE FOR SPECIAL EVENTS

During natural or human-made disasters, real-time and comprehensive knowledge of public health conditions is critical to inform response and recovery activities. Priority health conditions include infectious disease cases, injuries, and mental health disorders.

In recent years, the world has been through a number of global scale deathly disasters. Some examples that have affected millions of lives include Hurricane Katrina in 2005, causing the most severe loss of life and property damage occurring in New Orleans, Louisiana; the outbreak of the

SARS pandemic in 2002. In addition to large scale disasters, special events such as the Olympic Games, FIFA World Cup, or G8 Summit often involve participation of large populations. The temporary and sudden surge of population density in the event location brings potential health hazards to the participants, such as intensified infectious disease transmission and surging healthcare utilization. For instance, the 2008 Olympics in Beijing brought a large influx of people into the metropolitan area for 2 weeks. Population surge caused by the influx of a large number of tourists would significantly alter healthcare utilization patterns. It is critical to quickly identify any localized infectious disease outbreaks and prevent them from taking place.

Therefore, in this section, we discuss the category of syndromic surveillance practice that is concerned with syndromic surveillance for special and large-scale events. Teams of public health officials often need to work together to monitor public health status for such events (e.g., the 2002 World Series in Phoenix (Das et al., 2003), the wildfire outbreak in San Diego, 2003 (Johnson et al., 2005)). During Korea-Japan FIFA World Cup 2002 in Japan (Suzuki et al., 2003) and Korea (Cho et al., 2003), syndromic surveillance systems also played a role in public health status monitoring. Another two examples are syndromic surveillance systems implemented for the 2002 Kentucky Derby (Goss et al., 2003) and the G8 Summit in Gleneagles, Auchterarder, Scotland in 2005 (2005a). Typically, during the events data from regional emergency departments will be collected. Information concerning a predefined list of symptoms and probable diagnoses will also b e collected manually using special-purpose forms or via a Web-based interface. Table 2-5 summarizes six representative efforts in this category.

Table 2-5. Six representative syndromic surveillance efforts for special events.

Syndromic surveillance systems for special events	**Stakeholders/location**
Syndromic surveillance for Korea-Japan FIFA World Cup 2002 in Japan	National Institute of Infectious Diseases, Japan
Communitywide syndromic surveillance for 2002 Kentucky Derby	University of Louisville Hospital and Jefferson County Health Dept.
Syndromic surveillance for Korea-Japan FIFA World Cup 2002 in Korea	Korea
Drop-in bioterrorism surveillance system for World Series 2002 in Phoenix, Arizona	Phoenix, Arizona
Syndromic surveillance during the wildfires outbreak in San Diego, 2003	San Diego County
Syndromic surveillance for G8 Summit in Gleneagles, Auchterarder, Scotland, July 2005	Scotland, UK

In addition to the surveillance efforts of varying scopes as summarized above, there has been an increasing need for the development of syndromic surveillance systems and efforts at the global scale. World Health Organization (WHO)'s Epidemic and Pandemic Alert and Response program represents one such effort toward global syndromic surveillance. Note that the challenge of implementing a global surveillance system is more of a policy and administration nature as opposed to technical.

Chapter 3

SYNDROMIC SURVEILLANCE DATA SOURCES AND COLLECTION STRATEGIES

In this and the ensuing two chapters, we will focus on three key technical aspects of modern syndromic surveillance systems: data sources and collection strategies; data analysis and outbreak detection; and data visualization, information dissemination, and reporting.

This chapter discusses syndromic data collection strategies and related data sources. Data collection is a critical early step when developing a syndromic surveillance system. It involves the selection of data sources, choices over vocabulary to be used, data entry approaches, and data transmission strategies and protocols. We will go through the related technical issues in the following sections. Towards the end of this chapter, we briefly summarize additional policy-related considerations that may impact data collection.

1. DATA SOURCES FOR PUBLIC HEALTH SYNDROMIC SURVEILLANCE

Syndromic surveillance is a largely data-driven public health surveillance approach. Data sources used in syndromic surveillance systems are expected to provide timely, prediagnosis health indicators and are typically electronically stored and transmitted. Note that most syndromic surveillance data were originally collected and used for other purposes and such data now serve dual purposes. Figure 3-1 depicts the conceptual timeline of prediagnosis data types and sources for syndromic surveillance.

H. Chen et al., *Infectious Disease Informatics: Syndromic Surveillance for Public Health and BioDefense*, Integrated Series in Information Systems 21, DOI 10.1007/978-1-4419-1278-7_3,

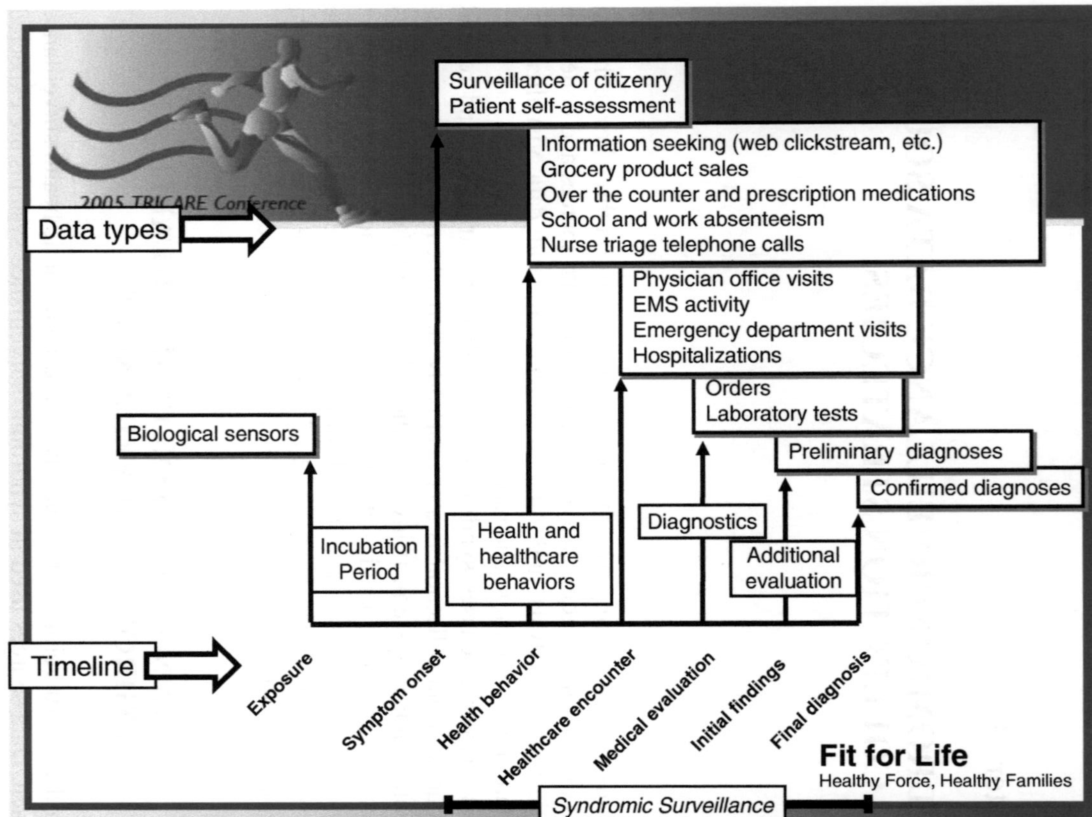

Figure 3-1. Conceptual timeline of collection and analysis of prediagnosis information for Syndromic Surveillance (2005c).

According to an empirical study conducted by Platt et al. (2003), most data collected for syndromic surveillance purposes include similar data elements: demographic data such as gender, age, area of residence; and data relevant to patient visits such as hospital name, the date of the visit, and the symptom set (chief complaints or admission status).

In this monograph, we identify the range of syndromic data sources and briefly summarize how they are used. Healthcare providers, schools, pharmacies, laboratories, and military medical facilities are all data contributors for syndromic surveillance. Specifically, data used for syndromic surveillance include emergency department (ED) visit chief complaints, ambulatory visit records, hospital admissions, OTC drug sales from pharmacy stores, triage nurse calls, 911 calls, work or school absenteeism data, veterinary health records, laboratory test orders, and health department requests for influenza testing (Ma et al., 2005).

Chief complaints record patient-reported signs and symptoms of their illness (e.g., coughing, headache, etc.) for ED or ambulatory visits. Chief complaints are among one of the most widely-used syndromic data sources in many syndromic surveillance systems. Figure 3-2 shows some sample chief complaint records collected from a hospital.

Chief complaints as a syndromic data source present many advantages as well as challenges for public health monitoring. Chief complaint records are routinely generated and become available typically on the same day the patient is seen. As a comparison, diagnostic data typically take a much longer time to be coded and transmitted due to various logistical and infrastructural issues and the lack of IT personnel at smaller hospitals (Travers et al., 2006). Chief complaint records are typically accessible in an electronic format. The wide availability and timeliness make chief complaints an ideal syndromic data source. However, as each chief complaint entry is a concise statement often in short free-text phrases that often contain misspellings and abbreviations, cleaning chief complaint data and mapping them into more meaningful representations are typically necessary before the analytical processes take place. In Chapter 4 we will further elaborate this problem as to processing chief complaints for syndromic surveillance.

date	MEDREC	AGE	SEX	RACE	ETHNIC	chief_complaint
09/01/2004	MA116315	78	F	H	1	OTH PULMON EMBOLISM
09/01/2004	MA216315	2	M	B	2	WHEEZING
09/01/2004	MA316315	15	M	W	2	SOB
09/01/2004	MA416315	75	M	W	2	DYSPNEA

Figure 3-2. Sample chief complaint records sheet.

OTC medication sales and prescription data are indicative of certain illness (e.g., influenza), which could be timelier than patient visits, as people may visit a drug store before considering seeing a physician. However, getting additional information about the purchasers such as demographical information is often not possible. ESSENCE and EARS are among the systems that utilize OTC sales data for surveillance purpose. The RODS laboratory has built the National Retail Data Monitor (NRDM) to monitor the sales of OTC medications as a public health surveillance tool. Thousands of retail pharmacies, groceries, and mass merchandise operations have participated in the program, where the data and analytical results are made accessible to public health officials across the nation.

School or work absenteeism reported by schools and workplaces can also be used as an indicator of public health status. As no disease characterization available with the absenteeism report, school or work absenteeism data have relatively limited use in syndromic surveillance. Systems (such as EARS, ESSENCE) monitor the school or work absenteeism data as a rough-cut early indication to generate alarms that "something might be wrong" instead of telling "what is going wrong."

Highly reliable disease diagnostic data are available as part of hospital admission record when hospitalization takes place. However, there could be 1–3 days between a patient's first healthcare visit and his or her possible hospitalization, making such data less timely than many other data types. The Hospital Admission Syndromic Surveillance (HASS) system implemented at Connecticut Department of Public Health utilizes hospital admission data for syndromic surveillance.

Triage nurse calls, 911 calls, and ambulance dispatch calls also have the potential of signaling possible events and changes in the public health status. Although the phone call data are relatively timely, information concerning symptoms or signs recorded during patient calls when the patient consults healthcare providers needs to be cleaned and extracted for the use of disease characterization. NHS Direct in the UK has been used for spatiotemporal analyses to initiate prospective geographical surveillance of influenza in England (Meynard et al., 2008), based on calls about fever and vomiting placed to a national telehealth system.

International Classification of Diseases 9th edition (ICD-9) codes and International Classification of Diseases, 9th edition, Clinical Modification (ICD-9-CM) codes assigned for diagnoses and procedures are often available in today's healthcare information systems used for billing or third-party insurance reimbursement purposes. ICD-9/ICD-9-CM codes are used as a syndromic data source in many systems because of their wide availability in an electronic format. Other data sources such as laboratory test orders and results, or even news reports, are also studied by researchers as feasible early public health indicators. For instance, researchers have studied how the mass media covered disease outbreaks and the media activity affected antiviral sales as monitored by syndromic surveillance techniques (Racer, 2007). Web-accessible information sources regarding infectious diseases such as discussion forums, mailing lists, and government Web sites, and news outlets have been found valuable in early public health event detection. As the rapid growth of Internet use and wide adoption of real-time online communication continues, more and more current, highly local information about outbreaks is available and accessible by Web crawling to support situational awareness (Brownstein et al., 2008a). Researchers also propose to monitor blogs, discussion sites, and listservs to complement news coverage and the use of click-stream data and individual search queries is also a promising new surveillance source (Eysenbach, 2006). However, because of the distributed and unstructured nature of these sources of information, monitoring public health related events through them becomes a challenge. Recently two global systems, HealthMap and Argus, were developed to provide real-time global information integration and public health status monitoring (Brownstein et al., 2008a). The systems have been discussed in previous sections, and dedicated chapters describing them can be found in Part II.

There are very few studies connecting environmental factors with public health status. Serious investigation is called for to determine whether monitoring environmental indicators can assist public health surveillance. In one such study (Babin et al., 2007), air quality measurements from the Environmental Public Health Tracking Program (EPHTP) are passed to the CDC, and the relationship between air quality and pediatric emergency department (ED) visits for asthma among DC residents are quantified over a 3-year period. Studying environmental factors could help understand background disease patterns so that unexpected fluctuations could be better detected (Zeng et al., 2008).

1.1 Comparison of Data Sources

A quantitative compilation of our research results shows that most of the syndromic surveillance systems monitor a combination of data sources from multiple sites instead of relying on a single data indicator. Out of the 56 systems numerated in Tables 2-1 through 2-5, wherein the details are known, 80% use ED chief complaints (both free text and ICD-9 coded chief complaints) as a timely public health indicator. Fifty percent of the systems monitor OTC drug sales. Thirty percent of the systems use hospital admission data as one of the inputs. Thirty of the systems also collect school/work absenteeism data. However, absenteeism or drugs sales are never used alone. Fourteen systems also connect to poison centers or laboratories for test orders, or monitor 911 calls. Additionally, most ED visits chief complaints are in free text (90%), which suggests the importance of free text processing or natural language processing techniques for medical information processing in this area.

ISDS (International Society for Disease Surveillance) also conducted a survey of state syndromic surveillance use including 46 respondents in 2008. The following figure (Figure 3-3) shows the distribution of use of data sources by the surveyed syndromic surveillance system (Mostashari et al., 2008). The numbers largely align with our quantitative findings above.

A major concern regarding the data used in the surveillance activities is about the effectiveness and validity of their usage for illness pattern detection. To be valid in the context of syndromic surveillance, evidence is needed that a data source may have value in identifying an outbreak or biological attack. A number of studies have examined to some degree whether and how effective the data sources are, as well as a possible time lead compared with diagnosis. Magruder's study (Magruder, 2003) about using OTC data/sales as a possible early warning indicator of human diseases revealed about a 90% correlation between flu-remedy sales and physician diagnoses of acute respiratory conditions together with a 3-day lead time reported. Another study (Doroshenko et al., 2005) shows that nurse-led helpline calls can also be used for early event detection. SSIC (Syndromic Surveillance Information

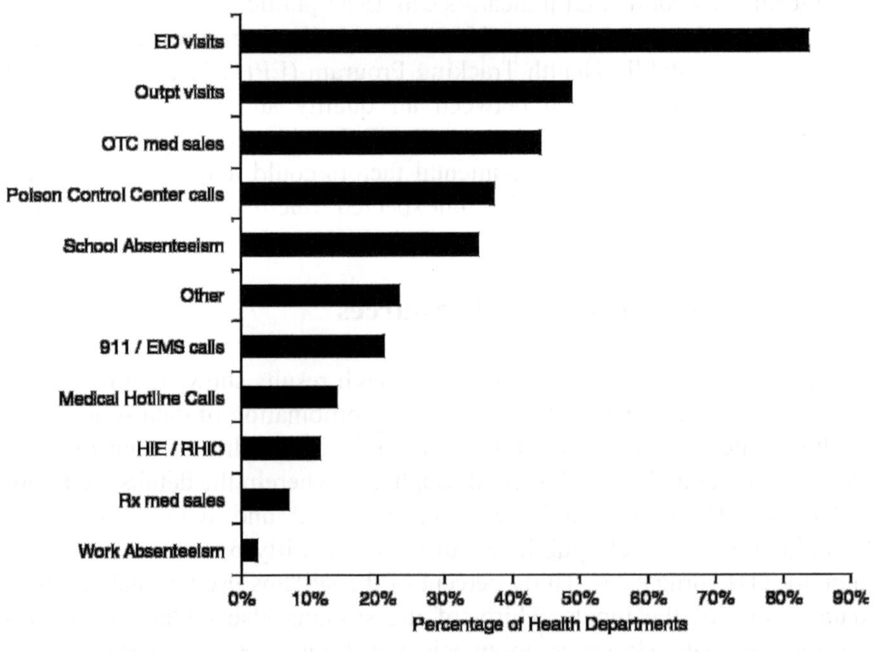

Figure 3-3. Syndromic surveillance data sources use survey by ISDS.

Collection) program tested the use of visit-level discharge diagnoses from several clinical information systems as a syndromic data source (Duchin et al., 2001; Lober et al., 2003). One limitation of using chief complaints as syndromic data is that they provide different predictive values from discharge diagnoses, as reported by (Begier et al., 2003). Generally, chief complaints best capture illnesses mainly characterized by nonspecific symptoms like fever, while discharge diagnoses appear better at tracking illnesses requiring brief ED clinical evaluation and testing, such as sepsis and possibly meningitis (Begier et al., 2003).

Although most of the syndromic surveillance systems use multiple data sources, further examination about whether the different data are telling the same story, i.e., flagging the possible outbreaks for certain illness with consistency, is necessary. Edge et al. (2004) reported correlations between OTC antinausea and antidiarrhea medication sales and ED admissions. However, in a study conducted by the Infectious Disease Surveillance Center, Japan (Ohkusa et al., 2005a), they found no evidence that sales of OTC medications used to treat the common cold correlated with influenza activities. It has been observed that as individuals may seek care in a variety of settings resulting in multiple reports for the same individual case in different data sources, combining these data sources properly presents major technical challenges due to dependencies existing among these data sources (Costa et al., 2007).

Preliminary investigations have evaluated the effectiveness of different data sources in syndromic surveillance and studied the differences among them in terms of information timeliness and characterization ability for outbreak detection, as they represent various aspects of patient healthcare-seeking behavior (Ma et al., 2005). For example, school/work absenteeism comes to notice relatively earlier as individuals take leave before seeking healthcare in hospitals or clinics, but specific disease evidence provided by the absenteeism type of data is limited. Table 3-1 provides a classification of different data sources used for syndromic surveillance organized by their timeliness and capability to characterize epidemic events.

Table 3-1. Data sources and their timeliness and disease characterization capability.

Data source	**Description**	**Specif-icity ***	**Timel-iness ****	**Advantages**	**Weaknesses**
Chief complaints from ED visits or ambulatory visits	Patient-reported signs and symptoms of their illness (e.g., coughing, headache, etc.) (Bradley et al., 2005; Espino and Wagner, 2001; Lombardo et al., 2004)	H	M-H	Routinely generated; available typically on the same day the patient is seen; and often available in electronic format	Available in short free-text phrases that contain mispellings and abbreviations; need to be cleaned; vocabulary differences across hospitals
ED diagnosis data	Diagnosis data available in electronic form from EDs (Travers et al., 2006)	H	L	Widely available in electronic format	Typically available a week after an encounter
OTC medication sales, prescription medication data	Medication sales data indicative of certain illness (e.g., influenza) as patients seek remedies (Besculides et al., 2004; Thomas et al., 2005)	M-H	H	Providing early signs and indications more timely than patient visits; data routinely generated and available in electronic format	Additional information about medication purchasers unknown
School or work absenteeism	Collected from school or workplace (Besculides et al., 2004; Thomas et al., 2005)	L-M	H	Timely	Lack of disease characterization (Quenel et al., 1994)
Hospital admission	Data are recorded when hospitalization takes place (Dembek et al., 2005; Dembek et al., 2004)	H	M	Highly reliable disease diagnosis	Generally an interval (1-3 days) exists between the first healthcare visit and admission (Buehler et al., 2003)

Data source	Description	Specif-icity *	Timel-iness **	Advantages	Weaknesses
Triage nurse calls, 911 calls	Symptoms of signs recorded during patient calls consulting healthcare nurses (Crubézy et al., 2005).	H	H	Relatively timely, as patients usually make phone calls before office visit	Need to be cleaned
ICD-9 (International Classification of Diseases, 9th edition) coded billing info	Preliminary diagnosis for billing (Begier et al., 2003; Espino and Wagner, 2001; Tsui et al., 2001)	H	M	May provide a better positive predictive value than chief complaints. available in most electronic medical systems	Often available after a relatively brief ED evaluation (days or weeks after an encounter)
ICD-9-CM (International Classification of Diseases, 9th edition, Clinical Modification)	Allow assignment of codes to diagnoses and procedures; often used for third-party insurance reimbursement purposes	H	M	Relatively timely and specific regarding illness characterization	Often assigned to patient visit days or even weeks after patient encounter
Laboratory test orders	Orders for laboratory tests (Wagner et al., 2001)	M	M-H	Relatively timely and specific regarding illness characterization	
Laboratory test results	Results of laboratory tests	H	L	Disease cases can be reported with high reliability	Lack of timeliness (test results may take more than a week)
Open source information (local or regional events)	Official or unofficial news reports, bulletin notification, Web forums and other online media	L	L	Tremendous amount of information that is freely available	Distributed and unstructured nature

*Disease characterization capability (Low-L, Medium-M, High-H)

**Timeliness of data to enable detection of outbreaks before confirmed diagnosis (Low-L, Medium-M, High-H)

2. STANDARDIZED VOCABULARIES

Data standard development, or more generally interoperability, is a key to successful, cross-jurisdictional syndromic surveillance. A standardized syndromic data representation would have a number of implications. First, a specialized vocabulary enables accurate representation for communicating information and events. Data formats and coding conventions that are inconsistent among different sites (e.g., laboratory tests and results can be reported in multiple ways) could be an obstacle in capturing illness cases.

More importantly, streamlining the delivery of electronic data across multiple sites saves time and eventually enables real-time reporting and alerting. Real-time data transmission and event reporting with a universal data format standard and messaging protocol is a primary motivator in the development of syndromic surveillance systems. Because of the varying internal data structures and database schema among various healthcare information systems, it takes a significant amount of time and processing resources for data conversion and normalization. According to an estimation in 2004, the use of data exchange standards in healthcare could save up to $78 billion annually (Pan, 2004).

In addition, syndromic surveillance systems that are more complex and geographically distributed need to be interoperable to enhance jurisdictional collaboration for timely event detection and response. Therefore, developing and imposing standards from programmatic, constructive, architectural, and managerial perspectives is especially addressed by the CDC-led syndromic surveillance initiatives. These initiatives are a collaborative effort involving the Public Health Information Network (PHIN) framework (CDC, 2006c), the National Electronic Disease Surveillance System (NEDSS) (CDC, 2004), the National Center for Vital Health Statistics, Department of Defense, Department of Veteran Affairs, and all National Institutes of Health.

This section discusses the development, adoption, and implementation of standard vocabularies for electronic emergency room records, laboratory testing, clinical observations, and prescriptions, along with the messaging standard to transport these records. Many available code standards currently used in syndromic surveillance have been borrowed from public health systems (Wurtz, 2004). Current efforts to standardize vocabulary are based on Logical Observation Identifiers Names and Codes (LOINC®), Systematized Nomenclature of Medicine (SNOMED®), International Classification of Diseases, Ninth Revision (ICD-9), and Current Procedural Terminology (CPT®) as core vocabularies. In addition, Unified Medical Language System (UMLS) has been used as cross reference ontology among the above coding systems. Health Level Seven (HL7) is used as a messaging standard in public health.

2.1 Existing Data Standards Used in Syndromic Surveillance

Here we provide a brief summary of each coding system to illustrate their scope and target medical domain.

UMLS: The Unified Medical Language System (UMLS) (Fung et al., 2006) provides a cross reference ontology among a number of different biomedical coding systems and standards, and a semantic structure defining relationships among different clinical entities. Its Semantic Network and Metathesaurus help facilitate system developers in building or enhancing electronic information systems that integrate and/or aggregate biomedical and health data and knowledge.

LOINC: LOINC codes are universal identifiers for laboratory and other clinical observations. Distinct LOINC codes are assigned based on specimen types (e.g., "ser" = serum) and methods of the test (e.g., immune fluorescence), with specific description for different conditions. As LOINC codes were originally developed for billing purposes, they do not convey information about the purpose or results of the test (Wurtz, 2004). The CDC has developed "Nationally Notifiable Conditions Mapping Tables" (http://www.cdc.gov/PHIN/data_models), which provide mappings from LOINC codes to nationally-notifiable (and some state notifiable) diseases or conditions.

SNOMED: SNOMED is a nomenclature classification scheme for indexing medical vocabulary, including signs, symptoms, diagnoses, and procedures. It defines code standards in a variety of clinical areas called coding axes. It can identify procedures and possible answers to clinical questions that are coded through LOINC.

ICD-9-CM: ICD-9-CM was developed to allow assignment of codes to diagnoses and procedures associated with hospital utilization in the United States and are often used for third-party insurance reimbursement purposes. Table 3-2 shows a partial code set used by ESSENCE for fever.

Table 3-2. ICD-9-CM coding examples.

ICD9CM	ICD9DESCR
020.2	PLAGUE, SEPTICEMIC
020.8	OTHER TYPES OF PLAGUE
020.9	PLAGUE NOS
021.8	TULAREMIA NEC
021.9	TULAREMIA NOS

An updated release of ICD-10-CM was made available in 2007 for public viewing. The codes of ICD-10-CM are now under testing and not currently valid for any purpose or use. A research study has been conducted to examine the usefulness of the ICD-10-CM system in capturing public health diseases, when compared with ICD-9-CM. The study also examined agreement levels of coders when coding public health diseases in both ICD-10-CM and ICD-9-CM. Overall results demonstrate that ICD-10-CM is more specific and captures more of the public health diseases examined than ICD-9-CM (Watzlaf et al., 2007).

HL7: HL7 (HL7, 2006; Hooda et al., 2004; Thomas and Mead, 2005) is the ANSI-accredited healthcare standard messaging format, used for transmitting information across a variety of clinical and administrative healthcare information systems. It specifies the syntax that describes where a computer algorithm can find various data elements in a transmitted message, enabling it to parse the message and reliably extract the data elements contained therein. HL7 Version 2.3 provides a protocol that enables the flow of data between systems. HL7 Version 3.0 (Beeler, 1998) is being developed through the use of a formalized methodology involving the creation of a Reference Information Model to encompass the ability not only to move data, but also to use it once it has been moved.

Development and adaptation of coding standards and standardized messaging formats are essential for information exchange and sharing, a prerequisite for public health surveillance. However, different standards and implementations exist for operational clinical, laboratory, and hospital information systems, which causes significant obstacles for information sharing. Nonetheless, standards are being developed, improved, and adopted increasingly widely.

Table 3-3. Adopted healthcare information standards in syndromic surveillance.

Clinical vocabulary	Main contents	Advantages	Limitations
UMLS	The UMLS Metathesaurus is a collection of different source vocabularies, organized according to meaning and lexical characteristics of terms. The Semantic Network contains explicit biomedical concepts and relationships.	Provides cross referencing between multiple vocabularies	Lacking granularity for medical diagnosis and syndromic surveillance (Lu et al., 2006)
LOINC	Laboratory results and observations. Could refer to a laboratory value (e.g., potassium, white blood cell count) or a clinical finding (e.g., blood pressure, EKG pattern)	Contains many genetic tests. It is mapped to UMLS and SNOMED RT and CT	Not suitable to capture the purpose or results of the test
SNOMED-CT (SNOMED-Clinical Terminology)	Used to distinguish concepts for the condition (e.g., pertussis) and the causative organism (e.g., *Bordetella pertussis*), suitable to code laboratory results, nonlaboratory interventions and procedures, and anatomy and diagnosis	Combines SNOMED RT and Clinical Terms Version 3	Proprietary
SNOMED-RT (SNOMED-reference terminology)	Includes concepts and terms for findings (disorders and clinical findings by site, method, and function), normal structures (anatomy/topography) and abnormal structures (pathology/morphology)	Well-tested and used in the field for decades	Proprietary
ICD-9-CM	Used to code morbidity data, final diagnosis, procedures, and reimbursement	Widely used (state-mandated)	Not suitable for clinical documentation of diagnoses, symptoms, signs and problem lists. (Hogan et al., 2002)
ICD-10-CM	ICD-10-CM represents a significant improvement over ICD-9-CM. Some specific improvements include: the addition of information relevant to ambulatory and managed care encounters; expanded injury codes; the creation of combination diagnosis/symptom codes to reduce the number of codes needed to fully describe a condition. It allows greater specificity in code assignment(2008)	Not deployed yet	Testing studies have demonstrated that ICD-10-CM is more specific and fully captures more of the public health diseases examined than ICD-9-CM. (Watzlaf et al., 2007)

In addition to leveraging existing healthcare standards, some groups have proposed additional coding and messaging standards tailored specifically for syndromic surveillance. For example, the Frontlines group (Barthell et al., 2002, 2004) is focusing on the development of standard reporting and coding structures specific to syndromic data. They defined the data elements in triage surveillance reports and a set of codified values for chief complaints. They also proposed a system to facilitate continuous flow of XML-based triage report data among hospital EDs, and state and local health agencies. The ongoing effort motivated to develop an electronic health record is largely relevant as well to public health surveillance from the point of view of coding and messaging standards. For instance, the Veterans Administration (VA) has been standardizing its clinical terminology to comply with industry-wide standards. In the National VA Health Data Repository (HDR), "Unique enterprise identifiers are assigned to each standard term, and a rich network of semantic relationships makes the resulting data not only recognizable, but also highly computable and reusable in a variety of applications, including decision support and data sharing with partners such as the Department of Defense (DoD)" (Bouhaddou, Lincoln et al., 2006).

In addition to technical considerations, regulatory and compliance issues also need to be examined carefully to address data standardization challenges. For instance, the US has implemented laws, such as HIPAA's Administrative Simplification, to enforce standardization in healthcare information by mandating, for example, health plans, healthcare clearinghouses, and providers that conduct certain transactions electronically comply with the HIPAA transaction standards.

Despite the availability of standard vocabularies discussed above, healthcare providers and public health researchers and practitioners often use natural language when describing biomedical concepts and constructs, even in the context of highly structured case report forms. Hunscher et al. (2006) described work in progress and lessons learned in translating complex natural-language concepts on case report forms into machine-readable format using the HL7 CDA, LOINC, and SNOMED-CT standards.

3. DATA ENTRY AND DATA TRANSMISSION

Syndromic data are being collected through various kinds of healthcare and public health information systems. Such data collection efforts often have to cross organizational boundaries and jurisdictions. This section discusses related data entry and transmission techniques.

3.1 Data Entry Approaches

Data entry approaches for syndromic surveillance fall into four categories: paper-based forms, Web-based interface, local data input software application, and hand-held devices (Zelicoff et al., 2001). Many systems support multiple data entry approaches as they involve multiple sites with possibly different IT infrastructure support (Espino et al., 2004; Lombardo et al., 2003). In general, the manual approach using paper-based forms can lead to unwanted delays as the records have to be converted later to an electronic format.

3.2 Secure Data Transmission

Secure data transmission is critical to data integrity and confidentiality. The specific challenges are as follows. How can a syndromic surveillance system retrieve syndromic data from data providers (e.g., hospitals and pharmacies)? How can data transfers be done securely over the communication channels such as the Internet?

The existing transmission approaches are either automated or manual. Automated transmission refers to transferring of data over a communication media where human intervention (e.g., to initiate each transmission transaction) is not required. Manual transmission entails significant human intervention. About 33% of the 50 systems surveyed rely primarily on automated data transmission, whereas the remaining 67% rely on human intervention in both data requesting and receiving. Email messages with text reports or data files as attachments, despite the security and data exposure risks, are still widely used to transfer syndromic data from clinical systems to syndromic surveillance systems.

The XML-based HL7 messaging standards play an important role in automated data transmission, since a significant portion of health systems support HL7. Among the systems surveyed, those capable of automated data transmission all use HL7 one way or another. For example, the RODS system and the BioPortal system use HL7 messaging protocols for automatic syndromic data transmission. In RODS, an HL7 listener implemented as Enterprise JavaBean (EJB) beans is used to receive HL7 messages from each underlying health system. The messages transmitted are first parsed by an HL7 parser bean before being loaded into the database. A configuration file written in XML is used to specify the hierarchical structure of the data elements in each HL7 message (Tsui et al., 2003). BioPortal also relies on an HL7-based approach to transmit data as HL7-compliant XML messages. This approach allows for dynamic changes in the message structure (Hu et al., 2005; Zeng et al., 2004b).

Compared with other approaches that mainly support file-based transmissions in a batch mode, HL7-based approaches are more efficient and effective. According to a RODS study (Tsui et al., 2005), they could reduce reporting latency by 20 hours. Secure networking techniques such as VPNs (Virtual Private Networks), SSL (secure socket layer), HTTPS, and SFTP (secure file transfer protocol) are now being increasingly utilized (Rhodes and Kailar, 2005).

Is there a best approach to transmit data from data providers to syndromic surveillance systems and the involved public health agencies? There is no simple answer to this question. Typically the IT infrastructure of the data providers (e.g., hospitals) needs to be upgraded to enable timely, reliable, and secure data collection.

Many practical challenges hindering the data collection effort also need to be addressed, including: (1) providing and transmitting data either requires staff intervention or dedicated network infrastructure, which often require extra costs; (2) data sharing and transmission must comply with HIPAA and other privacy regulations; (3) reducing data acquisition latency has important implications to syndromic surveillance yet is difficult and can be costly; (4) data quality concerns (e.g., incompleteness and duplications) often pose additional challenges. In particular, data ownership, confidentiality, security, and other legal and policy-related issues need to be closely examined. When infectious disease datasets are shared across jurisdictions, important access control and security issues should be resolved in advance between the involved data providers and users (Hu et al., 2005).

Chapter 4

DATA ANALYSIS AND OUTBREAK DETECTION

The analysis components of a syndromic surveillance system focus on detecting the changes in public health status, which may be indicative of disease outbreaks. At the core of these analysis components is the automated process of detecting aberration or data anomalies in the public health surveillance data, which often have prominent temporal and spatial data elements, by statistical analysis or data mining techniques. These methods are also capable of dealing with various common problems in epidemiological data such as bias, delay, lack of accuracy, and seasonality. These techniques are the focus of this chapter.

When processing public health surveillance data streams, it is often necessary to map the collected syndromic data into a small set of syndrome categories to facilitate follow-up analysis and outbreak detection. Section 4.1 discusses related syndrome classification approaches. In Section 4.2, we provide a taxonomy of anomaly analysis and outbreak detection methods used for biosurveillance. Sections 4.3–4.6 summarize various specific detection methods spanning from classic statistical methods to data mining approaches, which quantify the possibility of an outbreak conditioned on surveillance data.

1. SYNDROME CLASSIFICATION

The onset of a number of syndromes can indicate certain diseases threatening public health. For example, the influenza-like syndrome could be due to an anthrax attack, which is of particular interest to biodefense. Syndrome

H. Chen et al., *Infectious Disease Informatics: Syndromic Surveillance for Public Health and BioDefense*, Integrated Series in Information Systems 21, DOI 10.1007/978-1-4419-1278-7_4,

classification thus is one of the first and important steps in syndromic data processing and analysis.

A substantial amount of research effort has been expended to classifying free-text chief complaints into syndromes. This classification task is difficult because different expressions, acronyms, abbreviations, and truncations are often found in free-text chief complaints (Sniegoski, 2004). For example, "chst pn," "CP," "c/p," "chest pai," "chert pain," "chest/abd pain," and "chest discomfort" can all mean "chest pain." On the basis of our summary findings reported in Section 3.1, a majority of syndromic surveillance systems use chief complaints as a major source of data. Therefore, the problem of mapping each chief complaint record to a syndrome category, referred to as syndrome classification, is an important practical challenge needing a solution. Another syndromic data type often used for syndromic surveillance purposes, i.e., ICD-9 or ICD-9-CM codes, also needs to be grouped into syndrome categories. Processing such information is somewhat easier as the data records are structured.

A syndrome category is defined as a set of symptoms, which is an indicator of some specific diseases. For example, a short-phrase chief complaint "coughing with high fever" can be classified as the "upper respiratory" syndrome. Table 4-1 summarizes some of the most commonly-monitored syndrome categories. Note that different syndromic surveillance systems may monitor different categories. For example, in the RODS system there are seven syndrome groups of interest for biosurveillance purposes, whereas EARS defines a more detailed list of 43 syndromes. Some syndromes are of common interest across different systems, such as respiratory or gastrointestinal syndromes.

Table 4-1. Diseases and syndrome categories commonly monitored.

Influenza-like	**Respiratory**	**Dermatological**
Fever	Neurologic	Cold
Gastrointestinal	Rash	Diarrhea
Hemorrhagic illness	Severe illness and death	Asthma
Localized cutaneous lesion	Specific infection	Vomit
Lymphadenitis	Sepsis	Other/none of the above
Constitutional		
Bioterrorism agent-related diseases		
Anthrax	Botulism-like/botulism	Plague
Tularemia	Smallpox	SARS (severe acute respiratory syndrome)

1.1 Syndrome Classification Approaches

The syndrome classification process can be either manual or implemented through an automated system. The BioSense system, developed by CDC (Ma et al., 2005), for instance, relies on a working group that develops syndrome mapping using CDC definitions. However, automated, computerized syndrome classification is essential to real-time syndromic surveillance. A software application that analyzes chief complaint records or ICD-9 codes and then determines appropriate syndrome categories is often known as a syndrome classifier.

Manual Grouping The BioSense system (Bradley et al., 2005; Sokolow et al., 2005) and the Syndromal Surveillance Tally Sheet program used in EDs of Santa Clara County, California, use a manual approach to classify the symptoms. They ask the medical experts in syndromic surveillance, infectious diseases, and medical informatics to perform the mapping of laboratory test orders into 11 syndromes categories defined by a multi-agency working group (Ma et al., 2005).

Automated Classification Existing automated classification methods can be roughly categorized into three groups: supervised learning, rule-based classification, and ontology-enhanced classification. The supervised learning methods require as input a set of CC records labeled with syndromes as learning samples before they can proceed to classify unlabelled CC records by syndromes. Naive Bayesian and Bayesian network-based methods are two examples of the supervised learning methods (Ivanov et al., 2002; Sniegoski, 2004). For instance, the CoCo chief complaints classifier developed as part of the RODS system is a Bayesian classifier (Chapman et al., 2003). Often, a learning approach has a natural language processing (NLP) component, which classifies free-text CCs with simplified grammar containing rules for nouns, adjectives, prepositional phrases, and conjunctions. As part of RODS, Chapman et al. adapted the MPLUS, a Bayesian network-based NLP system, to classify the free-text chief complaints (Wagner et al., 2004a; Chapman et al., 2005). Implementing learning algorithms is straightforward; however, collecting training records is usually costly and time-consuming. Another major disadvantage of supervised learning methods is the lack of flexibility and generalizability. Recoding for different syndromic definitions or implementing the CC classification system in an environment that is different from the one where the original labeled training data were collected could be costly and difficult.

In contrast, rule-based classification does not require labeled training data. A text string searching process for syndrome category classification is a typical rule-based approach. In general, the CC records are first cleansed and then mapped to the syndrome categories according to a set of rules often predefined by medical experts following the definitions of syndromes of interest. For instance, an example rule could be "fever, if NOT *animal* and NOT *environmental* and *fever.*" Many applications, for example, EARS (Hutwagner et al., 2003), ESSENCE (CDC, 2003), and the National Bioterrorism Syndromic Surveillance Demonstration Program (Yih, Abrams et al., 2005), make use of such rules. Rule-based methods are relatively flexible, as the inference rules can be easily modified and updated. A major problem with rule-based classification methods is that they cannot handle symptoms not covered in the set of predefined rules.

The third category of automated approaches, ontology-based classification, utilizes relations between medical concepts (Leroy and Chen, 2001). Two representative methods are the BioPortal CC Classifier, which relies on Unified Medical Language System (UMLS) vocabularies and semantics (Lu et al., 2006, 2008), and the BioStorm approach, which uses a vocabulary abstraction method (Crubézy et al., 2005). BioPortal CC Classifier uses UMLS's Meta-thesaurus and SPECIALIST Lexicon to suggest a symptom grouping (as an intermediary representation) for a given CC record and then classify it using rules. It is able to provide a flexible architecture that supports easy adaptation to new syndromic categories. The BioStorm approach creates a series of intermediate abstractions up to a syndrome category from the primitive data (e.g., signs, lab tests) for syndromes indicative of illness due to an agent of bioterrorism.

We summarize representative syndrome classification methods in Table 4-2.

Table 4-2. Representative syndrome classification approaches.

Category	Example approaches	Application
Manual grouping	Medical experts perform the mapping of laboratory test orders into syndrome categories (Ma et al., 2005).	The BioSense system (Bradley et al., 2005; Sokolow et al., 2005) and Syndromal Surveillance Tally Sheet program in EDs of Santa Clara County, California.
Natural language processing (NLP)	NLP-based approaches classify free-text CCs with simplified grammar containing rules for nouns, adjectives, prepositional phrases, and conjunctions. Critiques of NLP-based methods include lack of semantic markings in chief complaints and the amount of training needed.	As part of RODS, Chapman et al. adapted the MPLUS, a Bayesian network-based NLP system, to classify the free-text chief complaints (Chapman et al., 2005; Wagner et al., 2004a).
Bayesian classifiers	Bayesian classifiers, including naïve Bayesian classifiers, bigram Bayes, and their variations, can classify CCs learned from the training data consisting of labeled CCs.	The CoCo Bayesian classifier from the RODS project (Chapman et al., 2003)
Text string searching	A rule-based method that first uses keyword matching and synonym lists to standardize CCs. Predefined rules are then used to classify CCs or ICD-9 codes into syndrome categories.	EARS (Hutwagner et al., 2003), ESSENCE (CDC, 2003), and the National Bioterrorism Syndromic Surveillance Demonstration Program (Yih et al., 2005)
Vocabulary abstraction	This approach creates a series of intermediate abstractions up to a syndrome category from the individual data (e.g., signs) for syndromes due to an agent of bioterrorism.	The BioStorm system (Crubézy et al., 2005; Buckeridge et al., 2002; Shahar and Musen, 1996)
Ontology-based classification	A rule-based system that can generalize symptoms grouping rules based on UMLS-derived vocabularies and semantics. It provides a flexible architecture for changing or adapting new syndromic categories.	The syndromic mapping component of the BioPortal system (Lu et al., 2008)

An interesting complementary method using both manual and natural-language processing techniques to create CC classifiers is presented by Halasz et al. (2006). They apply an *n*-gram text processing program to build an ICD9 classifier to a training set of ED visits for which both the CC and ICD9 code are known. A collection of CC substrings with associated probabilities was constructed and used to generate a CC classifier program. This approach allows the rapid automated creation and updating of CC classifiers based on ICD9 groupings.

Researchers have also started working on a CC classifier for non-English CCs. It is noted that there is a critical need for the development CC classification systems capable of processing non-English CCs as syndromic surveillance is being increasingly practiced around the world. One design first maps non-English CCs to English CCs and then use well-tested English CC classification systems to process translated CCs (Lu et al., 2007a).

1.2 Performance of Syndrome Classification Approaches

On the basis of our survey, about 40% of syndromic surveillance systems use automated syndrome classification, while the other 40% rely on a manual approach (details are unknown for the remaining 20%). There is clearly room for improvement and adoption of automated methods.

Evaluation studies have been conducted to compare various classifiers' performance for selected syndrome types (Travers and Haas, 2004). For instance, experiments comparing two Bayesian classifiers for the acute gastrointestinal syndrome showed a 68% mapping success against expert classification of ED reports (Ivanov et al., 2002). In general, however, it is difficult to paint a general picture of how well syndromic classifiers perform and how they fare against each other as many systems have not been evaluated on classification accuracy. In addition, the performance of these classifiers varies with different syndrome categories, further complicating the evaluation task.

Many prior studies show that a considerable portion (30–40%) of the chief complaints data is not classifiable because they are too noisy. However, combining chief complaints with the diagnostic codes (such as ICD-9) during the same visit can achieve a better classification accuracy (Reis and Mandl, 2004).

Another challenge facing syndrome classification is that there are no universally-accepted, standardized syndrome definitions. As a result, significant rewriting/fine-tuning efforts are needed when applying a classification approach in particular application contexts. One possible approach to deal with these difficulties is to create intermediary representations (such as symptom groups) and create explicit rules that map these intermediary representations into customized syndrome categories (Lu et al., 2006).

2. A TAXONOMY OF OUTBREAK DETECTION METHODS

Syndromic surveillance systems typically make available multiple outbreak detection algorithms, as no single method can deliver superior performance across a wide range of scenarios or meet different surveillance objectives (Buckeridge et al., 2003).

Many statistical and data mining techniques for syndromic surveillance have been proposed in the literature. These methods can be generally divided into retrospective and prospective approaches. If instead we consider the characteristics of the surveillance data analyzed, another orthogonal classification scheme is possible, dividing the outbreak detection methods into temporal analysis, spatial analysis, and spatial-temporal analysis approaches. This subsection focuses on both schemes.

Interested readers are referred to http://statpages.org/, which provides tutorials for various kinds of parametric and nonparametric statistical tests that form the statistical foundation of outbreak detection, and http://www.autonlab.org/tutorials/, which includes statistical data mining and machine learning tutorials. The review articles on data mining and its application in health and medical information (Bath, 2004; Benoit, 2002) are also good references to provide in-depth background for the material presented in this section.

2.1 Retrospective vs. Prospective Syndromic Surveillance

A number of surveillance approaches fall under the general umbrella of *retrospective* models, which aim at testing statistically whether events are randomly distributed over space and time for a predefined geographical region during a predetermined time period (Kulldorff, 2001). Some examples of retrospective methods include space scan statistic (Kulldorff, 1997), Nearest Neighbor Hierarchical Clustering (NNH) (Levine, 2002), and Risk-adjusted Support Vector Clustering (RSVC) (Zeng et al., 2004a). When applying retrospective methods, there is usually a clear distinction between the baseline data points and the observations of interest, where the baseline data correspond to known "normal" health status and the observations of interest are case reports to be examined for surveillance purposes. In applications where the separation between the baseline data and observations of interest can be cleanly and meaningfully done, retrospective methods can be effectively applied.

One major limitation of retrospective methods is that they are slow in detecting emerging clusters when the separation between the baseline data and observations of interest is not obvious. The resulting manual trial-and-error interventions severely limit the applicability of retrospective methods.

Prospective surveillance often entails repeated analyses performed periodically on incoming surveillance data streams to identify statistically significant changes in an online context (Chang et al., 2005). Using such a method, the separation of the baseline data and observations of interest is no longer needed as the system automatically tries various combinations of having some time windows as the baseline and some periods after them as the time of interest.

Prospective analysis has long been used in disease surveillance applications. The CUSUM method is one of the most established methods. Other examples include Rogerson's approaches (Rogerson, 1997), Kulldorff's prospective version of time-space scan statistics (Kulldorff, 2001), and the Prospective Support Vector Clustering (PSVC) method (Chang et al., 2005).

2.2 Temporal, Spatial, and Spatial-Temporal Outbreak Detection Methods

Table 4-3 summarizes a wide range of outbreak detection methods, all of them implemented in one or more syndromic surveillance systems surveyed. They are divided into three groups: temporal, spatial, and spatial-temporal (Buckeridge et al., 2005b; Mandl et al., 2004). Note that this table does not attempt to exhaustively list every detection algorithm proposed in the literature. Interested readers can refer to (Brookmeyer and Stroup, 2004; Lawson and Kleinman, 2005) for recent in-depth reviews of a more comprehensive set of algorithms. The methods listed in Table 4-3 are chosen because of their connection with the syndromic surveillance systems surveyed. Although not exhaustive, it covers most of the detection method types and provides a useful snapshot of the state of the art. Sections 3-5 provide additional analysis of these three groups of detection methods, respectively.

Table 4-3. Outbreak detection algorithms.

Algorithm	Short description	Availability and applications	Features and problems
Temporal analysis			
Serfling method	A static cyclic regression model with predefined parameters optimized through the training data	Available from RODS (Tsui et al., 2001); used by CDC for flu detection; Costagliola et al. applied Serfling's method to the French influenza-like illness surveillance (Costagliola et al., 1981)	The model fits data poorly during epidemic periods. To use this method, the epidemic period has to be predefined.
Autoregressive Integrated Moving Average (ARIMA)	A linear function learns parameters from historical data. Seasonal effect can be adjusted.	Available from RODS	Suitable for stationary environments.
Recursive Least Square (RLS)	A dynamic autoregressive linear model that predicts the current count of each syndrome within a region based on the historical data; it continuously adjusts model coefficients based on prediction errors	Available from RODS	Suitable for dynamic environments.
Exponentially Weighted Moving Average (EWMA)	Predictions based on exponential smoothing of previous several weeks of data with recent days having the highest weight (Neubauer, 1997)	Available from ESSENCE	Allowing the adjustment of shift sensitivity by applying different weighting factors.

Algorithm	Short description	Availability and applications	Features and problems
Cumulative Sums (CUSUM)	A control chart-based method to monitor for the departure of the mean of the observations from the estimated mean (Das et al. 2003; Grigoryan et al., 2005). It allows for limited baseline data.	Widely used in current surveillance systems including BioSense, EARS (Hutwagner et al., 2003) and ESSENCE, among others	This method performs well for quick detection of subtle changes in the mean (Rogerson 2005); it is criticized for its lack of adjustability for seasonal or day-of-week effects.
Hidden Markov Models (HMM)	HMM-based methods use a hidden state to capture the presence or absence of an epidemic of a particular disease and learn probabilistic models of observations conditioned on the epidemic status.	Discussed in (Rath et al., 2003)	A flexible model that can adapt automatically to trends, seasonality covariates (e.g., gender and age), and different distributions (normal, Poisson, etc.).
Wavelet algorithms	Local frequency-based data analysis methods; they can automatically adjust to weekly, monthly, and seasonal data fluctuations.	Used in NRDM to indicate zip-code areas in which OTC medication sales are substantially increased (Espino and Wagner 2001; Zhang et al., 2003)	Account for both long-term (e.g., seasonal effects) and short-term trends (e.g., day-of-week effects) (Wagner et al., 2004b).
Spatial analysis			
Generalized Linear Mixed Modeling (GLMM)	Evaluating whether observed counts in relatively small areas are larger than expected on the basis of the history of naturally occurring diseases (Kleinman et al., 2005a; Kleinman et al., 2004)	Used in Minnesota (Yih et al., 2005)	Sensitive to a small number of spatially focused cases; poor in detecting elevated counts over contiguous areas when compared with scan statistic and spatial CUSUM approaches (Kleinman et al., 2004).

SMall Area Regression and Testing (SMART)	An adaptation of GLMM that takes into account multiple comparisons and includes parameters for ZIP code, day of the week, holiday, and seasonal cyclic variation.	Available from BioSense and National Bioterrorism Syndromic Surveillance Demonstration Program (Yih et al., 2005)	Seasonal, weekly effects, and other parameters under consideration can be adjusted during the regression process.
Spatial scan statistics and variations	The basic model relies on using simply-shaped areas to scan the entire region of interest based on well-defined likelihood ratios. Its variation takes into account factors such as people mobility	Widely adopted by many syndromic surveillance systems; a variation proposed in (Duczmal and Buckeridge 2005); visualization available from BioPortal (Zeng et al., 2004a).	Well-tested for various outbreak scenarios with positive results; the geometric shape of the hotspots identified is limited.
Bayesian spatial scan statistics	Combining Bayesian modeling techniques with the spatial scan statistics method; outputting the posterior probability that an outbreak has occurred, and the distribution of this probability over possible outbreak regions	Available from RODS (Neill et al., 2005)	Computationally efficient; can easily incorporate prior knowledge such as the size and shape of outbreak or the impact on the disease infection rate.
Spatial-temporal analysis			
Space-time scan statistic	An extension of the space scan statistic that searches all the sub-regions for likely clusters in space and time with multiple likelihood ratio testing (Kulldorff 2001).	Widely used in many community surveillance systems including the National Bioterrorism Syndromic Surveillance Demonstration Program (Yih et al., 2004)	Regions identified may be too large in coverage.

Algorithm	Short description	Availability and applications	Features and problems
What is Strange About Recent Event (WSARE)	Searching for groups with specific characteristics (e.g., a recent pattern of place, age, and diagnosis associated with illness that is anomalous when compared with historic patterns) (Kaufman et al. 2005)	Available from RODS; Implemented in ESSENCE	In contrast to traditional approaches, this method allows for use of representative features for monitoring (Wong et al. 2003; Wong et al. 2002). To use it, however, the baseline distribution has to be known.
Population-wide ANomaly Detection and Assessment (PANDA)	A causal Bayesian network approach to model a population and infer the spatial-temporal probability distribution of disease for the entire population or individual patients	Available from RODS (Cooper et al. 2004; Moore et al. 2002)	Extensive computational effort
Prospective Support Vector Clustering (PSVC)	This method uses the Support Vector Clustering method with risk adjustment as a hotspot clustering engine and a CUSUM-type design to keep track of incremental changes in spatial distribution patterns over time	Developed in BioPortal (Chang et al. 2005; Zeng et al. 2004a)	This method can identify hotspots with irregular shapes in an online context

Because of the importance of outbreak detection algorithms for syndromic surveillance, we review some of the critical methods adopted in more detail below. The readers should note that the models we are about to discuss can be written in a number of mathematically equivalent ways, while the ones presented in the text are one of the representations.

3. TEMPORAL DATA ANALYSIS

This section discusses representative temporal anomaly detection methods. Temporal anomaly detection belongs to the vast domain of time series analysis. It monitors public health events or incidences as a sequence of data points, measured typically at evenly-distributed successive times. Temporal anomaly detection methods attempt to identify unusual patterns, smooth out naturally-occurring (or known) variations, and distinguish the variations caused by a possible outbreak from natural variations. Such methods either study the event frequency or the intensity of adverse event occurrences (time intervals between occurrences) to detect changes. These changes could follow different trends (e.g., linear, exponential).

3.1 Statistical Process Control (SPC)-Based Anomaly Detection

A majority of the systems surveyed employ statistical process control (SPC)-based algorithms. These algorithms were originally developed to monitor a process and its mean in industrial settings. The ability to differentiate the "out-of-control" mean from the "in-control" mean makes these methods readily applicable for anomaly detection.

The basic idea behind SPC-based algorithms is as follows. A small random sample $x = (x_1, \ldots x_t, \ldots)$ is drawn repeatedly at certain time intervals. The sample mean is compared against given thresholds; alarms are triggered at $t_A = \min\{s; \text{sample\_mean}(x_s) > G(s)\}$, if the sample mean exceeds the control limit *G(s)*. The alerting threshold is either theoretically defined, or dynamically estimated through historical data. The later one is proved to be more robust than the former (Buckeridge et al., 2005a). The single time-series analyzed often exhibits substantial day-of-week or seasonal patterns. As such, it is a common practice to estimate the incidence rate using a linear or Poisson regression model, and then to apply a SPC-based method to the regression residuals (Buckeridge et al., 2005a).

The Control Statistical Cumulative Sums (CUSUM) and Exponentially Weighted Moving Average (EWMA) methods are two standard SPC-based methods that have been widely applied for outbreak detection. CUSUM keeps track of the accumulated deviation between observed and expected values. Formally, the accumulated deviation is defined as $S_t = \max(0, S_{t-1} + z_t - k)$, where k is a control parameter and z_t models the distribution of the variable of interest (e.g., $z_t = \frac{x_t - \mu_t}{\sigma_t}$, if the variable is normally distributed) (Rogerson, 2005). Different forms of CUSUM have been developed, which assume that the underlying distribution could be Poisson or exponential (Rogerson, 2005). Nonparametric models have also been developed, removing the need for knowledge of the underlying distribution. A deployed SPC method often incorporates a short guard band (e.g., 2 days) between the baseline period and the day to be monitored. The guard band may lift the sensitivity by avoiding a gradually increasing outbreak contaminating the baseline with the outbreak signal. CUSUM methods have been specifically designed to deal with limited availability of historical data. Three CUSUM algorithms used in the EARS system require less than 10 days as the baseline period. They differ from each other by the different settings of the baseline period and the threshold levels, resulting in different levels of sensitivity (Hutwagner et al., 2003).

The Shewhart method is another simple form of SPC-based methods. It can be viewed as performing repeated significance tests on deviations of an observation from a target constant. The Shewhart method performs poorly for small and moderate shifts, but for large shifts, CUSUM actually converges to the Shewhart method (Lawson and Kleinman, 2005). One study used a Shewhart control chart to detect epidemics of Influenza A (Quenel et al., 1994).

Instead of considering only the last observation in the Shewhart method, the exponentially weighted moving average (EWMA) method monitors all the previous observations, summing up the multiple deviations in a weighted scheme, giving the most recent observation the greatest weight, and all the previous observations geometrically decreasing weights (Neubauer, 1997).

SPC-based methods are widely used in surveillance due to their simplicity. Their performances have been tested in many real settings. BioSense, EARS, and ESSENCE syndromic surveillance systems among others implemented either CUSUM or EWMA or both, and reported their early aberration detection capacity for influenza-like illness and other diseases (Hutwagner et al., 2005a; Zhu et al., 2005). The details of the performance evaluation can be found in Chapter 6.

3.2 Serfling Statistic

Serfling's method uses cyclic regression to model the normal pattern of the numbers of patients susceptible to death for pneumonia and influenza when there is not an epidemic with the objective of determining an epidemic threshold. Its use requires a clear definition of the disease, the selection of data to identify a normal pattern of susceptible patients, and the assumption that the normal pattern is periodical.

The Serfling statistic was originally proposed by Serfling for statistical analysis of weekly pneumonia and influenza deaths in 108 US cities in 1963 (Serfling, 1963). Serfling's method uses cyclic regression to establish an expected threshold for daily statistic based on history data excluding the epidemic weeks, accounting for seasonal variations. It requires a clear definition of the disease and the assumption that the normal pattern is periodical (Mandl et al., 2004). A theoretical form of this method is formulated as:

$$y(t) = c_1 + c_2 t + c_3 \sin(2\pi \frac{t}{52}) + c_4 \cos(2\pi \frac{t}{52})$$

Serfling's method is regarded as a traditional modeling technique applied to a number of disease surveillance practices such as the French influenza-like syndrome data (Costagliola et al., 1981). Serfling's method has also been used by RODS system to model hospital visitation data for influenza (Tsui et al., 2003).

3.3 Autoregressive Model-Based Anomaly Detection

The autoregressive integrated moving average (ARIMA) method is a class of time-series analysis models that are typically specified by three parameters: the order of autocorrelation (AR), the order of integration (I), and the order of moving average (MA) (Box et al., 1994). These parameters determine two things: how much of the past should be used to predict the next observation and how much do the past observations weigh in predicting the next observation. The higher-order models are more complex and can usually achieve a better fit of the training data set, while the simpler low-order models are usually less likely to over-fit to training dataset (Reis and Mandl, 2003). Description of the class of ARIMA methods in full details can be found in (Box et al., 1994). We here give an example ARIMA (1, 1, 1) model to simply show the notations. In the following equation, μ is a constant term, $(Y(t-1) - Y(t-2))$ represents a first-order "autoregressive" term, and the forecast error – first-order moving average at period $t-1$ is $e(t-1)$. ϕ and θ are coefficients.

$$\widehat{Y}(t) = \mu + Y(t-1) + \phi(Y(t-1) - Y(t-2)) - \theta e(t-1)$$

ARIMA models have been applied to pneumonia and influenza deaths for detection of outbreaks (Reis and Mandl, 2003). In the Automated Epidemiologic Geotemporal Integrated Surveillance (AEGIS) program at Children's Hospital Boston and Harvard Medical School, a hybrid of ARIMA with cyclic regression was found to have excellent predictive ability (Mandl et al., 2004). These models are available in many common statistical software packages (e.g., SAS Time Series Forecasting module). One drawback of the ARIMA models is that there is no systematic way to update model parameters when new data points arrive.

The Recursive Least Square (RLS) algorithm is another method based on autoregressive linear models and is implemented as part of RODS (Wong et al., 2002, 2003). It learns from the time series but does not need a large learning sample. Also it is more sensitive to recent historical data to predict outcomes, so it is well suited to surveillance for short-term events. Unlike ARIMA or the Serfling method, RLS continuously updates its parameters. RLS operates by converging on a set of coefficients (for a weighted linear equation) that best predicts historical values. The algorithm uses these coefficients to predict the current value. It calculates the prediction errors between the predicted values and the time series values. Using the prediction errors and algorithm threshold (expressed in number of standard deviations), RLS computes a threshold value. This algorithm is ideal for detecting spikes of cases when there is little historical data. Using these models implies that transformation of the data leads to a stationary time series, for which a single underlying probability distribution is assumed. These two hypotheses are not necessarily true, however; the data may present abrupt and wide changes of magnitude as well as irregular periodicity, in situations such as epidemics, modifications of the case-definition, screening, or vaccination (Le and Carrat, 1999).

3.4 Hidden Markov Model (HMM)-Based Models

The SPC-based models and the cyclic regression methods need nonepidemic data to model the baseline distribution, which is not always available without data preprocessing. This makes it an obstacle for automated surveillance. Researchers, therefore, have proposed to use Hidden Markov Models (HMM) to segment the time series of influenza indicators into epidemic and nonepidemic phases. Hidden Markov models have found major success in temporal pattern recognition such as speech and handwriting recognition, and bioinformatics. The basic idea behind HMM-based models is to add another layer of random signal generation process conditioned on the state of a hidden Markov process to determine the conditional distribution of each observed data point.

The sequence of state transitions in HMM is reconstructed using statistical methods to calculate the most likely trends of the surveillance data. HMM-based models are flexible enough to be easily adapted automatically to trends, seasonality, covariates (e.g., gender and age), and different distributions (normal, Poisson, Gaussian, Gamma, etc.). HMM-based models have been applied in a number of surveillance data time series analysis studies. For example, Le Strat and Carrat applied a univariate HMM to ILI time series surveillance in France (Le and Carrat, 1999). More technical details of HMM in disease surveillance can be found in (Madign, 2005). The author further discussed the proper number of hidden states, multivariate extensions to the above univariate HMM, as well as HMMs with random observation times. Madigan also pointed out that a key extension to the existing research on HMM-based surveillance would be to incorporate a spatial component in the hidden layer of the models.

4. SPATIAL DATA ANALYSIS

Spatial analysis techniques are used to find the extent of "clustering" of cases across a map and have long been an important component of the surveillance analysis toolset. More specifically, spatial clustering analysis aims to detect and locate the anomalies in disease occurrences or outbreaks by examining the surveillance data's spatial distribution, as clusters might be of insufficient size to be detected in analyses that consider only an entire region. This would also allow for the possibility that some areas contained populations more likely to become sick, such as older people, or more likely to seek healthcare, as might be the case for certain cultural groups. It thus provides the capability of tracking the progression of disease outbreaks and identifying the population at risk for proper treatment and prevention.

The rationale behind spatial surveillance is that natural disease outbreaks or biological attacks are typically localized at some spatial scale. Spatial analysis in syndromic surveillance uses spatial information residing in the data, such as the patient's home residence, sometimes the work place, and the location of the hospital where the illness is reported. Temporal analyses we discussed in the earlier section are capable of detecting elevated rates across an entire region, but would be less sensitive to a smaller number of spatially focused cases. Furthermore, spatially correlated random effects are often ignored by pure time series methods, thus it is assumed that all tests are independent.

Investigations of clusters in space often associate the varying population density with the null hypothesis. Denote the intensity of the disease cases (the number of expected events per unit area) by $\lambda_0(s)$, where s represents a location in the study area. Also denote by $\lambda_1(s)$ the intensity function of the population at risk. The null hypothesis of normal spatial distribution is in fact a proportional intensity function, $H_0 : \lambda_0(s) = \rho\lambda_1(s)$, where ρ is the expected number of cases divided by the expected number at risk.

One widely-used spatial analysis algorithm is SMART, made available through the BioSense system and the National Bioterrorism Syndromic Surveillance Demonstration Program. Other popular methods include the GLMM algorithm (Kleinman et al., 2004); spatial scan statistics (Kulldorff, 1999) and a number of its variations such as Modified spatial scan statistics (Duczmal and Buckeridge, 2005); and the Risk-adjusted Support Vector Clustering (RSVC) method (Zeng et al., 2004a).

Temporal analysis methods such as CUSUM can also be adapted to analyze spatial information by maintaining CUSUM charts for the surrounding neighborhood of each individual region as local spatial statistics or by maintaining multivariate CUSUM charts for all regions in a global setting (Lawson and Kleinman, 2005). Vice versa, spatial clustering techniques could be adapted to temporal surveillance, if considering time as one-dimensional space.

4.1 Generalized Linear Mixed Models and SMART Algorithm

Kleinman et al. (2005a) proposed the use of Generalized Linear Mixed Model (GLMM) statistics based on a logistic regression model to estimate the probability that each subject under surveillance is a case, in each area, on a given day. The simple logistic regression model introduces "shrinkage" estimators showing the density of population in each area, as the size of the population under surveillance in each area often varies. The proposed method treats each small area as if it was an individual, and the relative locations of the small areas are not taken into account by the model. This method in essence ignores much spatial information and cannot detect elevated counts over several contiguous areas.

SMART is an adaptation of the GLMM method, taking additional parameters into account to adjust for seasonal, weekly, social trends, and holiday status (Bradley et al., 2005). In such an approach, generalized linear models are used to establish the expected count per ZIP code per day based on regressing historical series of counts in each small area. The established distribution of case counts are then refined to account for multiple ZIP codes through multiple testing. One experimental study suggested that SMART delivered slightly inferior results to the spatial scan statistic method. However, both methods achieved good performances (Kleinman et al., 2005a).

4.2 Spatial Scan Statistic and Its Variations

Most syndromic surveillance systems make use of spatial scan statistic and its variations. Using such methods for spatial analysis, a large set of circular windows with varying sizes is imposed on the map in different locations to search for clusters over the entire region. As the cluster size is unknown a priori, the scan statistic method uses a likelihood ratio test where the alternative hypothesis is that there is an elevated rate within the scanning window when compared with outside. The most likely clusters can then be identified based on the likelihood-ratio test if the null hypothesis is rejected. For each distinct window, the likelihood ratio is proportional to: $(\frac{n}{\mu})^n(\frac{N-n}{N-\mu})^{N-n}$, where n is the number of cases inside the circle, N is the total number of cases, and μ is the expected number of cases inside the circle (Kulldorff, 1997). Other probability models, i.e., distribution from which the case incidence are generated, have also been used for scan statistics. Poisson model is commonly seen. Bernoulli model can be used for on-off case-control type data, and exponential model is for survival data.

There are several advantages with scan statistic methods. First, they avoid preselection bias regarding the size or location of clusters. Second, they can be easily adjusted for nonuniform population density as well as other factors such as age.

The spatial-temporal version of the scan statistic uses cylinders instead of circles, where the height of the cylinder represents time. Still, the circular base defines a geographic area with a varying radius. The size of the area that is circled could be from zero to hundreds of kilometers or everything in between. The height of the cylinder can represent a time of day or years. The rest of the process is largely unchanged. A moving cylindrical window with variable sizes in both space and time visits all spatial-temporal locations to identify a significant excess of cases within it, until it reaches a predetermined size limit (Kulldorff, 1999, 2001). On the basis of the flexible purely spatial scan statistic, Takahashi et al. proposed a flexibly shaped space-time scan statistic for detecting irregularly-shaped clusters, which may not be detected by the circular spatial scan statistic (Takahashi et al., 2008). The performance of the flexibly-shaped space-time scan statistic is compared with the cylindrical scan statistic with a space-time power distribution developed by extending the purely spatial bivariate power distribution (Takahashi et al., 2008).

SaTScan is a freely-available software package that implements various types of spatial and space-time scan statistics (2006j). It has been used in more than 10 syndromic surveillance systems, according to our survey. Two commercial products, WpiAnalyst extension for ArcView GIS from the Public Health Research Laboratories (2003d) and ClusterSeer developed by TerraSeer (2006c) contain both spatial and spatial-temporal scan statistics together with many other statistical clustering methods. The SaTScan Macro Accessory for Cartography (SMAC) package consists of four SAS macros and was designed as an easier way to run SaTScan multiple times and add graphical output. The package contains individual macros, which allow the user to make the necessary input files for SaTScan, run SaTScan, and create graphical output all from within SAS software. The macros can also be combined to do this all in one step (Abrams and Kleinman, 2007).

A modified spatial scan statistic proposed by Duczmal and Buckeridge considers work-related factors. A factor reflecting the number of "contaminations" from workers at the nearest neighbors is added to the observed cases in the residential zones (Duczmal and Buckeridge, 2005). Their simulation shows that their approach can achieve greater detection power than the scan statistics that do not consider people movements. To apply their approach, workplace location information is required, which unfortunately is not commonly available in surveillance data sources.

There are a few known problems with spatial scan methods. First, they can only identify clusters in simple regular shapes. Second, it is difficult to incorporate prior knowledge, such as the size or shape of the outbreaks or the impact on disease infection rate. Third, exhaustive searches over a large region to perform statistical tests could be computationally expensive.

The method summarized in the next subsection deals with the first problem. To address the second and third problems, Neill et al. (2005) proposed a Bayesian spatial scan statistic that is computationally more efficient and capable of combining the a priori knowledge of the investigated outbreak. A conjugate Gamma-Poisson model, as opposed to the Poisson model in Kulldorff's original spatial scan statistic, is used to produce a spatially smoothed map of disease rates, with a focus on computing the posterior probabilities to determine the outbreak likelihood and to estimate the location and size of potential outbreaks.

4.3 Risk-Adjusted Support Vector Clustering (RSVC) Algorithm

Zeng et al. developed an approach called RSVC that combined the risk adjustment idea with a robust Support Vector Clustering (SVC) method to improve the quality of retrospective spatial-temporal analysis. Specifically, for regions with prior dense baseline data distribution, data points are less likely to be grouped to form anomaly clusters. Several steps are involved in the clustering process. First, the input data are implicitly mapped to a high-dimensional feature space defined by a kernel function (typically the Gaussian kernel). Second, the algorithm finds a hypersphere in the feature space with a minimal radius to contain most of the data. The problem of finding this hypersphere can be formulated as a quadratic or linear programming problem depending on the distance function used. Third, the function estimating the support of the underlying data distribution is then constructed using the kernel function and the parameters learned in the second step. The width parameter in the Gaussian kernel function is dynamically adjusted based on kernel density computed using background data. When mapped back to original space, the hypersphere splits into several clusters, which indicated high risk outbreak areas (Zeng et al., 2004b).

5. SPATIAL-TEMPORAL DATA ANALYSIS

5.1 Rule-Based Anomaly Detection with Bayesian Network Modeling

The "What's Strange About Recent Events" (WSARE) algorithm performs a heuristic search over combinations of temporal and spatial features to detect irregularities in space and time. The case features analyzed by WSARE include syndrome category, age, gender, and geographical information. For example, a two-term case feature could be "Gender = Male AND Home Location = NW." The number of the cases satisfying and those not satisfying the case feature are computed to be used to determine whether there is significant discrepancy between the observed statistic of the current day and the baseline.

Historic data (e.g., recent weeks before the day of analysis) is fed to a Bayesian network to create a baseline distribution. The network is constructed using an algorithm called optimal reinsertion (Moore et al., 2003) based on ADTrees (Moore and Lee, 1998). The benefit of the approach relies on Bayesian network's generalization capability that is able to predict the probability of a situation that may not have been encountered in the past. The network structure is rebuilt every month, while the parameters are updated daily. Environmental attributes such as season and day of week can be incorporated in the model as conditional probability.

All feature-value combinations are then searched and scored exhaustively. The scores are generated by conducting hypothesis testing for each feature-value combination against the baseline distribution. Instead of exhaustively searching for *i*-term feature-value combinations with an exponential complexity (i = 1, 2, …, n, suppose that there are n features in total), a greedy search approach is designed by searching the best 1-term case feature first and then adding another term to it to compose a 2-term case feature, and so forth. Compared with several other algorithms that do not examine covariate information, WSARE performed better as measured by timeliness at the expense of slightly higher false-positive rate (Wong et al., 2002).

5.2 Population-Wide Anomaly Detection and Assessment (PANDA)

Population-Wide Anomaly Detection And Assessment (PANDA) is a causal Bayesian network-based model constructing and inferring the spatial-temporal probability distribution of disease in a population as a whole. The causal Bayesian network consists of a large set of inter-linked patient-specific probabilistic causal models, each of them including variables that represent risk factors (e.g., infectious disease exposures of various types), disease states, and patient symptoms (Cooper et al., 2004). Simulation conducted by the RODS team showed that the model can handle a population size of 1.4 million (Cooper et al., 2004).

6. MONITORING MULTIPLE DATA STREAMS

In Sections 6 and 7, we discuss two specific sets of issues concerning outbreak detection that are worth separate treatments.

In disease surveillance, multiple data sets (data are collected simultaneously from pharmacies, hospitals, nurse help telephone calls, and clinics) are usually available for surveillance. However, the majority of implemented detection algorithms monitor individual data sources and do not cross reference between them. The problem is that no single data source captures all the individuals in the outbreak (Kulldorff et al., 2005). One potentially fruitful detection approach is a data-fusion approach using multiple sources of data (e.g., ED visits and OTC sales data) to perform outbreak detection. For example, MCUSUM and MEWMA (Yeh et al., 2003, 2004) were developed to increase detection sensitivity while limiting the number of false alarms. Multiple univariate statistical techniques and multivariate methods have also been used in prior studies based on different independence assumptions among the data streams. Multiple univariate methods assume independence among the data; while multivariate methods establish the covariance matrix typically estimated from a baseline period (Buckeridge et al., 2005a). In the ESSENCE II project, chief complaints data and sales of OTC medications are treated as covariates (Lombardo et al., 2004). However, to model the multiple univariate signals from different data streams, an in-depth investing-ation and characterization of health-care-seeking behavior is necessary.

Another approach is to monitor stratified data (e.g., based on syndrome type or age group, counties, or treatment facilities) in parallel. The WSARE (What is Strange About Recent Events) system proposed by Wong et al. (2003) is one example, which searches for outbreaks in various groupings of age, gender, or census tracts. Kulldorff et al. (2003) developed a tree-based scan statistic to do surveillance on groupings that can be preclassified into a hierarchical tree structure.

In addition, during major public events, unpredictable shifts in the healthcare data may occur due to changes in healthcare utilization patterns. This problem is addressed by Reis et al. Instead of monitoring different healthcare data streams individually, they proposed a class of epidemiological network models that monitor the interrelationships among these data streams. The integrated network-based modeling of the interrelationships among the epidemiological data streams allows more robust performance in the face of shifts in healthcare utilization during epidemics and major public events (Reis et al., 2007).

Simultaneous wavelets analysis over multiple time series are practiced by Dillard and Shmueli (Shmueli and Fienberg, 2006). Rigorous comparative evaluations to quantify the gain of using covariates from multiple data sources in surveillance are needed.

7. SPECIAL EVENTS SURVEILLANCE

Another challenging issue for real-time outbreak detection is that the surveillance algorithms often rely on historic datasets that span a considerable length of time. Few methods demonstrate reliable detection capability with short-term baseline data. This is a particular concern for surveillance systems for special events (also referred to as drop-in models), which are implemented against bioterrorism attacks or natural disease outbreaks in settings such as international and national sports events or meetings that involve many participants in a short time window.

EARS was used for syndromic surveillance at several large public events in the United States, including the Democratic National Convention of 2000, the 2001 Super Bowl, and the 2001 World Series (Hutwagner et al., 2003).

The RODS system was used during the 2002 Winter Olympic Games (Gesteland et al., 2002). The LEADERS system often serves as a drop-in surveillance system intended to facilitate communication and coordination within and between public health facilities (Ritter, 2002).

8. SUMMARY OF DATA ANALYSIS PROCESS FOR SYNDROMIC SURVEILLANCE

In this chapter, we first introduce syndrome classification as the first step of syndromic data analysis. We then summarize a large number of disease surveillance algorithms. These algorithms are organized in two dimensions. In the first dimension, a surveillance method is either retrospective surveillance or prospective. Retrospective analysis focuses on analyzing historical data, whereas prospective analysis is more useful for processing online data streams. In the second dimension, a surveillance method can be seen as either a temporal, spatial, or spatial-temporal analysis method. Methods designed for special events are discussed separately due to their unique characteristics. We also examine methods that monitor multiple data streams, which warrant further exploration due to their importance and applicability. We conclude this chapter by pointing out some technical issues to watch for while applying these surveillance methods.

First, the outbreak detection methods make a number of assumptions about the analyzed data. The distribution of the disease events are in many cases assumed, so before the application of any surveillance methods to the disease data, there should be analysis regarding disease behaviors such as the outbreak patterns and events distribution. Second, an algorithm's performance is related to a number of settings: (1) the availability of historic data; data collection process as discussed in Chapter 2 is thus closely related to a surveillance algorithm performance; (2) the type of outbreak signals (e.g., slow-building or surge outbreak); (3) the spatial granularity of the data in spatial analysis.

All the complications due to the dynamics of different diseases need to be considered and well investigated before applying a detection algorithm. In (Burkom and Murphy, 2007), the authors propose a data-adaptive method selection scheme to "suit the remedy to the case," by first evaluating a number of data discriminates such as mean, variance, and skewness before selecting a detection algorithm for analysis. The BioStorm research group developed an ontology-based method to incorporate the a priori knowledge so that different analytical methods are assigned to different types of surveillance data in different settings (Crubézy et al., 2005).

Chapter 5

DATA VISUALIZATION, INFORMATION DISSEMINATION, AND ALERTING

Syndromic surveillance systems are critical for public health surveillance because they often provide epidemiologists and public health officials the visual analytics tools and techniques to synthesize information and detect the data anomalies (possible outbreaks) from massive, dynamic, and often ambiguous surveillance data. Represented visually, the assessments of public health status are better understood and also more effectively communicated for action. The geographic or spatial components of the surveillance data enable the natural application of visualization techniques for computerized assistance for decision making in spatial (and often spatial-temporal) analytics (e.g., clustering detection and resource logistics). In addition, the interplay between simulation and visualization provides a powerful combination. Visualization techniques can be used to analyze simulation output and analysis results, and can drastically improve the understandability and accessibility of the model to both technical and nontechnical audiences. Virtually all simulation software packages have some level of visualization, ranging from basic diagrams to full animation.

This chapter provides a systematic summarization of data visualization techniques that are employed in the surveyed syndromic surveillance systems. Taxonomy of the visualization techniques procedes the discussion of the two classes of visualization technologies: visual information display and interactive visual data exploration. A number of example screenshots from the surveyed syndromic surveillance systems visualizations are shown along with the text.

H. Chen et al., *Infectious Disease Informatics: Syndromic Surveillance for Public Health and BioDefense*, Integrated Series in Information Systems 21, DOI 10.1007/978-1-4419-1278-7_5,

1. SCOPE AND TAXONOMY

Visualization technology and user interface design involve a vast literature in HCI, computing graphics, psychology, database organization, dynamic query, and display algorithms, as well as screen management algorithms. But we are not targeting a complete scientific discussion of visualization technologies, but instead, we identify the different visual representations of the syndromic surveillance data in the public health context and examine how to advance the relevant applications of user interface design methods.

Shneiderman (1996) identified two aspects of visualization technology that can be directly applied to a given structure. One focuses on mapping abstract information to a visual representation and the other provides user-interface interactions for effective navigation over displays on a screen. Our focus of the discussion accordingly includes two pieces of visualization techniques: visual information display and interactive visual data exploration. By and large, the visual information display includes temporal, spatial, and temporal-spatial information display exploring different dimensions of the information.

The readers should also be reminded that data analysis technologies serve as back-end support for visualization functions. As noted by Chen (1999), data analysis technology as a "third-dimension" of the information visualization technology serves to create structures that characterize the data set, abstract the unstructured or high-dimensional information. The data analysis technologies as discussed in the previous chapter are important back-end methods that drive many of the visualization approaches discussed in this chapter.

2. VISUAL INFORMATION DISPLAY

Visual information display techniques aim to present visually either raw surveillance data or analysis results (e.g., from the data anomaly detection algorithms) (Zhu and Chen, 2005). Visual representation techniques are applied to either time-series data or spatial/geographical data. The traditional methods of information display are multidimensional tables (line listing), and various static statistical graphics, such as line graphs, scatter plots, bar charts, and pie charts. Color-coded maps are often used to represent disease cases and clusters with case locations. Geographical Information Systems (GIS) are now being widely used for spatial information representation and cluster detection. Graphs with nodes and links, such as trees and networks, are not seen in the surveillance information display, but they might be viewed as promising tools for disease modeling based on spreading patterns.

2.1 Visualization of Time-Series Data

Line chart is a popular method to visualize time-series data as it can help identify temporal patterns such as spikes or clusters. Usually one curve represents the observed data, and the other curve is the normal pattern plotted by the temporal analysis algorithms. Line charts and other plotting methods for time-series analysis are supported by most statistical analysis packages (e.g., SAS and SPSS). The example view of the interface of BioSense application shown in Figure 5-1 is a line chart and a line listing of the fictional time-series syndromic data in a metropolitan area. Figure 5-2 shows a screenshot from the EARS system (Hutwagner et al., 2003), visualizing daily data feed from a hospital and the results of applying the CUSUM algorithm.

Other types of plots such as candlestick plot and density ratio map are also seen in syndromic surveillance applications. Figure 5-3 shows a density ratio map visualizing data aggregated by patient age in several influenza seasons (DIMACS, 2006).

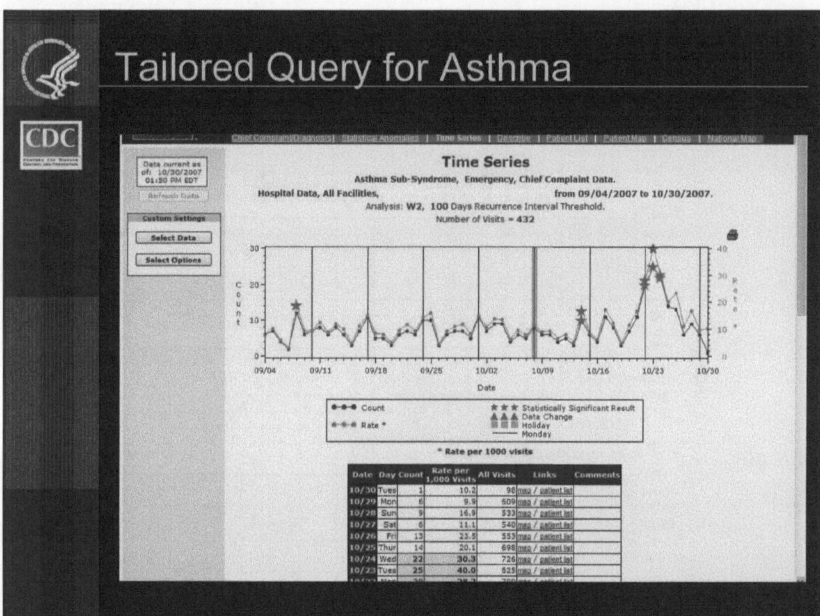

Figure 5-1. Example views available in the BioSense application (source: Biosence Website).

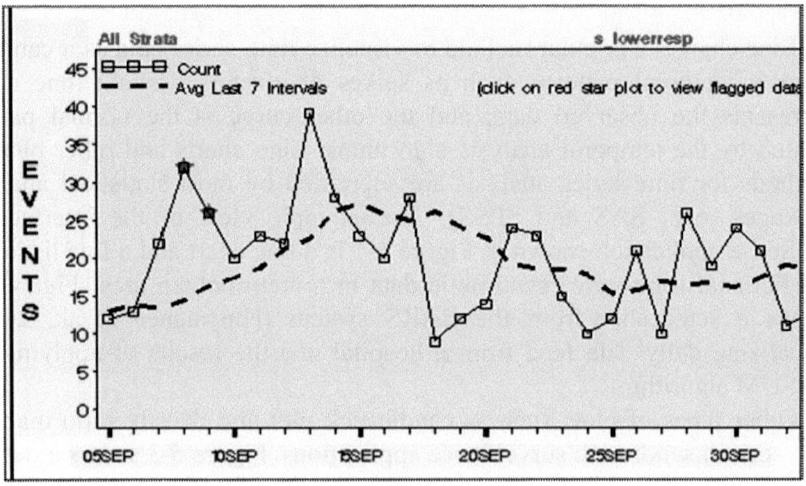

Figure 5-2. Line charts plotting temporal patterns of disease cases (EARS system).

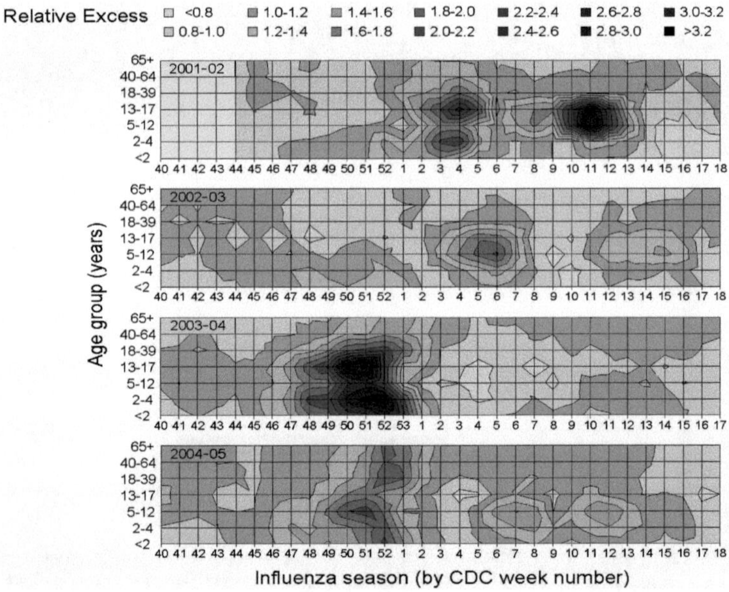

Figure 5-3. Density ratio maps visualizing data aggregated by patient age (DIMACS, 2006).

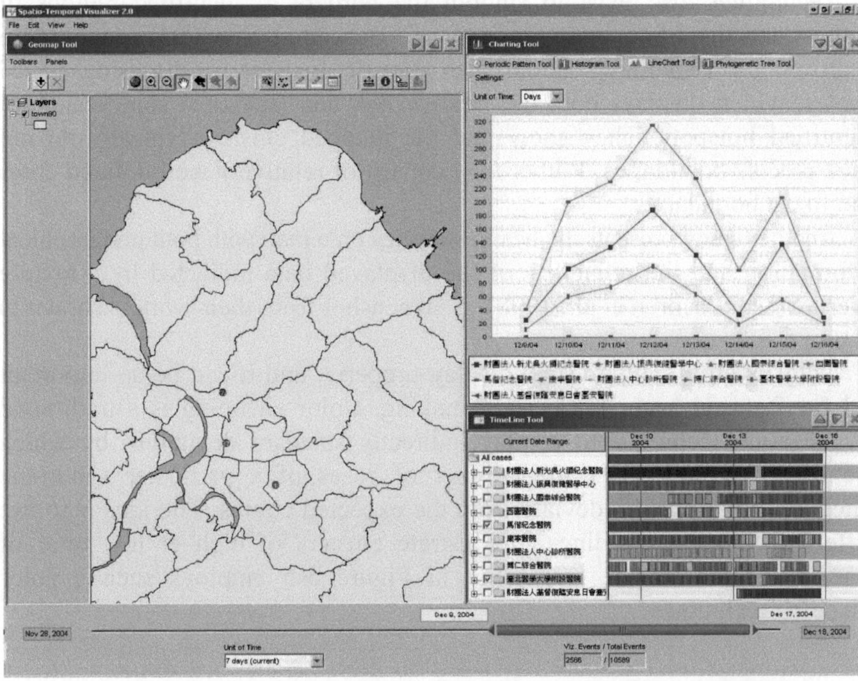

Figure 5-4. Selected Taipei hospitals CC spatial temporal patterns (2006a).

2.2 Visualization of Spatial Information

Visualizing disease cases or surveillance-related events on a map can help identify case clusters (typically indicative of outbreaks), investigate possible causes of a disease or an outbreak, and study an outbreak's dissemination and evolutionary patterns. One major objective of visualization is to identify geographical areas with unusually high numbers of cases or events to serve surveillance purposes and inform outbreak response decisions. Another objective is to determine high-risk areas for a disease under investigation and help analyze correlations between disease occurrences, various types of environmental factors, and social-demographic variables.

There are several techniques for displaying spatial information contained in syndromic data. Printed maps are often used to identify geographic clusters or hotspots (Figure 5–4). CDC and the National Center for Health Statistics support research to investigate the design and display for disease atlases (Lawson and Kleinman, 2005). Geographical display of disease statistics in real time is also widely used for situation awareness and incident response (Kulldorff, 2001).

Techniques also exist to smooth the borders of identified regions of interest and display overlapping clusters. Boscoe et al. (2003) proposed an approach for visualizing spatial scan statistic analysis results using nested circles, which displays both the relative risk and statistical significance of identified hotspots. They show that the mapped clusters typically do not have precise boundaries. Rather they consist of relatively well-defined cores and fuzzy boundaries.

Another study presents the health statistics on a map with both geographical information and the reliability of the displayed data indicated by a texture overlay (MacEachren et al., 1998). A screenshot from their work is shown in Figure 5-5.

Color is an effective visual display property, and it can be an important aid for fast and accurate decision making. Color encoding is a traditional visualization technique to display indirectly standard deviations by which the observed data (e.g., the number of cases of a particular syndrome category in a zip code) deviate from the expected counts. The idea is to use different colors or shadings to illustrate clusters of high or low rates of disease incidence. The screenshot in Figure 5-5 employs such a color encoding technique.

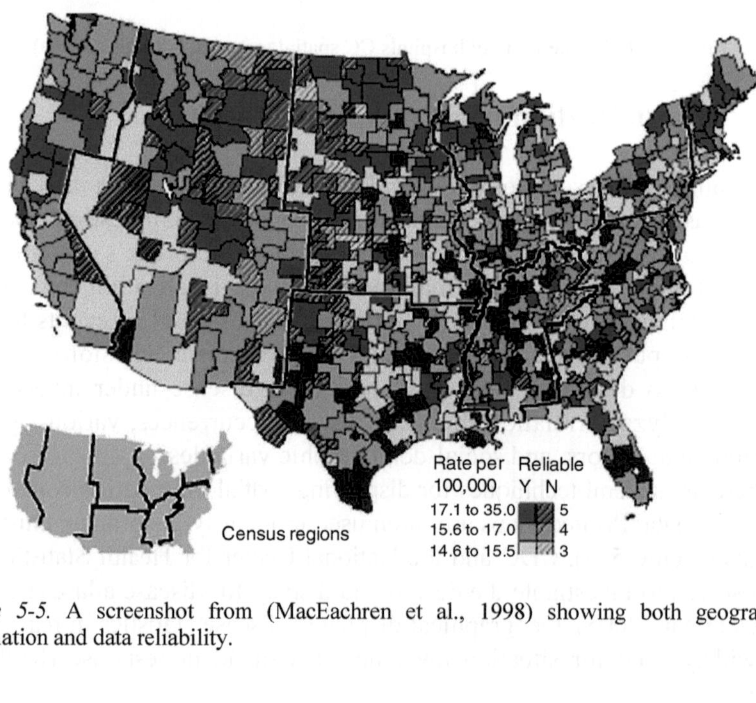

Figure 5-5. A screenshot from (MacEachren et al., 1998) showing both geographical information and data reliability.

2.3 GIS for Disease Event Visualization

Geographic Information System (GIS) is a powerful spatial information visualization tool and has found important applications in public health surveillance (2003c; Hurt-Mullen and Coberly, 2005; Lombardo et al., 2003). Most of the individual records registered into syndromic surveillance systems can often be georeferenced to a range of geographic areas such as blocks, tracts, county subdivisions, and other geographic units. Many syndromic surveillance systems (e.g., BioSense, RODS, ESSENCE, BioPortal, and RSVP) in the survey interface with GIS for disease visualization and spatial analytics.

The strength of GIS lies in its ability to integrate different types of data onto a common spatial platform. The integration of the environmental factors (e.g., groundwater contamination), demographical data and remote sensing data (e.g., satellite data) such as vegetation, land-use patterns and soil types, climatic changes, and so on, helps to identify and track the environmental characteristics and risks for epidemiological studies. First, GIS is a powerful tool for disease mapping and spatial visualization of environmental factors. In addition to visualization, disease outbreak detection and prediction based on the GIS analytical tools has been studied widely.

Geostatistical functions are provided in many statistical software packages. To date, the GIS softwares are capable of disease mapping, geographical correlation studies, disease clustering, spatial-temporal analysis, disease data visualization. S+SpatialStats, available from Mathsoft, implements lattice model estimators. Matlab has a Mapping Toolbox (Matlab), a collection of Matlab functions, user interfaces, sample data sets, and demos that read, write, display, and manipulate geospatial data, that contains Kriging functions and SpaceStat (TerraSeer) provides tools for exploratory spatial data analysis such as Moran's I, Geary's C and spatial regression methods including trend surface regression, spatial analysis of variance among others. The SAS Bridge from SAS bridges SAS and ESRI's ArcGIS9 by linking spatial, numeric, and textual data through a single interface, saving the efforts of customizing data transformation and transfer. In addition, GSLIB and GEOEAS among others are also serving the market. GEOEAS is a collection of interactive software tools for geostatistical analysis. The principal functions of the package are the production of grids and contour maps of interpolated (Kriged) estimates from sample data. GEOEAS can produce data maps, univariate statistics, scatter plots/linear regression, and variogram computation and model fitting. GSLIB (Geostatistical Software Library and related software) maintains a collection of geostatistical programs developed at Stanford University over the years. GSLIB provides variogram analysis and Kriging techniques. It also analyzes three-dimensional data sets.

ESRI is a leading GIS modeling and mapping software and technology provider. The Spatial Analyst, 3D analyst with ArcGIS, Geostatistical Analyst and Tracking Analyst tools have found their applications in disease monitoring, tracking and outbreak detection for various types of disease data [e.g., West Nile Virus (WNV)] (ESRI). Geostatistical Analyst provides ESDA (Exploratory Spatial Data Analysis), Deterministic interpolation methods and Kriging interpolation methods. Tracking Analyst of ArcGIS can map objects that move or change status through time. Figure 5-6 shows the screenshot when executing spatial-temporal Analysis using tracking analyst in ArcGIS, illustrating the evolvement of Hepatitis B in China during 1999–2001 (Zhong et al., 2005). In another application, the Missouri Department of Health and Senior Services employs ArcGIS for disease and bioterrorism surveillance by tracking syndromic information.

GeoMedStat is another GIS application developed at ESRI. Using GeoMedStat, real-time syndrome data (typically visits for each syndrome) can be mapped at the ZIP Code level within the state over a Web-based interface (Li et al., 2006).

By integrating GIS and the city's standardized location data with various agency-wide databases, the New York City Department of Health and Mental Hygiene (DOHMH) is able to analyze a range of health data and evaluate disease trends and their relationship with environmental conditions.

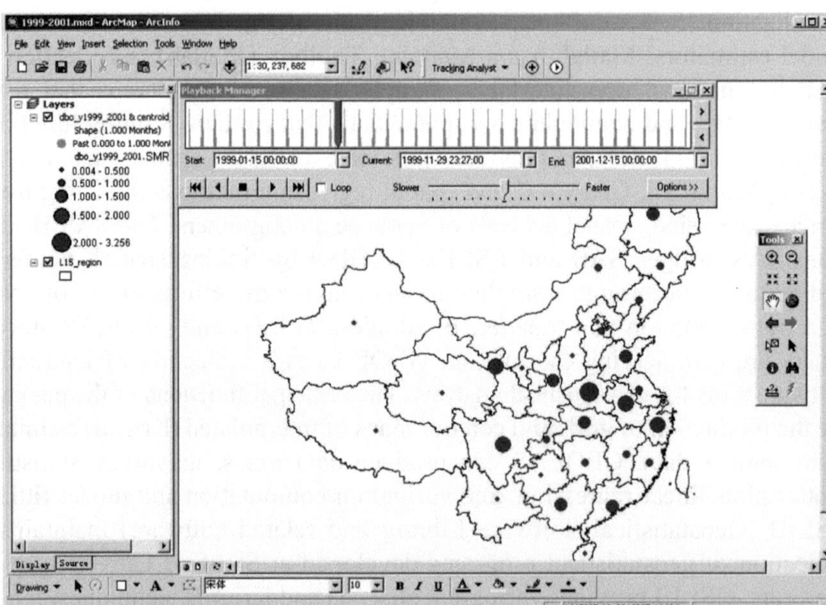

Figure 5-6. GIS application for disease incidence tracking (Zhong et al., 2005).

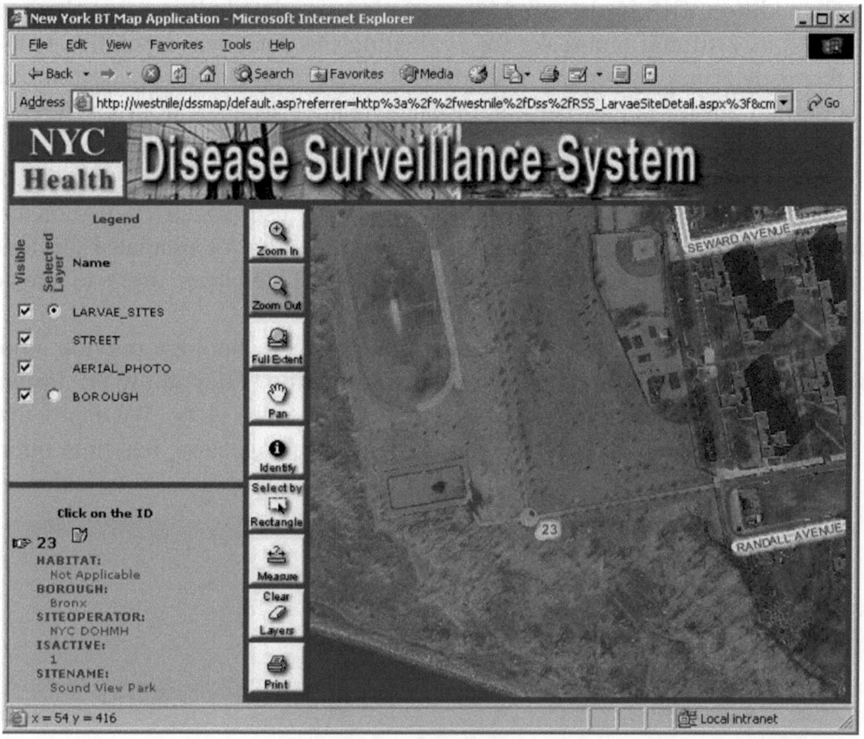

Figure 5-7. NYC disease surveillance system GIS view (2003a).

After West Nile Virus first appeared in the United States in the summer of 1999, DOHMH developed a vector and avian (mosquito and bird) tracking system using a GIS-enabled database and Intranet application. "The database is implemented with both spatial (ArcSDE) and relational (SQL Server) database management system software that allows staff to collect incoming information from the public through an ArcIMS software-enabled Web site" (Mostashari, 2002). The city's Bioterrorism Response Geographic Information System (BTRGIS) is also based on GIS technology.

GIS maps are also supported by Spatial Temporal Visualizer (STV) available from BioPortal disease surveillance system. The STV GIS view displays cases and sightings on a map, allowing the user to select multiple data sets (e.g., disease cases, natural land features, land-use elements) to be shown on the map in a layered manner using the checkboxes. It also supports dynamically generated views, zooming, brushing, and animation. In addition, it allows the user to invoke advanced spatial temporal analysis methods such as Prospective Support Vector Clustering (PSVC) (see Chapter 4 for details) and visually inspect their results through STV. A screenshot of GIS views from STV is shown in Figure 5-8.

In addition, GIS is also used in generating simulated cluster data that can be used as artificial outbreaks for evaluating the detection capability of the outbreak detection algorithms. The artificially generated clusters are customized for desired cluster radius, density, distance, relative location from a reference point, and temporal epidemiological growth pattern to explore a variety of the uncertainties for disease detection algorithm to test (Cassa et al., 2005; Watkins et al., 2005). For instance, based on user-specified parameters describing the location, properties, and temporal pattern of simulated clusters, the AEGIS Cluster Creation Tool (AEGIS-CCT) enables users to create simulated clusters with controlled feature sets.

Internet-based GIS technology and mobile GIS technology provide innovative mechanisms to facilitate flow of information. They allow the instant availability and accessibility of the information across the globe. We expect that the technologies can further facilitate the field data collection, real-time information sharing, and event investigations in the domain of disease surveillance.

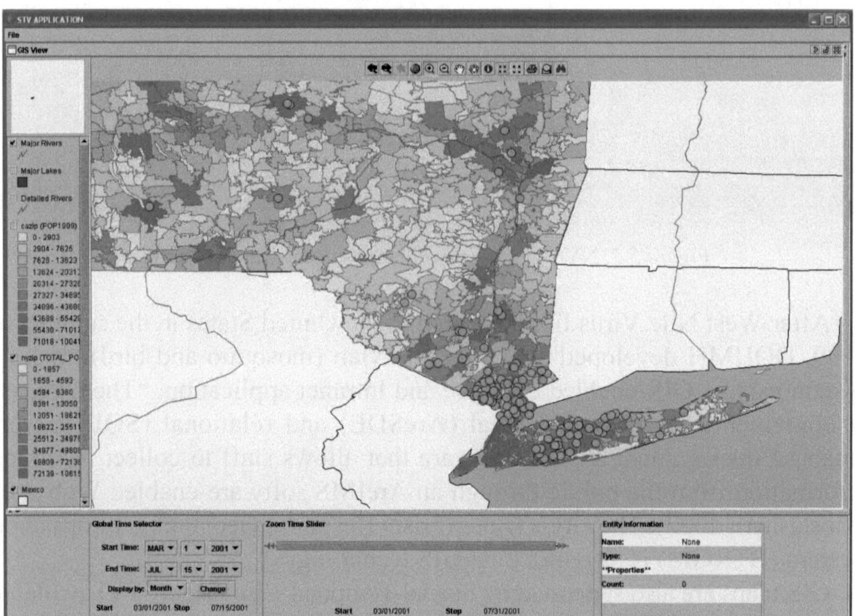

Figure 5-8. Visualization of dead bird cases distributed along populated areas near Hudson River by BioPortal STV (2006a).

2.4 Spatial-Temporal Disease Modeling and Other Visualization Examples

As an ongoing research project, IBM has developed a Spatio-temporal Epidemiological Modeler (STEM) to model and visualize the spatial and temporal models of emerging infectious diseases. The tool has built in GIS data and it integrates with Susceptible/Infectious/Recovered (SIR) and Susceptible/Exposed/Infectious/Recovered (SEIR) models.

The STEM model is one of the few works on visualizing the infectious disease spreading models. An example from STEM is shown in Figure 5-9.

"Policymakers responsible for creating strategies to contain diseases and prevent epidemics need an accurate understanding of disease dynamics and the likely outcomes of preventive actions. In an increasingly connected world with extremely efficient global transportation links, the vectors of infection can be quite complex. STEM facilitates the development of advanced mathematical models, the creation of flexible models involving multiple populations (species) and interactions between diseases, and a better understanding of epidemiology. The STEM application has built in GIS data for every county in the United States. It comes with data about county borders, populations, shared borders (neighbors), interstate highways, state highways, and airports" (Ford et al., 2005).

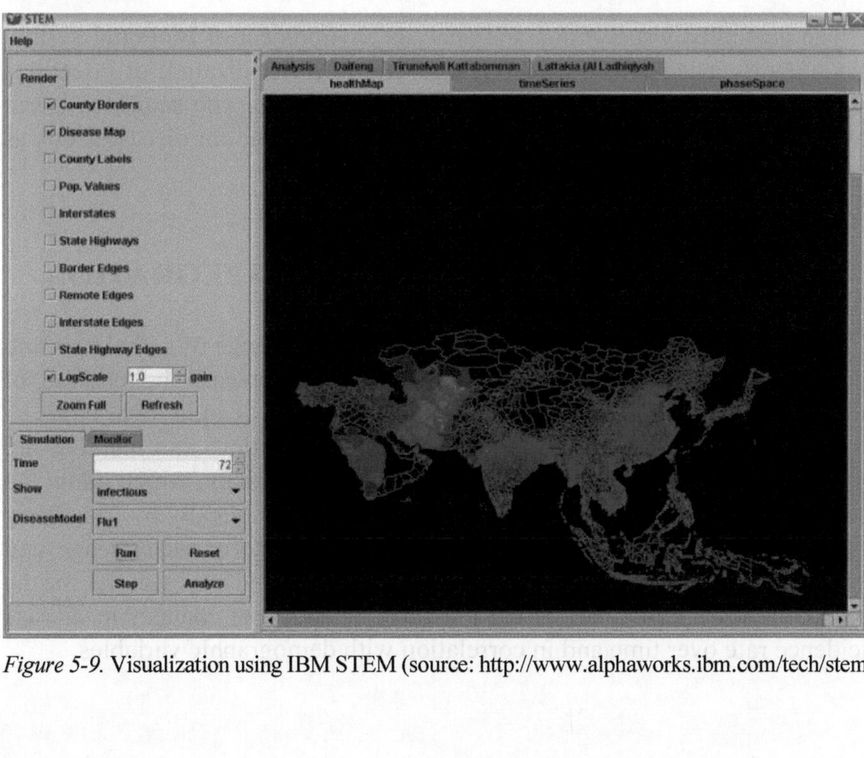

Figure 5-9. Visualization using IBM STEM (source: http://www.alphaworks.ibm.com/tech/stem).

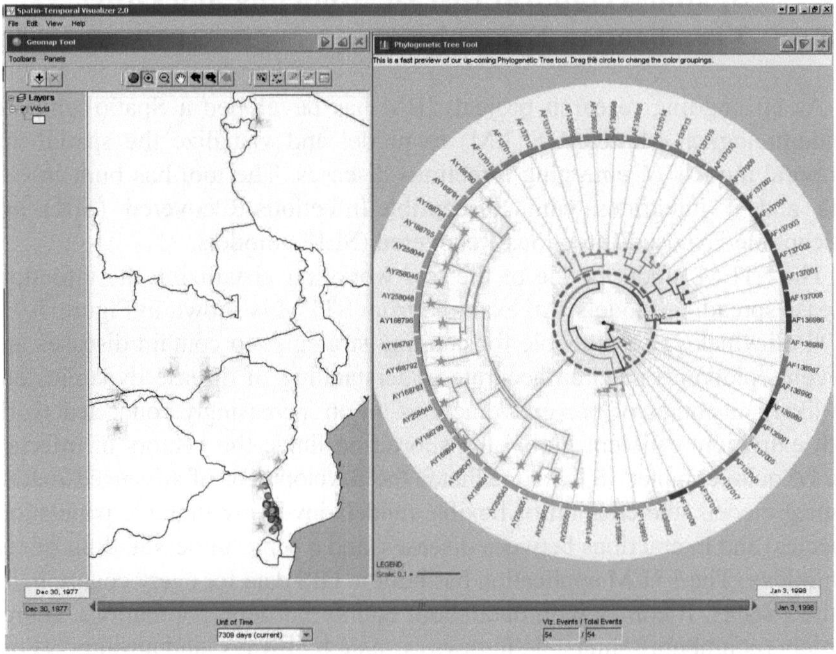

Figure 5-10. BioPortal visualizer with phylogenetic tree representation (2006a).

The integrated visualization and analysis environment of BioPortal system also supports a sequence-based phylogenetic tree visualization of infectious disease when gene sequence information is available. The sequence-based phylogenetic tree visualizer has been recently developed for diseases such as the Foot-and-Mouth disease as shown in Figure 5-10.

3. INTERACTIVE VISUAL DATA EXPLORATION

Interactive visual data exploration entails a wide range of techniques and operations for effective navigation on computer screens, the process of information query and, if needed, close examination of individual cases or patterns (Shneiderman, 1998). In particular, the operations and methods are expected to provide support for flexibility and interactivity, which allow the users to explore the information (e.g., a database) dynamically by specifying a year, a county, and the demographic querying criteria such as age and gender. Rapid, smooth screen changes on users' demand are essential for the perception of patterns, facilitating the early detection of changes in disease incidence rate over time and in correlation with demographic variables.

There are generally six types of interface functionality in syndromic surveillance applications: overview, zoom, filtering, details on demand, relate, and history (MacEachren et al., 1998). A typical surveillance task always involves a continuous combination of a set of functionalities of the six types.

As an example, the interactive visual data exploration environment from the BioPortal project, called the Spatial-Temporal Visualizer, supports all six elements to display disease hotspots (see Figure 5-11). This environment consists of a GIS display, a Gantt-chart temporal display, statistical plottings, and a time-range filter, which are all user controllable and synchronized.

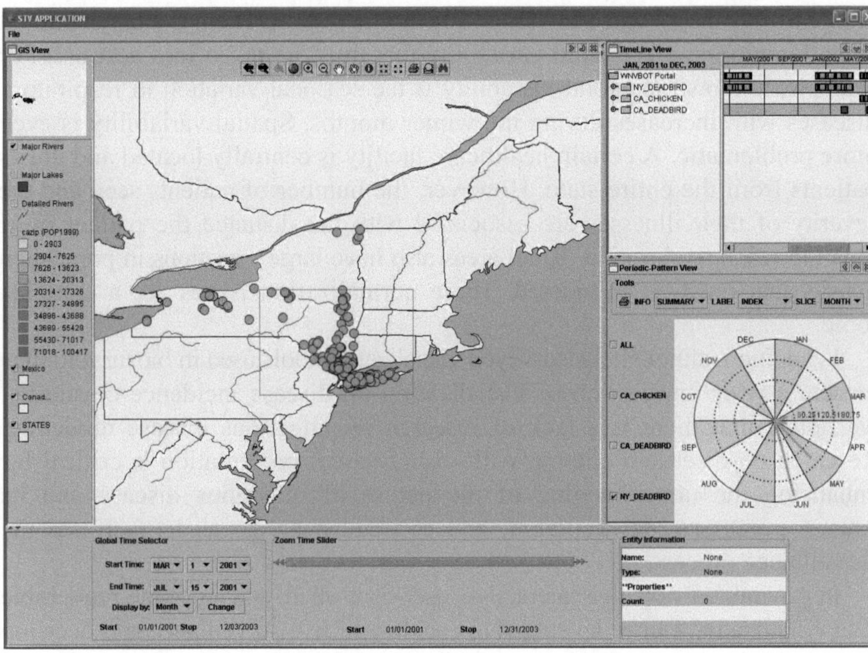

Figure 5-11. A screenshot of BioPortal's Spatial-Temporal Visualizer (2006a).

4. SUMMARY OF DATA VISUALIZATION IN SYNDROMIC SURVEILLANCE APPLICATIONS

In summary, we found that very few systems (e.g., BioPortal) support dynamic GIS functions or a full-blown interactive visual data exploration environment. Systems including RODS, ESSENCE, and BioSense provide limited support for interactive data exploration. Most syndromic surveillance systems support geographic displays of a local region with vector maps. All systems offer time-series plottings, arranged or aggregated by syndrome categories, ages, and other covariates.

There are several challenges with data visualization in syndromic surveillance. First, the number of maps generated daily for review is often large (Wagner et al., 2004b). For example, if there are 8 syndrome categories and 10 geographical regions, at least 80 maps need to be generated for daily review. If other parameters such as age and gender are also included in the analysis, the number of the maps generated quickly becomes unmanageable.

Therefore, automatic screening of the maps (e.g., based on anomaly detection algorithms) is critical.

Next, when the current research is focused around the best methods for automating the visual presentation and interpretation of the data, a major problem with spatial data analysis is data normalization. There is a large amount of both temporal and spatial variability that must be taken into account. For example, a known temporal variability is the seasonal variation in respiratory diseases with increases during the winter months. Spatial variability is even more problematic. A certain healthcare facility is centrally located and draws patients from the entire state. However, the number of patients seen and the severity of their illnesses are associated with the distance the patient must travel to reach the hospital. Rural areas also have large variations in population density that must be considered. These normalization issues are a complex topic.

In addition, although the surveyed visualization tools used in biosurveillance present a wide application of visualization on disease incidence clustering, we notice that there is a lack of research on infectious disease modeling. Research on disease modeling with visual model presentation is critical for enhancing the understanding of the nature of infectious disease and its causes, processes, development, and consequences, so as to facilitate the surveillance process.

In general, we note that interactive, user-controlled, and real-time renderable data visualization can be leveraged to enable effective surveillance and decision support, and represents an important research direction.

5. INFORMATION DISSEMINATION AND REPORTING

We summarize below some existing work on information dissemination channels for real time alerting and investigation process triggering. Information dissemination and alerting are concerned with managing and distributing daily or weekly public health updates and outbreak alerts for involved parties such as public health officials, analysts, primary care providers, and possible public safety and homeland security officials.

Existing syndromic surveillance information dissemination approaches include email, FAX, pager, phone calls, Web, and dedicated communication networks. These approaches differ greatly in their level of security, labor, and resources involved in the procedure, and delay in processing time.

A few nation-wide secure networks have been built for public health information dissemination and alerting. The CDC's Health Alert Network (HAN) serves as a communication backbone, linking public health departments in 37 states to CDC headquarters in Atlanta, and now is being expanded nationwide (2004b). The Epidemic Information Exchange (Epi-X) system is the CDC's secure, Web-based communications network that serves as an exchange between the CDC, state and local health departments, poison control centers, and other public health professionals (CDC, 2006b). Epi-X provides rapid reporting, immediate notification, and coordination of health investigations. The Public Health Information Network Messaging System (PHINMS) provides a secure and reliable messaging system for the PHIN (2003b; Barry and Kailar, 2005). PHINMS implements ebXML standard (Kotok, 2003) for bidirectional data transport, which offers high-quality encryption and authentication. An implementation of HAN- and PHINMS-based syndromic surveillance is described in (Daniel et al., 2005).

Most syndromic surveillance systems support multiple dissemination channels. The most commonly used methods, such as Email notification and voice communications, are relatively fast. Web-based messages and alerting networks are used less frequently. Secure network alerting with automatic role-based personnel directory access can be very useful in automatic and real-time alert distribution and is increasingly gaining acceptance.

Chapter 6

SYSTEM ASSESSMENT AND EVALUATION

Knowing how systems perform under various scenarios is important. We need to examine with which level of sensitivity and how quickly they can detect an outbreak or recognize a bioterrorism attack. Knowing the error rate of a system can help make decisions regarding how much effort is needed to investigate an alarm. The performance of the algorithms for outbreak characterization determines the amount of information they provide (e.g., sets of affected individuals, the outbreak size, and disease spreading rate), which provide important input for response planning.

Substantial costs can be incurred when developing or managing syndromic surveillance systems and investigating possible outbreaks based on the outputs of these systems (Reingold, 2003). For example, as reported in (Doroshenko et al., 2005), the annual cost of the NHS Direct Syndromic Surveillance System is about $280,000 and the usefulness of surveillance systems for early detection and response is yet to be established. Assessing the performance of surveillance systems is of significant importance for improving the efficacy of the investment in system development and management (Buehler et al., 2004).

As we discussed Chapter 4, dozens of different data analytical methods have been developed in the literature, and each method has its own limitations and strengths in different circumstances. One algorithm might work better when the size of the outbreak infected population is in a particular range. Another algorithm might have the lowest error rate in a slow-building but not a sudden-surge outbreak. Most researchers agree that no single algorithm can effectively cover the wide spectrum of all possible situations (Aamodt et al., 2006; Siegrist et al., 2004). As such, thoroughly evaluating different systems

H. Chen et al., *Infectious Disease Informatics: Syndromic Surveillance for Public Health and BioDefense*, Integrated Series in Information Systems 21, DOI 10.1007/978-1-4419-1278-7_6,

and analytical methods can provide important clues about their strengths and weaknesses, and their applicability in various application scenarios.

However, there fundamental difficulties in the evaluation of outbreak detection methods. The difficulties involve specification of the aberration of interest, and determining whether the aberration is of public health importance, caused by an infectious disease outbreak or not. In short, outbreaks are difficult to define precisely. Measurement of the validity of an outbreak detection method can be very complicated.

In this chapter, we first present a system evaluation framework that outlines three linked pieces of work evaluating communication components, outbreak detection algorithms, and system interface features. We then focus on evaluating outbreak detection algorithms along with syndrome classification algorithms. We then discuss the evaluation of data collection and information dissemination components and the system interface features. For each evaluation task, we introduce the commonly used measurement metrics. We also report representative evaluation results from a number of system evaluation studies employing the discussed measures.

1. SYNDROMIC SURVEILLANCE SYSTEM EVALUATION FRAMEWORK

CDC's Guidelines for Evaluating Surveillance Systems aim to address "the need for (a) the integration of surveillance and health information systems, (b) the establishment of data standards, (c) the electronic exchange of health data, and (d) changes in the objectives of public health surveillance to facilitate the response of public health to emerging health threats (e.g., new diseases)" (Buehler et al., 2004).

Many existing evaluation studies follow the guidelines of CDC's evaluation framework. This evaluation framework consists of a series of steps requiring the involvement of stakeholders, the description of system components, and the gathering of credible evidence regarding the system performance. It can serve as a checklist to guide the design and implementation of an evaluation procedure. Along with the description of the step-by-step tasks, relevant standards are also provided for each of the tasks for assessing the quality of the evaluation activities. Simplicity, flexibility, data quality, acceptability, sensitivity, predictive value positive (PVP), representativeness, timeliness, and stability need to quantified or described. These standards will be further developed later in this chapter when we discuss evaluation of specific components of syndromic surveillance systems.

Our evaluation framework in general follows the CDC evaluation framework but treats major system components separately for the purpose of performance analysis, considering their differences in terms of performance metrics, and visibility to different set of users. The specific evaluation tasks include evaluation of outbreak detection algorithms, data collection and information dissemination components, and system interface features.

2. EVALUATION OF OUTBREAK DETECTION ALGORITHMS

2.1 Evaluation Methodology

Simulation is one of the well-developed computational methodologies that can be applied to testing outbreak detection algorithms' validity and reliability. Different types of simulated signals, different days of duration, and different case distributions need to be specified in a simulation study, representing a realization of the system dynamic behavior. Tunable replications of simulation also enable the examination of alternative solutions. In addition, because of its flexibility and direct mapping to real-world entities, simulation can be used for training purposes and produce useful animated visual outputs.

On the basis of the extent of data authenticity, three types of simulation are possible. One is to use real data collected from real outbreaks. However, because the number of real outbreaks is small (Siegrist and Pavlin, 2004), it is very difficult to test outbreak detection algorithms using completely authentic data. Simulated outbreaks can also be superimposed on real data to provide additional tests for model validity. There are fully synthetic data-based simulation and semisynthetic data-based simulation. Without actual outbreak data, simulation-based evaluation, in particular, the fully synthetic data-based simulation, often demonstrates only limited validity (Kleinman et al., 2005b).

2.2 Real Data Testing

Running outbreak detection algorithms on real data provides the strongest and most direct validity tests. But the lack of surveillance data with real disease outbreaks makes it difficult for real data testing. There are very few published evaluation works that use real data with sufficient sample size to test outbreak detection algorithms. These few studies include the retrospective analysis by Hogan et al. (2003), a retrospective evaluation study (Ivanov et al., 2003), and the Bio-ALIRT Biosurveillance Detection Algorithm Evaluation program (Siegrist and Pavlin, 2004).

In Hogan et al.'s study, two types of real data – sales of electrolyte products and hospital diagnoses – were collected from six urban regions in three states for the period 1998 through 2001. The gold standard outbreaks are 18 significant increases in respiratory and diarrheal disease in the data. Time gain using the sales of electrolyte products to signal outbreaks of respiratory and diarrheal diseases in children compared with the hospital diagnoses were seen.

Ivanov et al. (2003) conducted a retrospective evaluation study evaluating chief complaints and the EWMA detection algorithm employing gold standard outbreaks obtained from a dataset derived from the Utah Hospital Discharge Database for the years 1998–2001 inclusive.

In the Bio-ALIRT Biosurveillance Detection Algorithm Evaluation program conducted by Siegrist et al., real historic deidentified data were obtained from five metropolitan areas over 23 months. Two natural disease outbreak cases in the data identified and labeled by an outbreak detection group were used as the gold standard. The study reports the difficulty in determining how quickly an algorithm might detect an attack is due to the fact that minimal data exists for an actual biologic attack. The limitations of real data testing are discussed, including the uncertainty about the exact start date and size of outbreaks and the inability to examine algorithm outbreak-detection capabilities under a substantial number of diverse conditions.

2.3 Fully Synthetic Data Testing

To address the data problem, synthetic data or semisynthetic data are often used in characterizing the performance of the outbreak detection algorithms.

Simulators are designed to generate the surveillance data such as illness incidences, drug purchases, physician visits that can best mimic the realization with careful characterization of an outbreak event and sick people's healthcare seeking behaviors.

A number of methods have been applied to generate these synthetic data. One is to use the outbreak detection algorithm itself by running it backwards to generate the illness incidence data. This kind of evaluation process was used to evaluate WSARE (Wagner et al., 2006).

Another method composes the shapes of outbreak signals by looking at the historical outbreaks. Figure 6-1 shows five temporal distributions used in one simulation study (Jackson et al., 2007). The temporal distributions are extracted from the epidemic curves of historic outbreaks, representing several ways in which a pathogen could spread through a community. They then specify the range of outbreak signal durations, and ranges of sizes of populations affected to generate a number of simulated outbreaks.

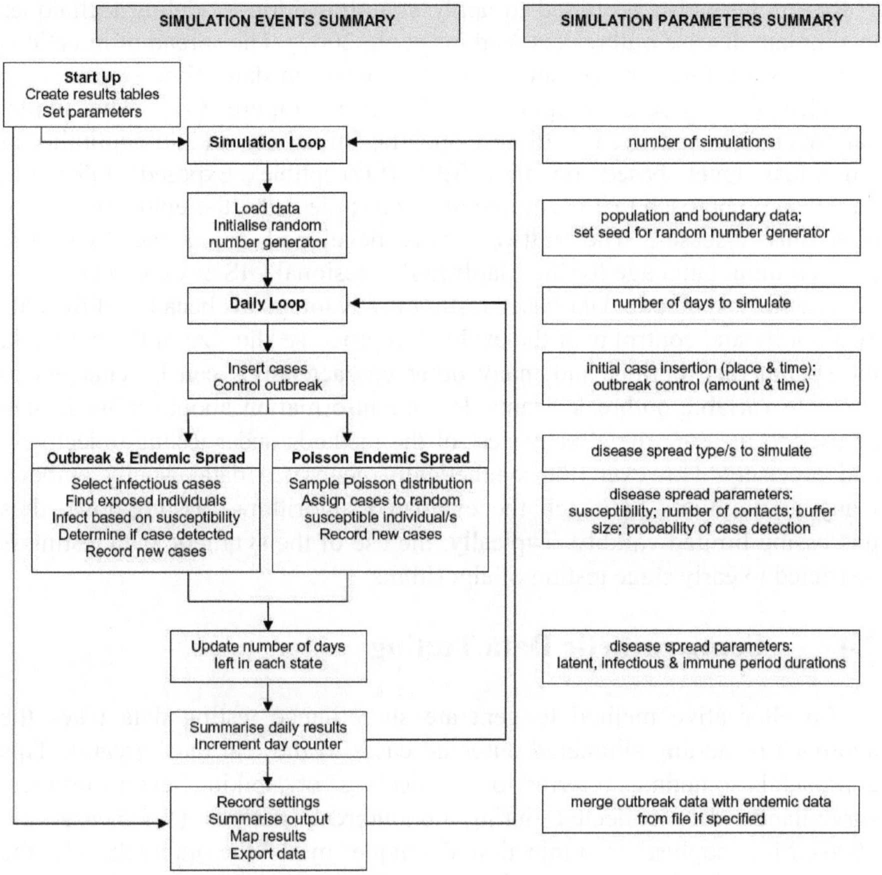

Figure 6-1. Simulation process diagram (Watkins et al., 2007).

A third method is agent-based method. Agent-based simulators (e.g., BioWar (Carley et al., 2003)) are also used to generate the surveillance data that best represent the realistic outbreak events by modeling the social and epidemiological characterization of public health status, which describes how people acquire diseases, manifest symptoms, seek information, and seek care. RODS also developed a CityBN (City Bayesian Network) simulator to validate the WSARE algorithm. The CityBN simulator runs on a large Bayesian network whose structure and parameters are created by hand. The Bayesian network introduces temporal dynamics based on a variety of factors such as weather and food conditions (Wong et al., 2005).

Researchers also proposed to apply state-transition modeling techniques to simulate disease outbreaks (Watkins et al., 2007). The spread of infectious diseases transmitted by person-to-person contact in daily time steps can be modeled (the process diagram is shown in Figure 6-1). The model parameters are specified as disease-specific infectivity and susceptibility at individual level based on the SEIR (Susceptible, Exposed, Infectious, Recovered) approach that is commonly used to describe the epidemiology of infectious diseases. The software was developed using the MapBasic programming language for the MapInfo Professional GIS environment.

The fully synthetic data-based testing is advantageous because of the data availability and control over the evaluation process. The size of the outbreak, the spatial distribution, and many other characteristics can be changed to simulate variable outbreak events. Precise information about outbreaks can be used to measure the effectiveness of the methods under testing objectively and precisely. However, the synthetically generated data usually embody many assumptions to match the evaluated algorithms' assumptions, thus possessing limited validity. Typically, the use of the synthetic data testing is restricted to early stage testing of algorithms.

2.4 Semisynthetic Data Testing

An alternative method to generate surveillance testing data takes the approach of adding simulated outbreak cases to the real data streams. This approach is sometimes referred to as "injecting" or "spiking" events into real surveillance data collected during nonoutbreak periods (Wagner et al., 2006). More sophisticated injection techniques model the outbreaks with the shape and noise level derived from surveillance data collected during real outbreaks. The high-fidelity detectability experiments (HiFIDE) are available for noncommercial use.

Most of the evaluation studies take this approach for system evaluation (Reis et al., 2003; Goldenberg et al., 2002). In the evaluation work of EARS (Hutwagner et al., 2005a), for instance, 56,000 sets of artificially generated case-count data are generated based on 56 sets of parameters using a negative binomial distribution with superimposed outbreaks. The ESSENCE II system is evaluated using simulated bioterrorism events with estimated patterns from the literature (Lombardo et al., 2003).

The semisynthetic approach provides greater validity than the fully synthetic data-based testing. It allows for flexible manipulation of outbreak sizes and the shapes of the spikes as well as the time courses of each injected event. In-depth understanding of the dynamics of real outbreaks is crucial for the fidelity of the injected outbreaks.

2.5 Evaluation Metrics for Outbreak Detection Algorithms

The main concerns regarding anomaly detection algorithms include how significant the signal needs to be to trigger an alarm, how early an outbreak can be detected, and how reliable the alarms are. Various aspects of outbreak detection algorithms need to be evaluated using different evaluation criteria. Such criteria include the quantification of sensitivity, predictive value positive, timeliness, false alarm rate, generalized ROC curves, and average run length. These criteria are in line with the CDC evaluation guidelines (CDC, 2001) and the prior literature (Buehler et al., 2004; Romaguera et al., 2000). Table 6-1 summarized the outbreak detection metrics in the most commonly used representations in the literature. A more detailed summary of detection algorithm evaluation metrics can also be found in (Buckeridge et al., 2005b).

Three metrics – sensitivity, false alarm rate or the alternative measure to the false alarm rate – predictive value positive and timeliness, are most commonly seen in the literature (Buckeridge et al., 2004; Sonesson and Bock, 2003). Sensitivity measures the probability that an alarm is correctly triggered when an outbreak indeed occurs. False alarm rate measures the

Table 6-1. Outbreak detection metrics.

Terms	Descriptions
Sensitivity	The proportion of outbreaks that an algorithm detected correctly (Wagner et al., 2006)
Specificity	The proportion of nonoutbreaks days without alarms (Wagner et al., 2006)
Predictive Value Positive (PVP)	The proportion of alarms signaled as outbreaks are truly outbreaks (CDC, 2001)
Timeliness (time-to-detection)	The difference between the date of the first true alarm and a reference date (e.g., a date established as a start date of an outbreak by expert consensus) (Wagner et al., 2006)
False alarm rate	The proportion of nonoutbreak time periods (days or weeks depending on the organization of the time series) on which an algorithm signals alarms (Wagner et al., 2006)
ROC curve	Plot of sensitivity versus false alarm rate
AMOC curve	Plot of timeliness against false alarm rate
ARL^0	Expected run length until the first false alarm (Sonesson and Bock, 2003)
ARL^1	Expected run length until an alarm (Sonesson and Bock, 2003)

ROC: Receiver Operating Characteristic

AMOC: Activity Monitoring Operating Characteristic

ARL: Average Run Length

probability that an alarm is triggered when there is no outbreak. The measurement of sensitivity and PVP for a syndromic surveillance system is often complicated by the absence of an appropriate gold standard (German, 2000). A gold standard is assumed to be accurate and can be used to validate the signals produced by an outbreak detection system.

There exists a tradeoff when trying to achieve good performance among multiple evaluation criteria (Buckeridge et al., 2004; Siegrist and Pavlin, 2004). The Receiver Operating Characteristics (ROC) curve and the area beneath it are further evaluation metrics that plot sensitivity against false alarm rate (Reis and Mandl, 2003). Through the AMOC (Activity Monitoring Operating Characteristic) curve plotting timeliness against false alarm rate, the evaluators can easily read the tradeoff between the false alarm rate and the timeliness.

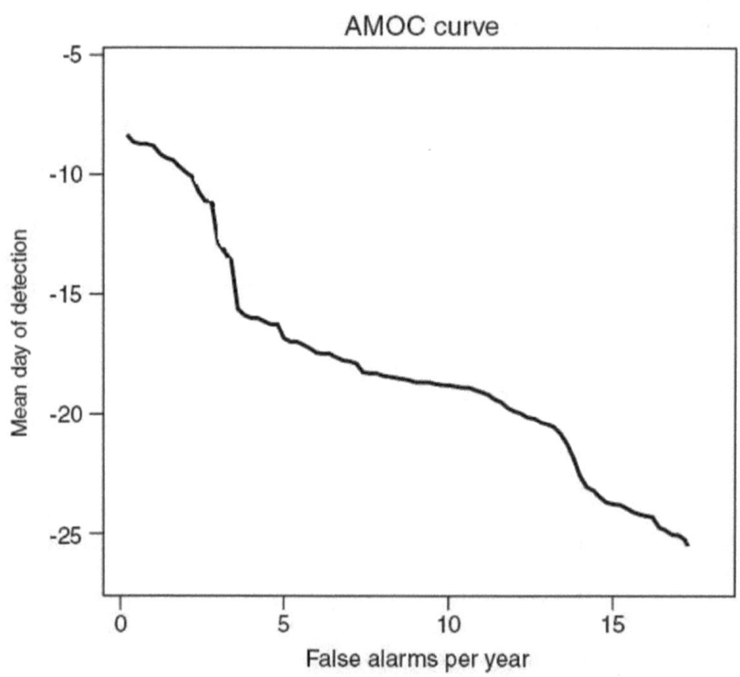

(a) Fictional AMOC curve.

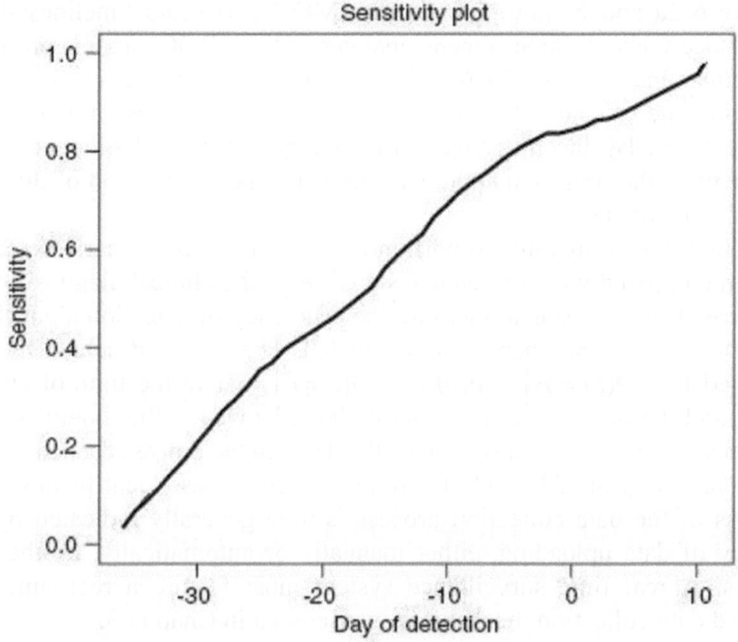

(b) Timeliness-ROC curve.

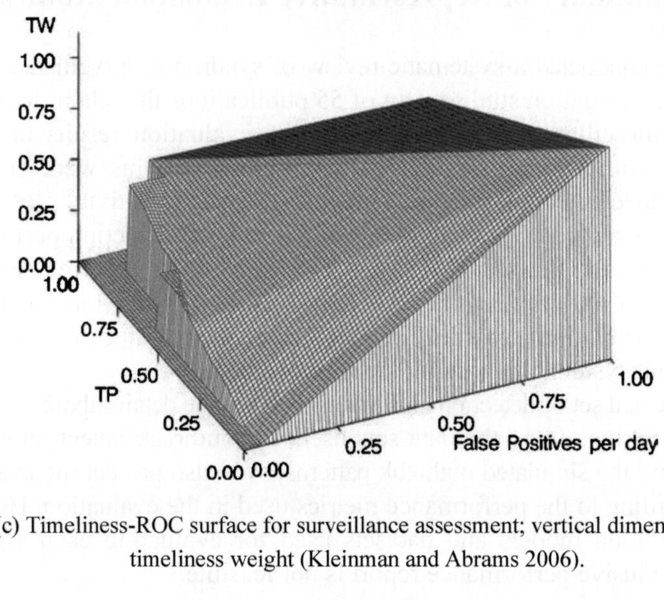

(c) Timeliness-ROC surface for surveillance assessment; vertical dimension is the timeliness weight (Kleinman and Abrams 2006).

Figure 6-2. Fictional AMOC curve, timeliness-ROC curve and timeliness-ROC surface.

Figure 6-2a and b show a fictional AMOC curve and timeliness-ROC curve, respectively. A three-dimensional generalized ROC curve is proposed by Kleinman and Abrams (2006). The 3-D ROC curve incorporates the time of detection and produces the timeliness-ROC surfaces (an example is shown in Figure 6-2c). By incorporating sensitivity, specificity and timeliness into single metrics, the proposed approach simplifies the comparison of different methods' performance.

Timeliness measures the proportion of time gained by an early detection algorithm compared with a reference signal (e.g., the clinical diagnosis of an anthrax case). As a means to measure the efficiency of detection algorithms, it refers to how fast an aberration is signaled. The expected delay time can be denoted by $ED(t) = E\left[\max(0, t_{\mathrm{A}} - t) \middle| \tau = t\right]$, where the time of change is $\tau = t$, and the time of alarm triggering is t_{A}. However, the timeliness of a surveillance process should also include the delay in the process data collection and case reporting in addition to the time for disease case identification. The timeliness of the data collection process is now generally indicated by the frequency of data uploading, either manually or automatically, by the data providers. A real time surveillance system must feature a real time and automated data collection mechanism as discussed in Chapter 3.

2.6 Summary of Representative Evaluation Studies

We have conducted a systematic review of syndromic surveillance system performance evaluation studies. Out of 55 publications that claim to evaluate syndromic surveillance systems, 32 reported evaluation results or system experiences with varying degrees of detail. Two systems were compared with a reference detection system. Timeliness versus sensitivity plotting was provided in 19 quantitative evaluations of algorithms' detection performance (e.g., WSARE, SaTScan, and RSVC). Twelve systems reported sensitivity and false alarm rate through the ROC curve. A few evaluations such as the BioALIRT evaluation program are conducted to examine the algorithms from different systems for side-by-side comparison.

For a selected set of detection algorithms, we provide details about evaluation design and settings (e.g., the data sets used, the outbreak detection methods evaluated, and the simulated outbreak patterns). We also present the evaluation results according to the performance metrics used in the evaluation. However, as the simulation models and datasets used for evaluating each algorithm differ, a conclusive performance report is not feasible.

Table 6-2. Summary of evaluation results on a selected set of syndromic surveillance systems.

Syndromes	Dataset	Evaluated system	Evaluated methods	Outbreak patterns	Criteria	Results
Respiratory infection	Daily hospital ED visit data (Mar. 2002–Dec. 2003) from Hillsborough County, Florida	EARS	P-chart C2 C3 MA [EARS] EWMA	Slow-building or sudden-surge trend	CARL ROC	The use of C2 and P-chart for timely surveillance is suggested when the syndromic data are moderately correlated (Zhu et al., 2005)
National and state pneumonia, influenza data and hospital influenza-like illness	56,000 sets of artificially generated case-count data based on 56 sets of parameters, with superimposed outbreaks	EARS (Hutwagner et al., 2005a)	C1-mild, C2-medium, C3-Ultra, the historical limits method and the seasonally adjusted CUSUM	Log normal, a rapidly increasing outbreak; inverted log normal, a slowly starting outbreak; a single-day spike	Sensitivity, specificity, time to detection	These simulations demonstrate that the methods for aberration detection that require little baseline data, C1, C2, and C3, are as sensitive and specific as the historical limits and seasonally adjusted CUSUM methods
Six syndromes (unspecified)	Simulated data generated from surveillance data in ED during several large public events in the United States	EARS (Hutwagner et al., 2005b)	C1-mild, C2-medium, and C3-ultra	The aberrations were added to the baseline data using a random binomial distribution	Levels of sensitivity, specificity, false positive rates	For the six syndromes, sensitivity for C1, C2, and C3-models averaged 48, 51, and 54%. The specificities averaged 98, 98, and 96%, respectively. The average false-positive rates were 32, 29, and 42%, respectively
Respiratory and gastrointestinal syndromes	Historic de-identified data obtained from five metropolitan areas over 23 months	2003 Bio-ALIRT algorithm evaluation	SPC, Bayesian change-point, wavelet methods, RODS, ESSENCE, EARS, and General Dynamics and IBM (Siegrist et al., 2004)	Actual outbreaks embedded in the data	Timeliness and sensitivity versus false-positive rates	The best algorithms (anonymous) were able to detect all of the outbreaks at false-alert rates of one every 2–6 weeks. However, whether certain algorithms were better overall than others was not determined

Syndromes	Dataset	Evaluated system	Evaluated methods	Outbreak patterns	Criteria	Results
Simulated data	Hospital ED respiratory syndrome counts, office visits, respiratory counts, OTC influenza medication sales, and school absentee totals.	ESSENCE II	Methods in ESSENCE II	Simulated bioterrorism events with estimated patterns from the literature	Sensitivity, specificity	The number of infected people is varied to achieve a detector performance with a sensitivity of 0.95 and a specificity of 0.97 (Lombardo et al., 2003)
Influenza	ICD-coded chief complaints (Dec 4, 1999 – Dec 1, 2000)	RODS	Serfling method [RODS]		Sensitivity, PVP, timeliness	For a one-year period, the detectors had sensitivity of 100% and PVP of 50% for RS and 25% for IS. The timeliness of detection using ICD-9–coded chief complaints was one week earlier than the detection using Pneumonia and Influenza deaths (Espino and Wagner, 2001; Tsui et al., 2001)
Influenza-like illness (ILI)	New York City Emergency Medical Services (EMS) ambulance dispatch data	New York City EMS	Data quality Case detection algorithm		Sensitivity, PVP	The selected call types had a sensitivity of 58% for clinical ILI, and a PVP of 22% (Greenko et al., 2003)

3. EVALUATION OF DATA COLLECTION AND INFORMATION DISSEMINATION COMPONENTS

The system components for data collection and information dissemination need to be evaluated in terms of HIPAA compliance, scalability, and flexibility.

HIPAA privacy rules govern the obligations and reporting requirements of healthcare data (CDC, 2003). HIPAA security regulations require methods that protect data from disclosure in transport. To be HIPAA compliant, data collection and dissemination components of syndromic surveillance systems need to provide security measures such as data encryption, secure sockets, secure shell tunneling, or the use of a virtual private network.

System scalability and flexibility indicate how scalable a syndromic surveillance system is in monitoring new diseases, accommodating new syndrome categories, or incorporating new types of data. Geographic coverage should be able to be expanded with small costs as additional healthcare facilities and jurisdictions participate. In addition, systems that use standard data formats (e.g., in electronic data interchange) can easily interoperate with other systems and thus might be considered more flexible and more scalable (CDC, 2001).

4. ASSESSMENT OF INTERFACE FEATURES AND SYSTEM USABILITY

4.1 System Usability Evaluation Methodology

To complete our discussion of system evaluation, the performance of operational systems bringing in the users' operation experiences need to be evaluated. The effectiveness (or value) of a syndromic surveillance system depends greatly on the outcome associated with their use of the system. The evaluation process usually employs two methodologies: controlled experiment and field testing. Controlled experiments consider the users' experience with the interaction with the system interfaces for completion of a particular operation. Field testing evaluates operational systems mainly for the measurement of the benefit, and the cost from a perspective of societal utility (Wagner et al., 2006). It takes into account how long it takes to deploy a system, what the system failure rate is, and so on.

4.2 System Usability Evaluation Metrics

In the evaluation work for the BioPortal system, Hu et al. (2005) applied a number quantitative or qualitative metrics for system usability evaluation. (1) Task accuracy: the correctness of the user generated analysis results using the system referenced to the experts' analysis results; (2) Task efficiency: measuring the amount of time a person needs to complete an analysis task; (3) User satisfaction: end-user satisfaction typically encompasses system content, accuracy, output format, use, and timeliness; (4) Perceived usefulness: it refers to the extent to which a person considers a system useful in his or her work role and has been shown to affect user adoption significantly; (5) Perceived ease of use: the ease of use of a system, as perceived by individual users refers to the degree to which a person believes that using a particular system will be free of effort.

Wagner summarized a group of measurable system benefits and cost related system features in his recent work on field testing of biosurveillance systems (Wagner et al., 2006). The metrics are: (1) Benefits from expected reductions in mortality and morbidity through earlier detection; (2) Benefits [usefulness, simplicity, representativeness (CDC, 2001)] from expected reductions in operational costs owing to policy improvements and workflow efficiency; (3) Costs to build or purchase and install, and costs of staff time on alarms monitoring and investigation and certain other metrics.

4.3 Summary of System Usability Evaluation Studies

The evaluation study conducted by Hu et al. (2005) is representative of research examining syndromic surveillance system usability issues, such as readability, learning curve, and decision making assistance. They used the User Interaction Satisfaction (QUIS) instrument by Chin et al. (1988) to evaluate the usability of the BioPortal system, based on the Object-Action Interface model developed by Shneiderman (1998). They examined the overall reactions to the system, the screen layout and sequence, the system's capability, the terminology/information used, and subjects' ease of learning, based on a 9-Point Likert scale (Hu et al., 2005).

From a user's perspective, all relevant data must be seamlessly integrated to support the surveillance and analysis tasks that are critical to the prevention of and alerts about particular disease events or devastating outbreaks. Data visualization support is also critical; the value of a syndromic surveillance system is greatly affected by the extent to which the system can present data and analysis results in an easily comprehensible, cognitively efficient manner. Ultimately, a syndromic surveillance system must facilitate and enhance the analysis tasks by public health professionals in terms of accuracy and time requirements, using their own heuristics and preferred analysis methods.

5. SUMMARY AND DISCUSSION

Evaluation of syndromic surveillance systems is confounded by a number of factors. First, few real-world datasets are available for evaluation and comparison purposes due to the low frequency or absence of outbreaks of most diseases. Second, timeliness of detection is closely related to the timing of patient visits or medication purchases, determined by individual patients' behavior. Third, data quality and availability are seldom considered in algorithm evaluations. Incomplete data from various healthcare participants can potentially impair algorithms' detection power.

Fourth, the criteria for optimized detection performance may vary for different illnesses. Different bioterrorism agents display different temporal and spatial patterns. Botulism and toxic shock syndrome are readily detected in relatively smaller clusters, whereas detection of SARS presents a greater challenge as the syndrome is relatively less specific and the impact may be more widely spread. The incubation time and the time between exposure and symptom onset could be longer or shorter depending on the type of biologic agent. The detection power of the algorithms for rare diseases (e.g., botulism-like illness or smallpox) is yet to be reported.

Lastly, the ability of an algorithm to identify the geographic location of an outbreak was rarely measured and reported. In spatial context, the signal extent is not usually considered. For example, in a scan-like method, the radius of a detected cluster could indicate a kind of accuracy of the detection method. The cluster validity measurement techniques discussed in a few works (Halkidi et al., 2002) seem ready to check the clustering algorithms' performance.

Part II

SYNDROMIC SURVEILLANCE SYSTEM CASE STUDIES

To better illustrate the earlier discussion on syndromic surveillance data sources, various technical components of syndromic surveillance systems, and related implementation issues, we present several case studies in Part II of this monograph. With case studies 1–6, we describe the system components in detail roughly following the structure of Chapters 3–5.

Increasingly, Web-based electronic information sources such as discussion forums, mailing lists, government Web sites, and news outlets are becoming major information sources for early infectious disease detection. Real-time data communication and advanced data mining technologies combined with interactive visualization technologies, provide unseen opportunities for accessing and integrating global information sources for disease surveillance. The following two cases are used to exemplify the efforts dedicated for global disease surveillance based on online information. Two systems, HealthMap and Argus, will be presented as cases 7 and 8, respectively.

In Chapters 7–14, we investigated eight biosurveillance systems in depth. They vary in operational coverage, some being national practice or functioning at an international scale, and the others being deployed locally.

Case 1: The first case study focuses on the BioSense system, which is a nationwide "safety net" for early detection in major cities, initiated and administrated by the US CDC. BioSense represents a major effort on infrastructure building targeted at near real-time data collection at local, state, and national levels.

During the wildfires in San Diego County in October 2007, the CDC BioSense system found a spike in respiratory illnesses that coincided with the wildfires in San Diego County. BioSense was set up to receive data from the emergency departments of six hospitals near the wildfire zones. BioSense identified significant increases in diagnoses of various respiratory syndromes ($p < 0.001$), particularly asthma ($p = 0.001$) and dyspnea ($p < 0.001$). Details of BioSense's use as a drop-in biosurveillance system during the San Diego wildfires are presented in Section 4 of Chapter 7.

Case 2: The second case study examines the Real-time Outbreak and Disease Surveillance (RODS) system, which has been deployed across the nation. The RODS project is a collaborative effort between the University of Pittsburg and Carnegie Mellon University. It provides a computing platform for the implementation and evaluation of different analytic approaches for outbreak detection, among other data collection and reporting functions. The National Retail Data Monitor (NRDM) monitoring anonymous sales of over-the-counter (OTC) healthcare products is part of the RODS project assisting with disease outbreaks identification. Thousands of retail pharmacy, grocery, and mass merchandise operations have participated in the NRDM nationwide.

RODS was implemented in Utah during the 2002 Winter Olympics. The implementation focused on the surveillance process automation and real-time communication that are essential for short-term drop-in situations such as international games or other gatherings. We discussed this implementation in detail as a RODS use case at the end of Chapter 8. Emphases are placed upon technical and operational aspects of the system implementation, including secure network infrastructure and messaging standards for automated data acquisition, data surveillance techniques including natural language processors, detection algorithms, notification systems, and user interfaces.

Case 3: The third case study examines the BioPortal system. Funded by the US National Science Foundation (NSF) and US Department of Homeland Security (DHS), the BioPortal project was initiated in 2003. This system is unique for its Web-based, highly interactive, and customizable spatial-temporal data visualization and analysis. This visualization and analysis environment provides integrated support for sequence-based phylogenetic tree visualization when sequence information is available. BioPortal enables epidemiological data sharing across jurisdictions. It also provides support for syndromic surveillance based on free-text chief complaints (in both English and Chinese). In addition to human infectious diseases, BioPortal has been applied to animal diseases such as Foot-and-Mouth disease (FMD).

FMD disease is a highly contagious and sometimes fatal viral disease of cloven-hoofed animals such as cattle, water buffalo, sheep, goats, and pigs. There were a number of epidemics and outbreaks in the US, UK, and Taiwan in recent history. In 2005, an Asia-I strain of FMD appeared in the eastern provinces of China. BioPortal collaborated with the FMD Laboratory at the University of California, Davis, which is dedicated to a global surveillance for FMD disease by gathering global FMD related information, identifying surrogates of risks and modeling and predicting FMD virus evolution. The detailed discussions about the FMD BioPortal in Section 4 of Chapter 9 highlight the significance as well as difficulties of operating a global surveillance system for animal diseases.

Case 4: The fourth example system is the Electronic Surveillance System for the Early Notification of Community-Based Epidemics (ESSENCE). The system monitors both military and civilian healthcare data daily for early outbreak detection and warning.

Case 5: We use the New York City syndromic surveillance systems as a case to illustrate the citywide surveillance activities in public health practice, discussing its uniqueness in the aspects of operational, response, and research components that are integrated within a health department. Field investigation experiences should be shared among the syndromic surveillance practitioners.

The NYC Emergency Department (ED) syndromic surveillance approach was practiced for respiratory illness in 2005. The practice focuses on not only detecting abnormal increases in respiratory illness visits but also determining and characterizing the cause of such increases. They took a "data fusion" approach, i.e., monitoring and investigating multiple data sources instead of relying on a single data source. This practice is presented in detail toward the end of Chapter 11.

Case 6: The Early Aberration Reporting System (EARS) of the US CDC is widely deployed in local and state public health departments and has helped public health officials to monitor, analyze, and report unusual trends or clusters in public health surveillance data. The aberration detection methods implemented in EARS are tested in a number of circumstances. Experiences of syndromic surveillance practices with EARS are accumulated regarding the tuning of the system, the interpretation of the output and the investigation process.

EARS was seen as a critical infectious disease surveillance system during the devastating hurricane disasters in Louisiana, Mississippi, and Texas in September and October of 2005. We present the implementation and operation of details as a use case of the EARS system for public health awareness preparedness during natural disasters.

Case 7: The Argus system has been developed to perform biological event detection and tracking on a global scale, by examining indications and warnings of social disruptions. It actively tracks avian influenza and 130 other infectious diseases.

Case 8: HealthMap is a Web application that automatically queries, filters, integrates, and visualizes unstructured electronic reports on disease outbreaks. It collects disease-related online information from around the world, including news media, expert-curated accounts, and validated official alerts. The system automatically classifies alerts by location and disease and then overlays them on an interactive geographic map.

In April 2009, a new strain of influenza known as H1N1 flu (swine flu) was first detected. HealthMap reported the detection of Swine Flu cases weeks before the news emerged in English-language resources. It is a real-time integrated news outlet to enhance the awareness of H1N1 flu outbreaks for the public around the world. Details of this practice are discussed as a HealthMap case study toward the end of Chapter 14.

Chapter 7

BIOSENSE

BioSense is part of the US CDC's Public Health Information Network (PHIN) framework managed through the CDC BioIntelligence Center. It supports early outbreak detection at the local, state, and national levels, by monitoring the size, location, and rate of spread of an outbreak; monitoring seasonal trends of influenza and other disease indicators; and assisting in case-finding for epidemiologic investigations.

In March 2005, BioSense had more than 340 state and local health department user accounts, representing 49 states. Its user base continues to expand. The current implementation status of BioSense (as of June 2008) is shown in Figure 7-1. The system has also been used in several high-profile events (e.g., the G8 meeting in 2004) (Bradley et al., 2005; Ma et al., 2005; Sokolow et al., 2005).

Figure 7-2 shows the BioSense system architecture. Specifically, BioSense consists of the following system components (BioSense, 2008):

- Data Transmission: assuring the secure, timely, and routine receipt of health data for public health surveillance. BioSense requires data to be transmitted over the PHIN Messaging System (PHINMS). PHINMS is an interoperable messaging system developed by CDC for data providers to transmit private data either as standardized messages and vocabulary securely over the Internet in real-time or in batches.
- Data Analysis: establishing a set of statistical methods and tools to assist public health analysts to detect potential public health events and make informed decisions. At the CDC BioIntelligence Center (BIC) each day, the public health analysts monitor, analyze, and interpret facility, state, and national trends or anomalies in the BioSense data and provide further analytic and reporting support to state and local public health departments.

H. Chen et al., *Infectious Disease Informatics: Syndromic Surveillance for Public Health and BioDefense*, Integrated Series in Information Systems 21, DOI 10.1007/978-1-4419-1278-7_7,

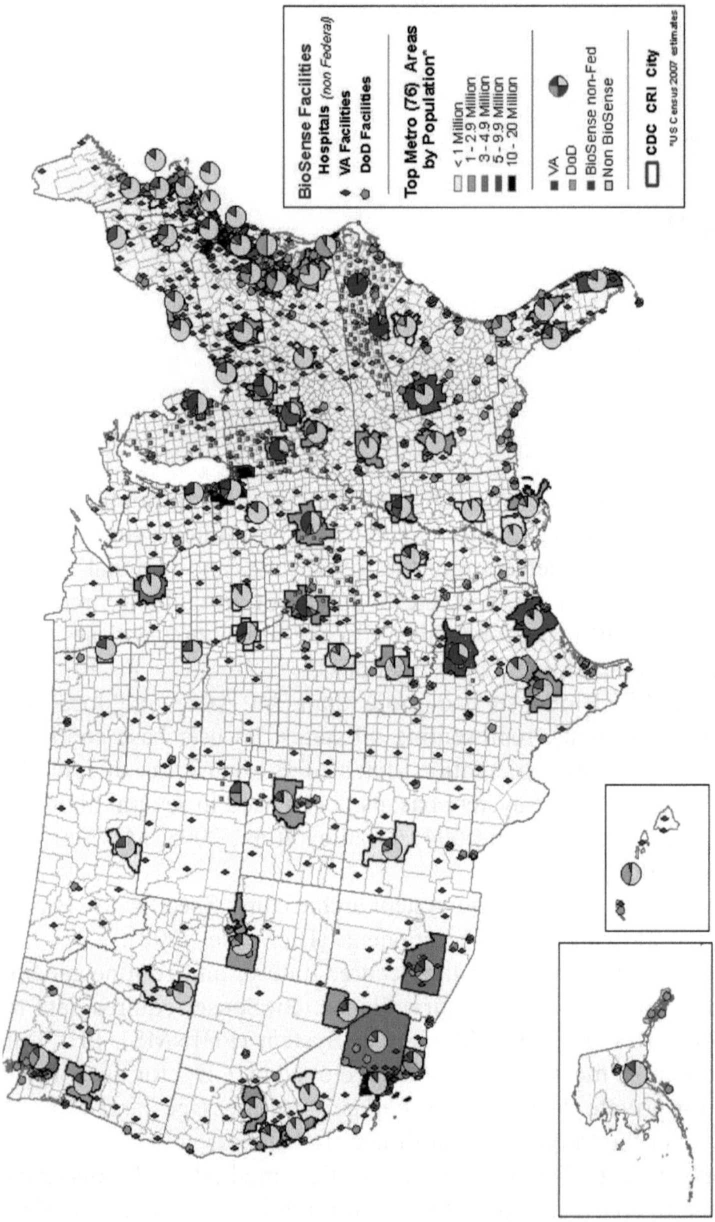

Figure 7-1. BioSense participation in top 76 MSAs as of June 2008 (BioSense, 2008).

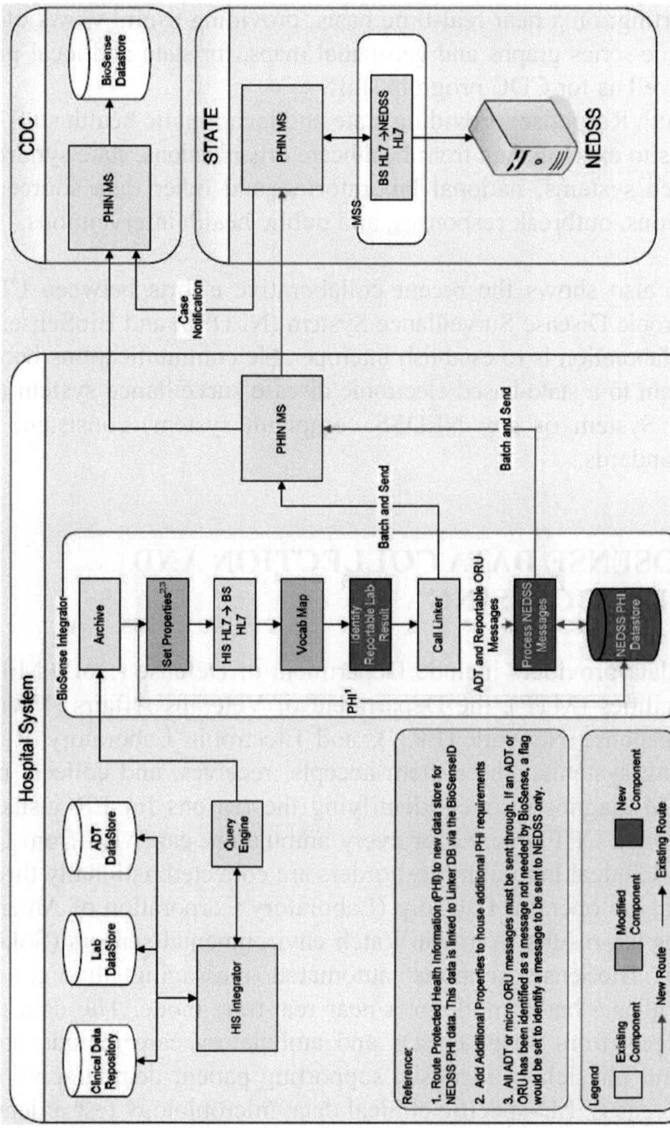

Figure 7-2. BioSense with ELR reporting intergration (source: BioSense Web site).

- Data Reporting: on a near real-time basis, providing useful views of data through time-series graphs and geospatial maps, for state and local public health as well as for CDC program staff.
- Public Health Response: providing state and local public health staff real-time access to existing data from healthcare organizations, state syndromic surveillance systems, national laboratories, and other data sources for investigations, outbreak responses, and public health interventions.

Figure 7-2 also shows the recent collaborative efforts between CDC's National Electronic Disease Surveillance System (NEDSS) and BioSense. The goal of the collaboration is to establish interoperable communications between a hospital system to a state-based electronic disease surveillance system (e.g., NEDSS Base System or any NEDSS compliant system) consistent with CDC PHIN standards.

1. BIOSENSE DATA COLLECTION AND PREPROCESSING

BioSense data providers include Department of Defense (DoD)-Military Treatment Facilities (MTF), the Department of Veterans Affairs (VA), the Laboratory Response Network (LRN), and Electronic Laboratory Results (ELR) reporting systems. The system accepts, receives, and collects up to four ICD-9-CM diagnosis codes identifying the reasons for ER visits and procedure-encoded CPT ordered for every ambulatory care visit from DoD-MTF and VA. Clinical laboratory test orders are collected nationally through the commercial lab operator LabCorp (Laboratory Corporation of America). It also receives lab results from BioWatch environmental sensors (Sokolow et al., 2005). BioSense supports automated messaging through HL7 protocols in either a batch mode or a near real-time mode. The data types BioSense collects from hospital EDs and ambulatory care include patient chief complaint, physician diagnosis, supporting patient demographic data, daily hospital census, ED-specific clinical data, microbiology test orders and results, radiology orders and results, and medication orders.

The 11 syndrome categories monitored by BioSense are shown in Table 7-1. To allow surveillance of more granular events than is possible using the 11 syndromes, BioSense medical expert staff developed 78 more subsyndromes. These subsyndrome definitions can be found at the BioSense project Web site (CDC, 2007).

Table 7-1. Eleven syndrome categories monitored by BioSense.

Fever	Neurologic
Gastrointestinal	Rash
Hemorrhagic illness	Severe illness and death
Localized cutaneous lesion	Specific infection
Lymphadenitis	Respiratory
Botulism-like/botulism	

Data in ICD-9-CM form are mapped to 11 syndromes based on a mapping schema created in 2003 by a multiagency working group (CDC, 2007). Free-text data are mapped to subsyndromes using the text word search. Most keywords in the chief complaint to subsyndrome mapping table were derived from the EARS system Text String Search method. It contains both English and certain Spanish keywords and includes regular terms, misspellings, word fragments, and abbreviations. The mapping is continually improving the keyword search list by examining the original free text and its corresponding mapping results. Keywords were modified during the initial implementation period. The majority of the keywords in the free-text physician diagnosis to subsyndrome mapping table were derived from terms that appeared in ICD-9-CM descriptions (CDC, 2007). At the same time, BioSense employs a Bayesian classifier – CoCo from the RODS laboratory – for syndrome classification.

2. BIOSENSE DATA ANALYSIS

BioSense uses the CUSUM algorithm for anomaly detection. The CUSUM algorithm is used as a short-term surveillance technique to indicate recent data changes through the comparison of moving averages (Bradley et al., 2005). Because of the high variability within the data, CUSUM values are computed for each date-source-syndrome combination at the state or metropolitan reporting area (MRA) level rather than for individual ZIP codes (Bradley et al., 2005).

The other detection algorithms available from BioSense include EWMA and SMART. EWMA and SMART algorithms are also used to predict the day-source-syndrome counts at the ZIP code level, with seasonality and day-of-week effects considered. The calculations are conducted on a daily basis. Spatial-temporal clustering methods such as various scan statistics are also being explored by the BioSense system. BioSense explored the use of SaTScan with a separate run for each month to detect spatial disease clusters. SaTScan is set to scan a maximum circle radius of 100 km with each ED facility as one geographic unit. Poisson probability model is used to model the disease rates, and clusters are identified by locating the geographic areas that do not conform to these model-predicted disease rates.

3. BIOSENSE DATA VISUALIZATION, INFORMATION DISSEMINATION, AND REPORTING

BioSense is an Internet-accessible, secure system. It displays data in multiple formats including line graphs, maps, tabular summaries, and case details. Graph plotting for individual data source, individual syndrome category,

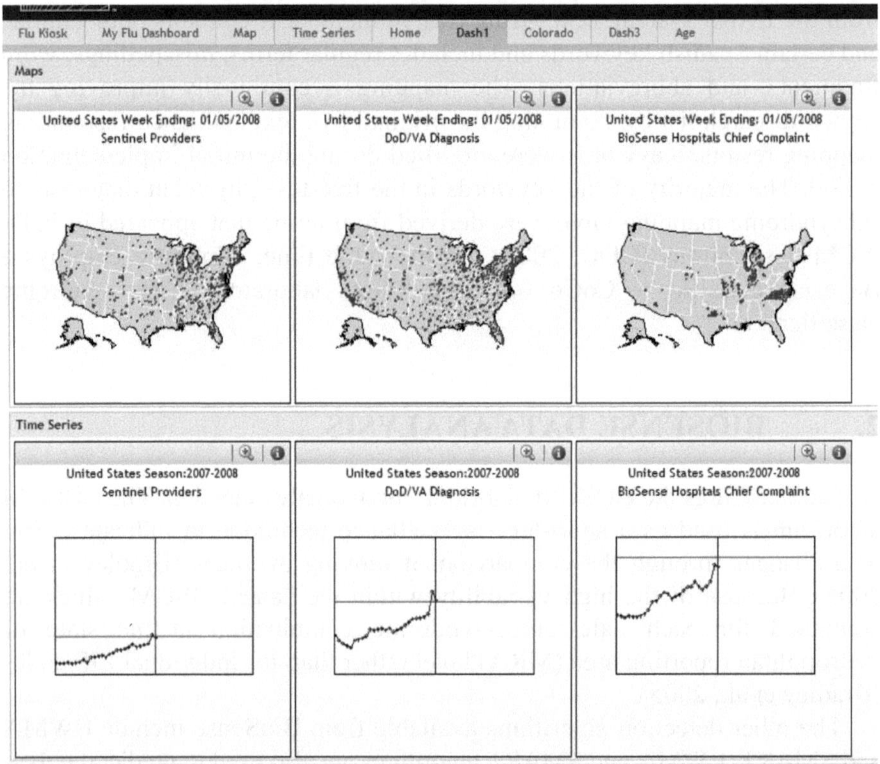

Figure 7-3. BioSense Influenza tool that merges multiple sources (source: BioSense Web site).

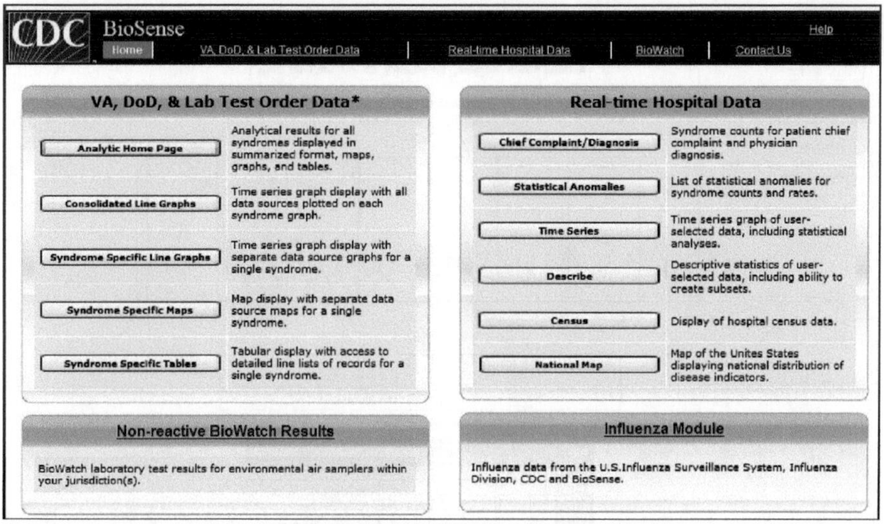

Figure 7-4. BioSense homepage showing available surveillance functionalities (source: BioSense Web site).

and different level of geographical regions is also available (Figure 7-3). On its homepage, as shown in Figure 7-4, it provides a collection of analysis and visualization functionalities. For VA, DoD, and Lab Test Order Data, (1) it can display time series graphs or map graphs of all data sources for each syndrome or a selected specific syndrome (the example of asthma time-series is shown in Figure 7-5); (2) it has tabular display with access to detailed line lists of records for a single syndrome; (3) infection alerts for several bioterrorism agents can also be reported. For real-time hospital data, a line list of statistical anomalies found by BioSense analysis, time series and map display for syndrome counts, and as well as drill-down patient details are all available.

CDC BioIntelligence Center is the agency responsible for monitoring anomalies detected by BioSense. The lightweight directory access protocol (LDAP) is employed for information reporting.

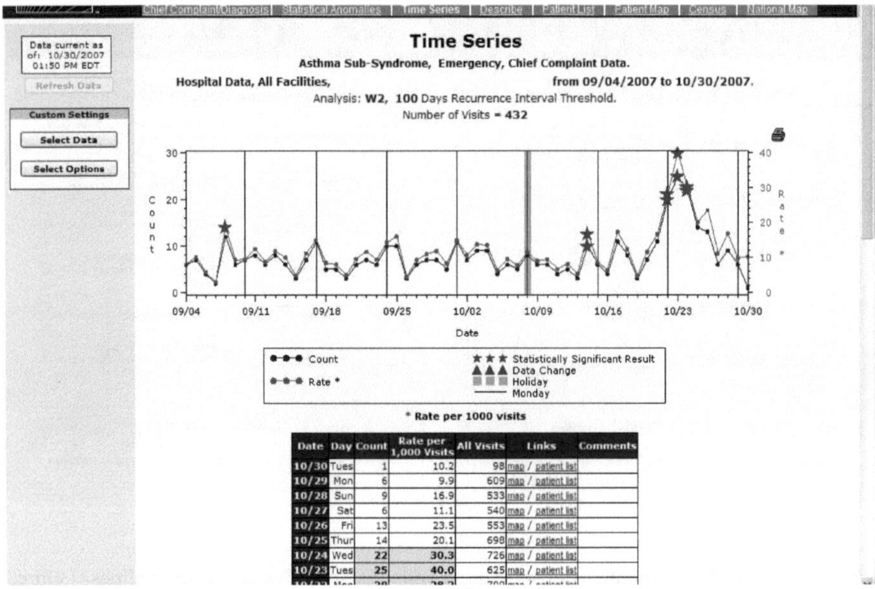

Figure 7-5. BioSense analysis page for Asthma query (source: BioSense Web site).

4. CASE STUDY: MONITORING HEALTH EFFECTS OF WILDFIRES USING BIOSENSE

From October 21 to October 26, 2007, wildfires spread across hundreds of thousands of acres of San Diego County, forcing the evacuation of more than 300,000 residents. During October 22–30, 2007, CDC personnel monitored BioSense for evidence of health effects possibly related to the wildfires in San Diego County.

In October 2007, data were being received from EDs at six of the 19 hospitals in San Diego County. These six hospitals were located near but outside the fire and evacuation areas (illustrated in Figure 7-6).

Data received by BioSense included age, sex, free-text patient-reported chief complaints, and diagnosis codes (usually ICD-9-CM codes). The first part of the standard procedure is syndrome classification. Diagnoses are assigned to one or more of the 11 general syndromes (shown in Table 7-1) and 78 more specific subsyndromes (e.g., asthma and dyspnea).

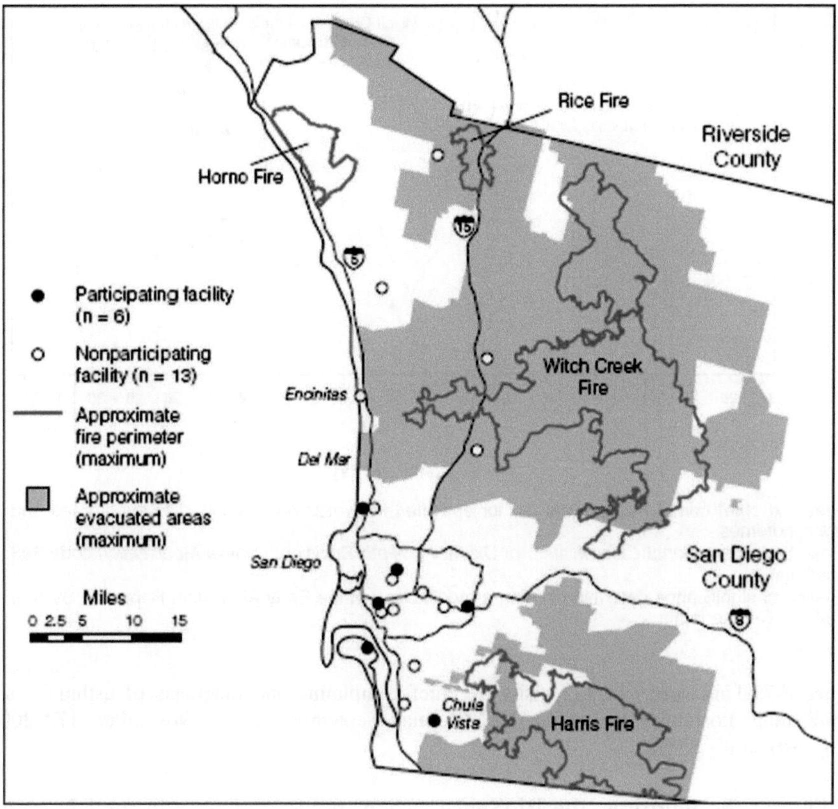

Figure 7-6. Hospital participation in BioSense, San Diego County, California, October 20-29, 2007 (Ginsberg et al., 2008).

These data are first centralized at CDC from hospital EDs. Within 2–3 hours, these data are processed at CDC and then made available in BioSense. The median time for chief complaints from patient visits to receipt of ED data at CDC is 8 hours. For diagnosis codes, the median time is 5 days.

For data analysis, the daily count of visits indicating diseases after the manual or automatic syndrome mapping is displayed on time-series graphs (Figure 7-7 shows an example time-series for counts of diagnoses and chief complaints of asthma) and compared with the predicted number based on a 7-day moving average. A modification of the EARS C-2 algorithm (Hutwagner et al., 2003) is used to determine statistical significance. A single-day visit count with a recurrence interval of ≥100 days (analogous to $p \leq 0.01$) is considered statistically significant.

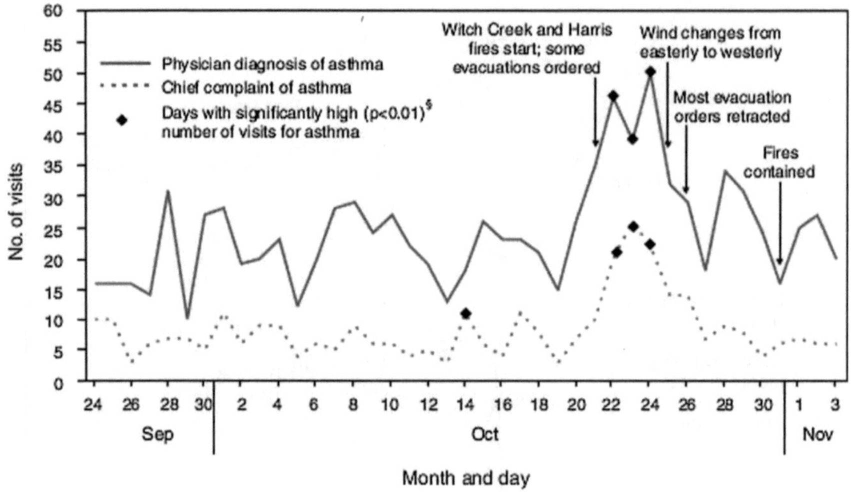

* Free-text chief complaints are parsed for specified keywords and assigned to syndromes and subsyndromes.
† Based on *International Classification of Diseases, Ninth Revision, Clinical Modification* code 493 (asthma).
§ Statistical significance determined using a modification of the Early Aberration Reporting System (EARS) C-2 algorithm.

Figure 7-7. Time-series of ED visits by chief complaints and diagnosis of asthma – six participating hospitals, San Diego, California, September 22 – November 17, 2007 (Gingsberg et al. 2008).

During the wildfires, the BioSense system noted increases in total hospital visit volume and large increases in respiratory visits to hospitals, especially visits for asthma and dyspnea (difficulty in breathing/shortness of breath). The BioSense system detected significant ($p < 0.01$) increases in visits for asthma from October 22 to 24. When the winds shifted on October 25, asthma complaints and diagnoses began to decline.

BIC and San Diego County public health officials also worked together to conduct retrospective analyses of BioSense post-wildfire data. These analyses helped to gain a better understanding of how cardiovascular and respiratory diseases develop before, during, and after the fire and how patients with chronic respiratory illness were affected by exposure to the wildfire smoke. The collaboration between BIC and San Diego County public health officials proved to be useful and has led to increasing collaborative activities across CDC and with state and local public health officials. Lessons learned from this experience will help not only the next time wildfires strike, but also in other large-scale exposures to environmental hazards.

5. FURTHER READINGS

We provide the following project link and some key readings for the readers who might be interested in learning more details about the BioSense project.

Project link:

http://www.cdc.gov/BioSense/

Important readings:

1. BioSense working group. (June 2008) "BioSense Technical Overview of Data Collection, Analysis, and Reporting." Available at http://www.cdc.gov/BioSense/files/BioSense_Techn_Overview_102908_webpage.pdf
2. Ginsberg, M., J. Johnson, J. Tokars, C. Martin, R. English, G. Rainisch, W. Lei, P. Hicks, J. Burkholder, M. Miller, K. Crosby, K. Akaka, A. Stock, and D. Sugerman. (2008). "Monitoring Health Effects of Wildfires Using the BioSense System – San Diego County, California, October 2007." MMWR July 11, 2008.
3. Bradley, C. A., and H. Rolka, et al. (2005). "BioSense: Implementation of a National Early Event Detection and Situational Awareness System." MMWR (CDC) 54(Suppl), pp 11–20.
4. Sokolow, Leslie Z., N. Grady, H. Rolka, D. Walker, P. McMurray, R. English-Bullard, J. Loonsk. "Practice and Experience: Deciphering Data Anomalies in BioSense." MMWR August 26, 2005.
5. Ma, H., J. Tokars, R. English, T. Smith, C. Bradley, L. Sokolow, and H. Rolka. 2006 Jul 7. "Surveillance of West Nile Virus Activity Using Biosense Laboratory Test Order Data." Advances in Disease Surveillance [Online] 1:1.
6. R. English, P. McMurray, L. Sokolow, H. Rolka, D. Walker, J. Quinn III, and K. Cox. 2006 Jul 7. "Geographic Categorization Methods Used in BioSense." Advances in Disease Surveillance [Online] 1:1.

Chapter 8

RODS

The Real-time Outbreak and Disease Surveillance (RODS) system was initiated by the RODS Laboratory at the University of Pittsburgh in 1999. The system is now an open source project under the GNU license. The RODS development effort has been organized into seven functional areas: overall design, data collection, syndrome classification, database and data warehousing, outbreak detection algorithms, data access, and user interfaces. Each functional area has a coordinator for the open source project, and there is an overall coordinator responsible for the architecture, overall integration of components, and overall quality of the JAVA source code. Figure 8-1 illustrates the RODS' system architecture.

The RODS system as a syndromic surveillance application was originally deployed in Pennsylvania, Utah, and Ohio. As of 2006, RODS performs emergency department surveillance for other states of California, Illinois, Kentucky, Michigan, New Jersey, Nevada, and Wyoming through an ASP model at the University of Pittsburgh, and through local installations in Taiwan, Canada, Mississippi, Michigan, California, and Texas. As of June 2006, about 20 regions with more than 200 healthcare facilities connected to RODS in real-time. It was also deployed during the 2002 Winter Olympics (Espino et al., 2004). It also serves as the user interface for national over-the-counter medication sales surveillance data collected through the NRDM.

The conceptual architecture of the RODS system is shown in Figure 8-1. Multiple data sources are collected and stored in a database and data warehouse where they are made available to outbreak algorithms and the RODS user interface.

H. Chen et al., *Infectious Disease Informatics: Syndromic Surveillance for Public Health and BioDefense*, Integrated Series in Information Systems 21, DOI 10.1007/978-1-4419-1278-7_8,

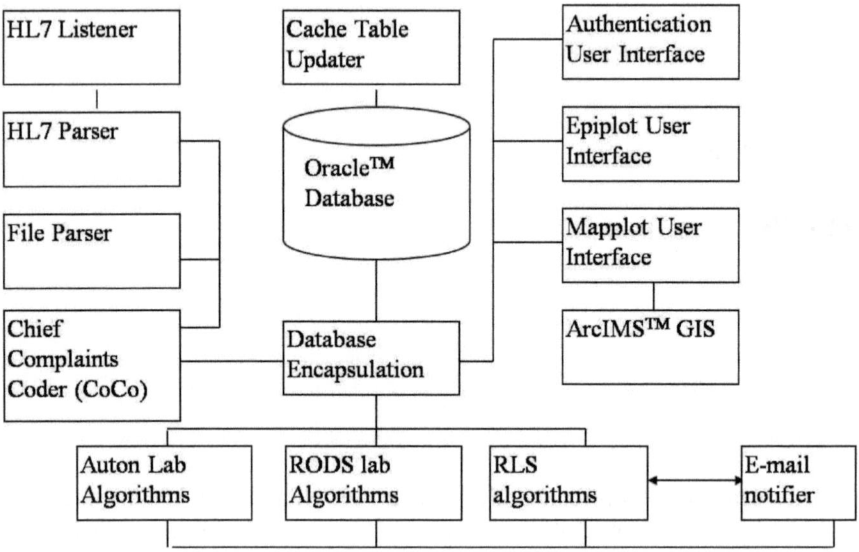

Figure 8-1. RODS system architecture (Espino et al., 2004).

The latest version of RODS system is RODS 6. RODS 6 is built from the ground up to be pluggable and part of a larger biosurveillance system as a biosurveillance grid node that incorporates as well as offers services. New data types and algorithms can be easily incorporated into the system without the need for database redesign or coding of the core software. RODS 6 also provides a robust API so that external applications can leverage the data collection, visualization, and data analysis capabilities of RODS.

1. RODS DATA COLLECTION

RODS collects healthcare registration data in real time from participating hospitals via a standard called HL7. Specifically, healthcare registration data consist of the age, gender, home zipcode, date/time of admission, and a free-text chief complaint of the patient.

The National Retail Data Monitor (NRDM) is a component of the RODS system, collecting and analyzing daily sales data for OTC medication sales. It also collects and analyzes chief complaints data from various hospitals. NRDM monitors more than 29,000 retail stores including stores from 12 big chains in the US and its territories for OTC medication sales 24 hours a day/ 7 days a week as of May 2009 (a screenshot of its deployment around the US is shown in Figure 8-2). Daily batch feeds of sales data from those stores are

received by NRDM everyday by midnight. Individual medication sales data are aggregated into one or more of the 18 OTC categories (Table 8-1) before being aggregated spatially by zip code according to store location.
There are plans to integrate laboratory orders, dictated radiology reports, dictated hospital reports, and poison control center calls in future versions.

The RODS system currently monitors 7 healthcare registration prodrome categories, as shown in Table 8-2.

Table 8-1. Eighteen over-the-counter medication categories monitored by NRDM.

Antidiarrheal	Cough syrup adult liquid
Antifever pediatric	Cough syrup adult tablet
Antifever adult	Cough syrup pediatric liquid
Bronchial remedies	Electrolytes pediatric
Chest rubs	Hydrocortisones
Cold relief adult liquid	Nasal product internal
Cold relief adult tablet	Thermometers
Cold relief pediatric liquid	Throat lozenges
Cold relief pediatric tablet	Others

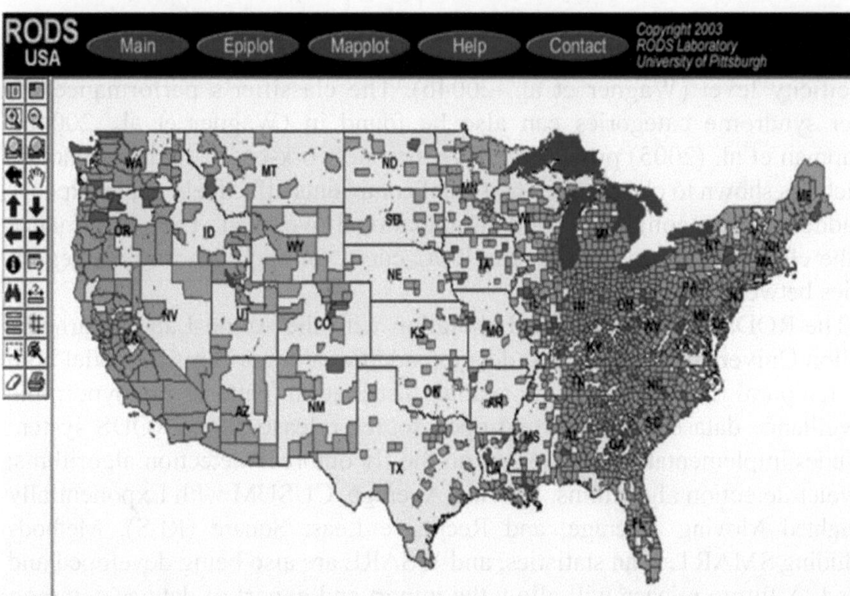

Figure 8-2. NRDM deployment at 20,000 stores as of 2002 (Wagner et al., 2003).

Table 8-2. Syndrome categories monitored by RODS.

Gastrointestinal	Rash
Hemorrhagic illness	Respiratory
Constitutional	Botulism-like/botulism
Neurologic	

The RODS data are collected in real-time through HL7 messages from other computer systems such as registration systems and laboratory information systems, over a Secure Shell–protected Internet connection in an automated mode.

2. RODS DATA ANALYSIS

One of the major strengths of RODS is in data analysis. Several syndrome classification approaches have been tested and implemented in the RODS system. It applies a keyword classifier and an ICD-9 classifier to chief complaint data. The CoCo module, a syndrome mapping component, has been tested in multiple settings (Olszewski, 2003). For the respiratory syndrome, based on manually-classified results, CoCo achieves a 77% sensitivity level and 90% specificity level (Wagner et al., 2004b). The classifier's performance for other syndrome categories can also be found in (Wagner et al., 2004b). Chapman et al. (2005) proposed a Bayesian network-based semantic model, which has shown to classify free-text chief complaints effectively at the expense of added system complexity and computational overhead. The performance of the classifier represented by the ROC curve for each syndrome category varies between 0.95 and 0.99.

The RODS laboratory, in collaboration with the Auton Lab at Carnegie Mellon University, continues to develop additional algorithms to model both the temporal fluctuations and spatial distribution patterns in syndromic surveillance datasets. The current open source release of the RODS system includes implementations of several on-the-fly outbreak detection algorithms: wavelet-detection algorithms, Moving Average, CUSUM with Exponentially Weighted Moving Average, and Recursive Least Square (RLS). Methods including SMART, scan statistics, and WSARE are also being developed and tested. A future release will allow the import and export of data as common text files such that stand-alone algorithms and statistical software packages can be used to analyze the data.

CUSUM and SMART are also used in the BioSense system. They were discussed in the previous section. What's Strange About Recent Events (WSARE) algorithm (Wong et al., 2003, 2005) evaluates all the possible rules that are made up of any data feature components (e.g., a two-component rule could be Gender = Male and Home = NW) in both recent data and baseline data. The rules that have the largest discrepancy of the proportions between the recent data and baseline data are detected as rules summarizing the most significant patterns of anomalies. WSARE 3.0 has been evaluated retrospectively using the data from the Israel Center for Disease Control and has shown its capability of detecting the outbreak on the second day from its onset (Kaufman et al., 2005).

In the latest release of RODS 6, high-fidelity injection detectability experiments (HiFIDE) are integrated for outbreak simulation and algorithm testing. HiFIDE enable public health officials to analyze the detectability characteristics of a surveillance system operating in their jurisdiction. HiFIDE inject synthetic outbreak data (spikes) into real surveillance data from a particular jurisdiction. The HiFIDE spike is both high-fidelity in contour and in scale by first deriving the spike shape and then rescaling the spike from real surveillance data collected during outbreaks that occurred in other regions. In particular, its interface focuses on depicting the expected sensitivity, specificity, and timeliness of detection for outbreaks of varying sizes, etiologies, and geographic and demographic scopes. A HiFIDE window is shown in Figure 8-3.

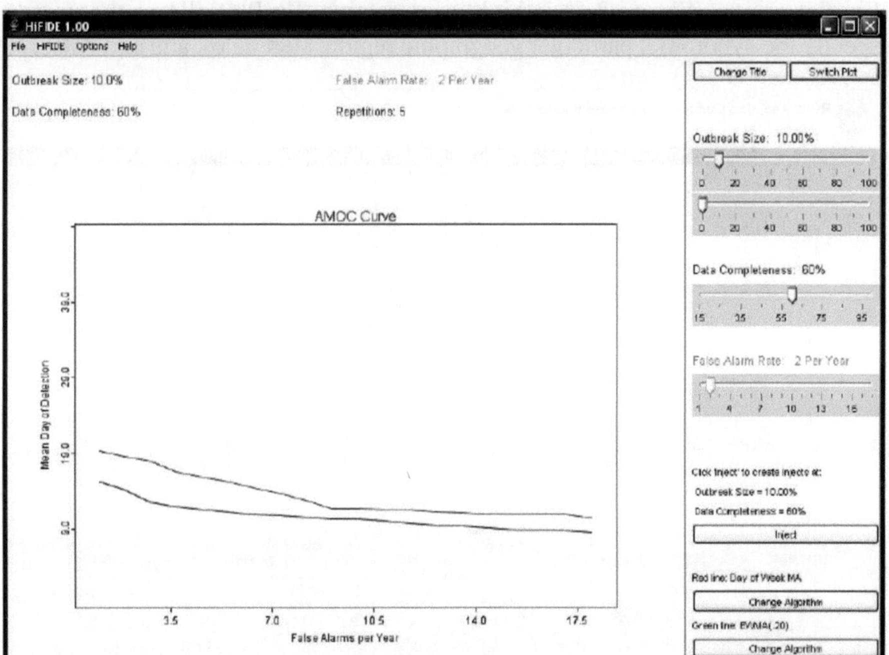

Figure 8-3. Sensitivity plots in HiFIDE (Wallstrom et al., 2005).

3. RODS VISUALIZATION, INFORMATION DISSEMINATION, AND REPORTING

The RODS system provides multiple graphing techniques with both time-series and geographical displays available via an encrypted, password-protected Web interface. Three different data views – Main, Epiplot, and Mapplot – are supported. Figures 8-4 to 8-6 are three example views of RODS user interface. These views are implemented using JFreeChart (an open-source graphing package) and ArcIMS (an Internet GIS server developed by the Environmental Systems Research Institute, Inc.).

The RODS Main screen (Figure 8-4) shows time-series plots updated on a daily basis for each syndrome. The intention of the Main screen is that of a "threat" board in a situation room. The Main screen refreshes itself every two minutes if left displayed. The graphs can be plotted with different event monitoring algorithms such as moving average and CUSUM. The user can choose to view these plots by county or for the whole state.

The RODS Main screen is limited to viewing six OTC (individual types of medication and prodrome categories cannot be selected from the OTC Main screen) or healthcare registration charts for the last seven days, whereas Epiplot screen (Figure 8-5) is highly interactive. EpiPlot allows the user to specify the syndrome, particular geographic region, start dates, and end dates, to

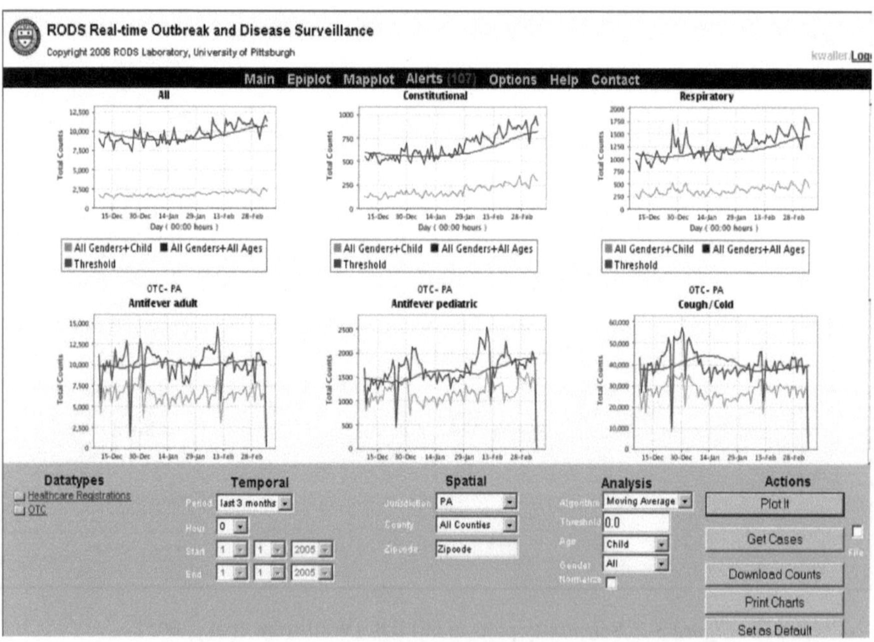

Figure 8-4. RODS system Main screen (source: RODS Laboratory, University of Pittsburg).

generate customized time-series plots. Users can choose to analyze the data using one of four on-the-fly analysis algorithms – CuSUM with EWMA, RLS, Wavelet or Moving Average. A "get cases" button allows users to view case-level detail for encounters making up the specific time-series.

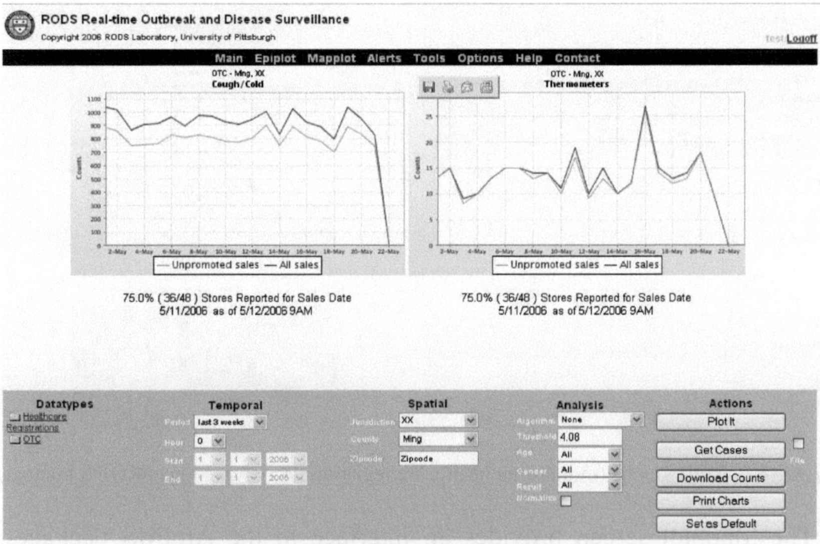

Figure 8-5. RODS Epiplot screen (source: RODS User Manual).

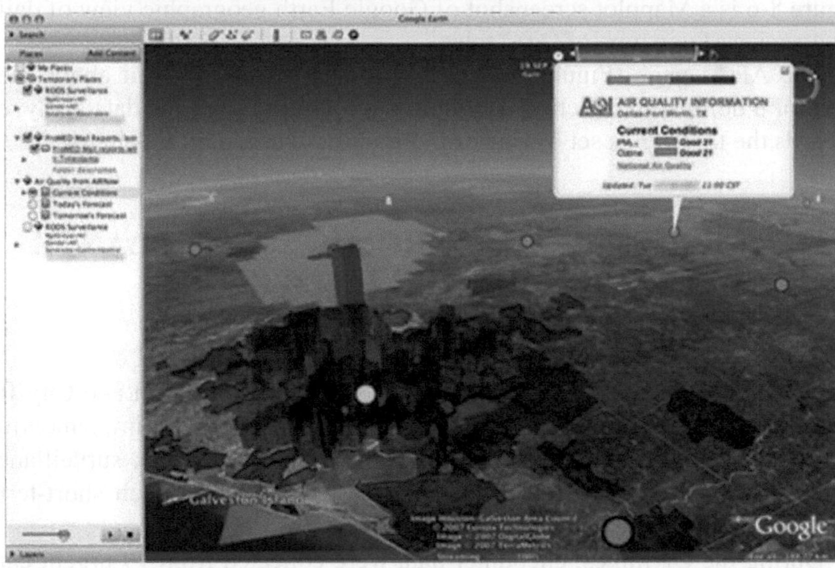

Figure 8-6. Mapplot output displayed in Google Earth (source: the RODS project at Source Forge.net).

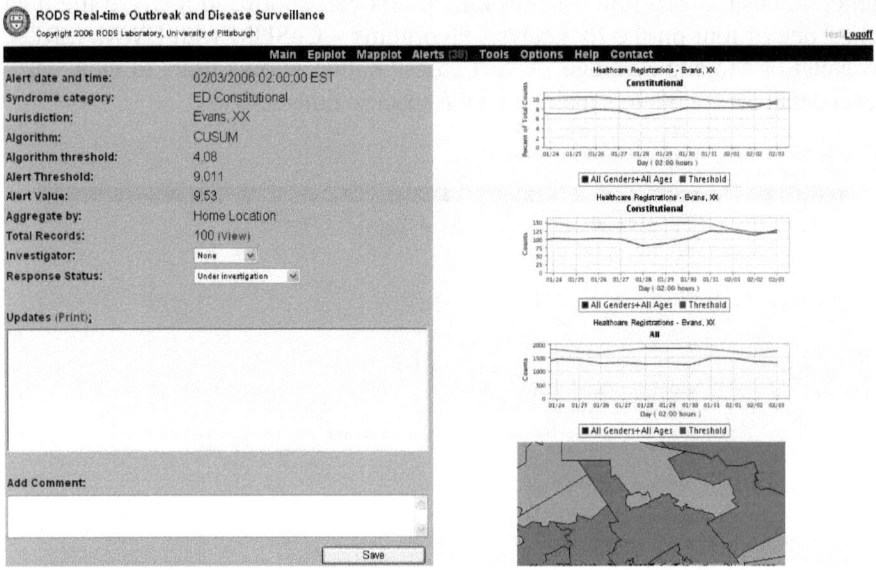

Figure 8-7. RODS alerts (monitoring healthcare registrations only) (source: RODS manual).

The Mapplot screen provides an interface to the ArcIMS package, to display disease cases' spatial distribution using patients' zip code information. Figure 8-6 is a Mapplot screenshot of Google Earth geographic view of daily frequencies of one type of OTC sales.

The Alerts page (Figure 8-7) provides detailed information about each alert for a defined jurisdiction. An alert is registered each time data analyzed exceeds the thresholds set by one or more of the four algorithms in use.

4. CASE STUDY: SYNDROMIC SURVEILLANCE WITH RODS FOR THE 2002 WINTER OLYMPICS

RODS was deployed at the 2002 Winter Olympics in Salt Lake City for bioterrorism and public health surveillance. The main purpose of implementing RODS was to automate an otherwise expensive, round-the-clock surveillance process. It was a successful test of RODS deployment in such short-term drop-in situations (Gesteland et al., 2003).

During the Olympics, encounter data were collected from 19 urgent care centers and nine emergency departments owned and operated by Intermountain Health Care (IHC), University of Utah Health Sciences Center (UUHSC) and from the University of Utah Hospital's emergency department and the

Polyclinic located in the Olympic Village. Together these emergency rooms and urgent care centers serve about 70% of the population of Utah.

RODS takes advantage of existing HL7 message routers in healthcare systems to receive admission, discharge, and transfer (ADT) data in real time from clinical information systems. HL7 message routers consist of HL7 data listeners and HL7 parsers. The HL7 listeners establish TCP/IP connections between RODS and IHC and UUHSC. The HL7 parser uses regular expressions to parse each data segment in an HL7 message. The parsed ADT messages are centralized into an Oracle8i database for data retrieval and analysis. Figure 8-8 shows a sample HL7 message from one of health systems. The primary keys for a HL7 ADT message contain sending facility, ADT message type, medical record number, patient class, and visit number (Tsui et al., 2003).

```
MSH|^~\&|HELP|xxx|COMMON|EXTERNAL|200202241715||ADT
^A04|2002022XXXXXXXX|P|2.3<CR>
PID||123456789||||^020|M||^^^^84204|||||<CR>
PV1||E|||||||||||||||98765432||||||||||||||||||||
|||200202XXXXXXX||<CR>
DG1||||SORE THROAT,COUGH<CR>
IN1||||||||||||||||||||||||||||||||||||||||||||||^^^^
84056<CR>
<ETX>
```

Figure 8-8. Sample HL7 ADT messages (Tsui et al. 2003).

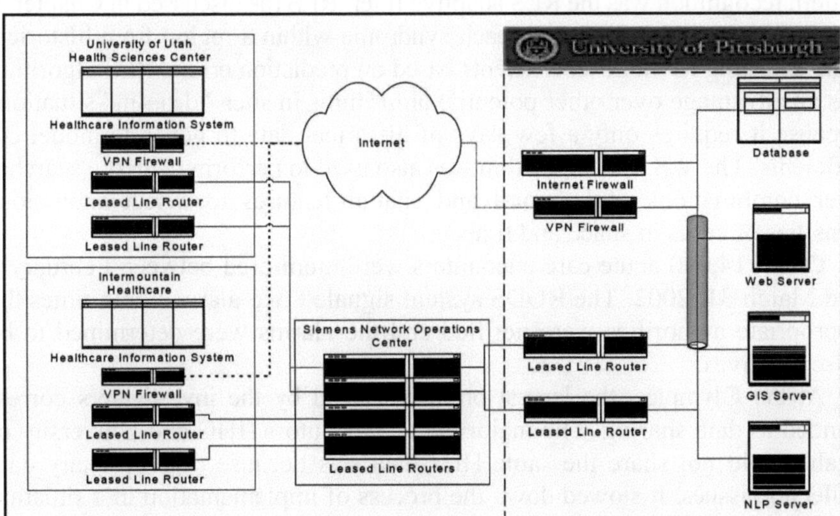

Figure 8-9. Network architecture of RODS implementation in Utah (Tsui et al. 2003).

The HL7 messages were communicated through a secure network infrastructure between Utah RODS and the data providers consisting of virtual private networks (VPN) and leased lines (Figure 8-9). Siemens Medical Systems (SMS) contributed to the initial establishment for the site-to-site VPNs. Utah RODS processes run on dedicated databases and servers including a Web server, a GIS server, and a natural language processing server, protected by Internet firewalls residing on separate servers.

To classify patients into a prodrome category utilizing free-text chief complaints as input, Utah RODS uses two Natural Language Processors (NLPS) – Bigram 8 and PLUSI0. They map a chief complaint into one of seven prodromes-respiratory, diarrheal, botulinic, viral, encephalitic, hemorrhagic, and rash. Bigram is a simple NLPS, developed at the University of Pittsburgh, computing the probability of a specific prodrome category of a patient based on pair of words in a free-text chief complaint. PLUS was developed at the University of Utah. PLUS classifies a free-text chief complaint using a more sophisticated Bayesian network. Both NLPS operate in real time using client-server TCP/IP socket connections. Whenever a chief complaint is available for processing, the RODS server sends a message to PLUS on the NLP server, and it returns the classification of the case based on the free-text chief complaint (Tsui et al., 2003).

RODS analyzes the data for anomalous densities of cases compared with historical patterns. The analyses were conducted every 4 h, and were frequently visually inspected by RODS staff through RODS user interfaces. The primary statistical tool used by RODS during the Olympics for automated pattern recognition was the RLS adaptive filter. RLS (as discussed in Chapter 4) computes an expected count of each syndrome within a region from historical data, adjusting its model coefficients based on prediction errors. RLS algorithm has an advantage over other potential algorithms in such "drop-in" situations because it requires only a few days of historical data to generate model coefficients. The WSARE algorithm was also used to perform heuristic searches over combinations of temporal and spatial features to detect anomalous densities of cases in space and time.

Over 114,000 acute care encounters were monitored between February 8 and March 31, 2002. The RODS system signaled two alarms; both times the appropriate authorities were notified and the alarms were determined to be false positives.

At the Olympics, the largest problems faced by the investigators corresponded to data sharing. The major data contributors (IHC and University of Utah) could not share the same HL7 data sets because of proprietary data collection issues. It slowed down the process of implementation in a situation where time was essential. RODS project spent a considerable amount of time during the 7 weeks in this project managing administrative issues instead of actually setting up the RODS system. Despite the inherent limitations of the 7-week establishment of the RODS system, the project was highly successful in proving how a computer-based, minimally invasive syndromic surveillance system can work.

5. FURTHER READINGS

We provide the following project link and some key readings for the readers who might be interested in learning more details about the RODS system.

Project link:

https://www.rods.pitt.edu/site/

Important readings:

1. Wu, T. S., F. Y. Shih, M. Y. Yen, J. S. Wu, S. W. Lu, K. C. Chang, C. Hsiung, J. H. Chou, Y. T. Chu, H. Chang, C. H. Chiu, F. C. Tsui, M. M. Wagner, I. J. Su, and C. C. King (2008), "Establishing a nationwide emergency department-based syndromic surveillance system for better public health responses in Taiwan," *BMC Public Health*, 8, p 18.
2. Shen, Y., C. Adamou, J. N. Dowling, and G. F. Cooper (2008), "Estimating the joint disease outbreak-detection time when an automated biosurveillance system is augmenting traditional clinical case finding," *Journal of Biomedical Informatics*, 41, pp 224–231.
3. Wallstrom, G. L., and W. R. Hogan (2007), "Unsupervised clustering of over-the-counter healthcare products into product categories," *Journal of Biomedical Informatics*, 40(6), pp 642–648.
4. Dara, J., J. N. Dowling, D. Travers, G. F. Cooper, and W. W. Chapman (2007), "Evaluation of preprocessing techniques for chief complaint classification," *Journal of Biomedical Informatics*, 41(4), pp 613–623.
5. Espino, J. U., M. M. Wagner, F. C. Tsui, H. D. Su, R. T. Olszewski, Z. Lie, W. Chapman, X. Zeng, L. Ma, Z. W. Lu, and J. Dara (2004), "The RODS Open Source Project: removing a barrier to syndromic surveillance," *Medinfo*, 11(Pt 2), pp 1192–1196.
6. Tsui, F.-C., J. U. Espino, M. M. Wagner, P. Gesteland, O. Ivanov, R. T. Olszewski, Z. Liu, X. Zeng, W. Chapman, W. K. Wong, and A. Moore (2002), "Data, network, and application: technical description of the Utah RODS Winter Olympic Biosurveillance System." *Proceedings of the AMIA Symposium*, pp 815–819.

Chapter 9

BIOPORTAL

The BioPortal project was initiated in 2003 by the University of Arizona Artificial Intelligence Lab and its collaborators in the New York State Department of Health and the California Department of Health Services to develop an infectious disease surveillance system. The project has been sponsored by NSF, DHS, DoD, Arizona Department of Health Services, and Kansas State University's BioSecurity Center, under the guidance of a federal inter-agency working group named the Infectious Disease Informatics Working Committee (IDIWC). Its partners include all the original collaborators as well as the USGS, University of California, Davis, University of Utah, the Arizona Department of Health Services, Kansas State University, and the National Taiwan University.

The BioPortal system provides distributed, cross-jurisdictional access to datasets concerning several major infectious diseases, including Botulism, West Nile Virus, foot-and-mouth disease, and live stock syndromes. Figure 9-1 shows the BioPortal system architecture. This portal system provides Web-based access to a variety of distributed infectious disease data sources including hospital ED free-text chief complaints (both in English and Chinese) as well as other epidemiological data. It features advanced spatial-temporal data analysis methods that include industry standard hotspot analysis algorithms and in-house developed innovative clustering-based techniques for retrospective and prospective data analysis. The analyses results are displayed via Spatio-Temporal Visualizer (STV). BioPortal also supports analysis and visualization of lab-generated gene sequence information. Its social network analysis module can be used to aid in the understanding of infectious disease transmission processes.

H. Chen et al., *Infectious Disease Informatics: Syndromic Surveillance for Public Health and BioDefense*, Integrated Series in Information Systems 21, DOI 10.1007/978-1-4419-1278-7_9,

The BioPortal system aims to improve the ability of public health practitioners to detect, and maintain situational awareness of outbreaks of emerging diseases and bioterrorist attacks, allowing for more timely and efficient deployment of resources for further investigation and response measures.

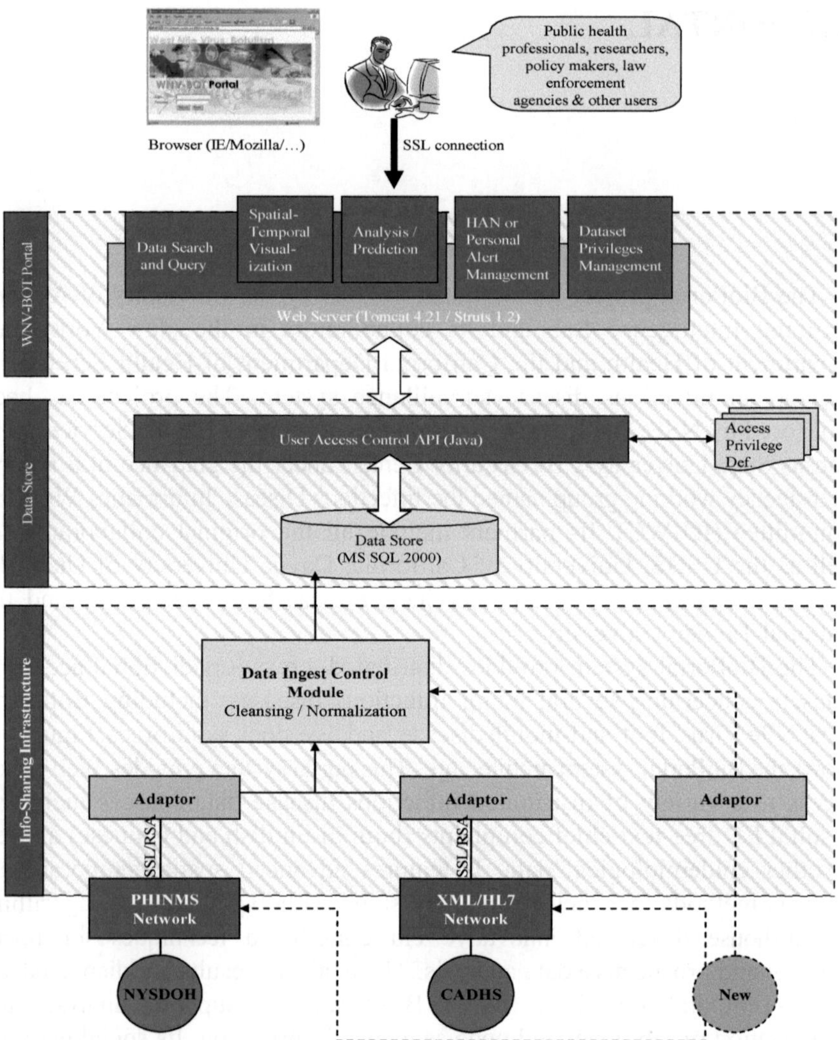

(a) BioPortal information sharing and data access infrastructure.

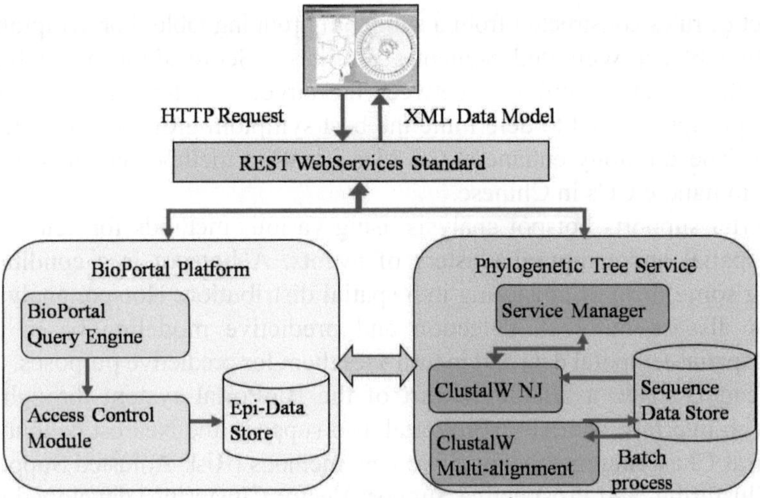

(b) BioPortal system architecture with epidemiological data and gene sequence data integrated.

Figure 9-1. BioPortal system architecture.

1. BIOPORTAL DATA COLLECTION

ED chief complaint data in the free-text format are provided by the Arizona Department of Health Services and several hospitals in a batch mode for syndrome classification. Various disease-specific case reports for both human and animal diseases are another source of data for BioPortal. It also makes use of surveillance datasets such as dead bird sightings and mosquito control information. The system's communication backbones, initially for data acquisition from New York or California disease datasets, consist of several messaging adaptors that can be customized to interoperate with various messaging systems. Participating syndromic data providers can link to the BioPortal data repository via the PHINMS and an XML/HL7 compatible network.

2. BIOPORTAL DATA ANALYSIS

BioPortal provides automatic syndrome classification capabilities based on free-text chief complaints. One method recently developed uses a concept ontology derived from the UMLS (Lu et al., 2008). For each chief complaint (CC), the method first standardizes the CC into one or more medical concepts in the UMLS. These concepts are then mapped into existing symptom groups using a set of rules constructed from a symptom grouping table. For symptoms not in the table, a Weighted Semantic Similarity Score algorithm, which measures the semantic similarity between the target symptoms and existing symptom groups, is used to determine the best symptom group for the target symptom. The ontology-enhanced CC classification method has also been extended to handle CCs in Chinese.

BioPortal supports hotspot analysis using various methods for detecting unusual spatial and temporal clusters of events. A hotspot is a condition indicating some form of clustering in a spatial distribution. Hotspot analysis facilitates disease outbreak detection and predictive modeling based on historical spatial-temporal data and in turn uses them for predictive purposes.

SaTScan is made available as part of the BioPortal system through a simple Web interface and STV. BioPortal also supports the Nearest Neighbor Hierarchical Clustering method, and two new methods (Risk-Adjusted Support Vector Clustering, and Prospective Support Vector Clustering) developed in-house (discussed in Chapter 4) (Chang et al., 2005; Zeng et al., 2004a). The version of SaTScan that is incorporated in the BioPortal system uses the Bernoulli method. The distribution of baseline observations (or controls) and the distribution of new observations (or cases) are compared and circular clusters are identified where the proportion of new observations is significantly higher than the proportion of new observations outside the circle. RSVC is a clustering-based, spatio-temporal hotspot analysis algorithm developed at the Artificial Intelligence Laboratory of the University of Arizona. It combines the power of support vector machines (SVM) with the risk adjustment approach from CrimeStat®. It clusters points with consideration for baseline information (data under normal conditions) to find the emerging at risk area. In addition, BioPortal uses the RNNH algorithm provided by CrimeStat® III. The Nearest Neighbor Hierarchical clustering (NNH) routine in CrimeStat identifies groups of incidents that are spatially close. It clusters points together and then proceeds to group the clusters together. The Risk-adjusted Nearest Neighbor Hierarchical clustering routine (RNNH) combines the hierarchical clustering capabilities with kernel density interpolation techniques.

3. BIOPORTAL VISUALIZATION, INFORMATION DISSEMINATION, AND REPORTING

Figure 9-2 shows the screenshot of the interactive Web-based surveillance portal. This application allows the user to explore the incidence of infectious diseases. The portal allows the user to: (1) select a disease of concern and access-related databases; (2) narrow the scope by time-frame and geographic area of interest; (3) view a variety of data aggregations; and (4) perform hotspot analysis to focus attention on critical areas.

	confirmed	probable	suspected	unknown	Total
1998	45	3	1	0	49
1999	122	15	8	6	151
2000	87	10	28	4	129
2001	60	11	11	0	82
2002	25	1	1	2	29
2003	14	0	1	0	15
Total	353	40	50	12	455

Hide chart Download CSV

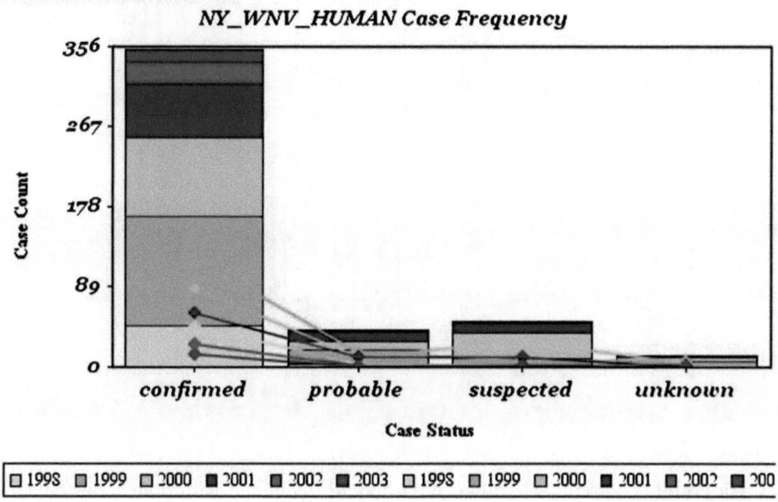

Hotspot Analysis -->

Figure 9-2. Interactive Web-based BioPortal surveillance portal.

Monitored disease incidence time series are shown on the surveillance dashboard for the participating hospitals and other healthcare organizations to view (Figure 9-3). The dashboard is integrated with time series detection capability and the BioPortal hotspot analysis and visualization tools. Detected abnormalities are alerted on the upper panel.

BioPortal makes available a visualization environment called the Spatial-Temporal Visualizer (STV), which allows users to interactively explore spatial and temporal patterns, based on an integrated tool set consisting of a GIS view, a timeline tool, and a periodic pattern tool (Hu et al., 2005).

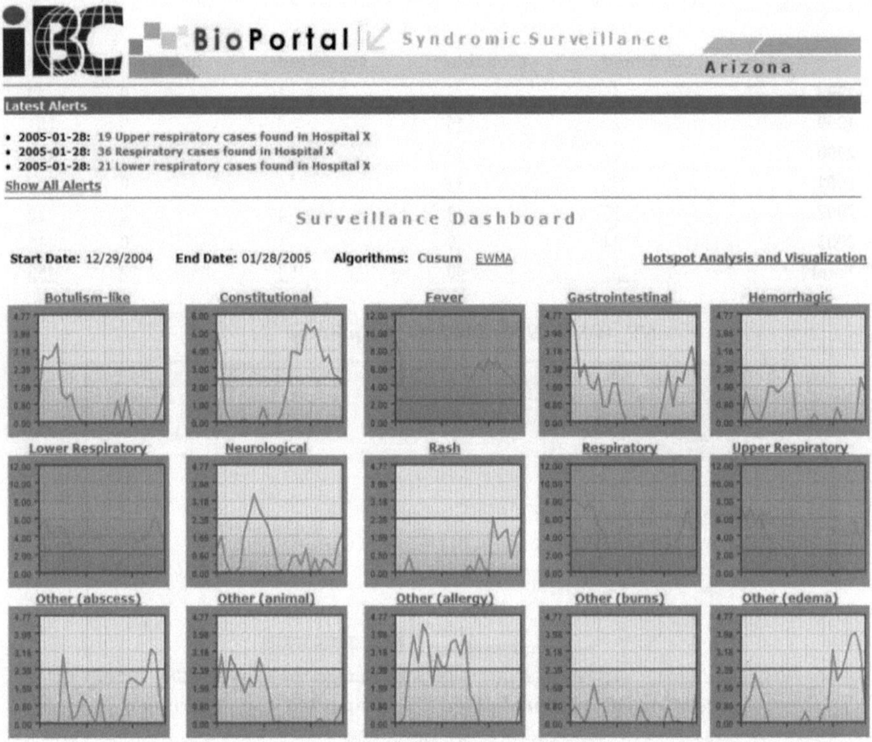

Figure 9-3. BioPortal syndromic surveillance dashboard integrated with time series detection capability and the hotspot analysis and visualization tools.

Figure 9-4 illustrates how these three views can be used to explore an infectious disease dataset. The GIS view displays cases and sightings on a map. The user can select multiple datasets to be shown on the map in different layers using the checkboxes (e.g., disease cases, natural land features, and land-use elements). Through the periodic view the user can identify periodic temporal patterns (e.g., which months or weeks have an unusually high number of cases). The unit of time for aggregation can also be set as days or hours. The timeline view provides a timeline along with a hierarchical display of the data elements, organized as a tree.

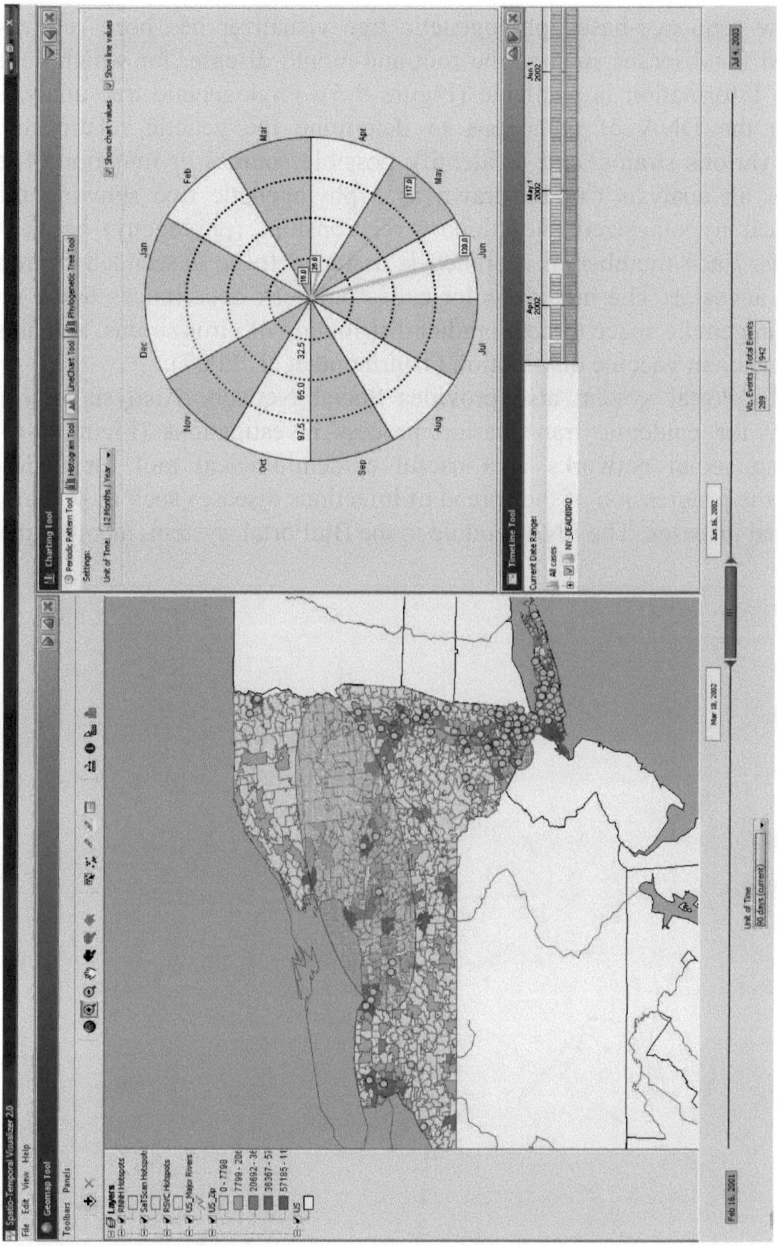

Figure 9-4. BioPortal Spatial-Temporal Visualizer.

A new sequence-based phylogenetic tree visualizer has been recently developed for diseases such as the foot-and-mouth disease, for which gene sequence information is available (Figure 9-5). Phylogenetic tree analysis examines the DNA of pathogens to determine the genetic relationship between various strains, and to identify possible sources or mutation. The results of an analysis can be drawn as a phylogenetic tree showing the hierarchical hypothesized evolutionary relationships (phylogeny) between organisms. Each member in a branch is assumed to be descended from a common ancestor. The module color-codes outbreak occurrences based on distance in genetic space to help predict distribution of virus strains, and aids in more efficient vaccine distribution (Thurmond et al., 2007).

The BioPortal system also provides Social Network Analysis (SNA) capability for epidemic transmission process investigations (Figure 9-6). Examining social networks is a useful epidemiological tool for understanding the progression of the spread of infectious diseases such as sexually transmitted diseases. The SNA module in the BioPortal system incorporates

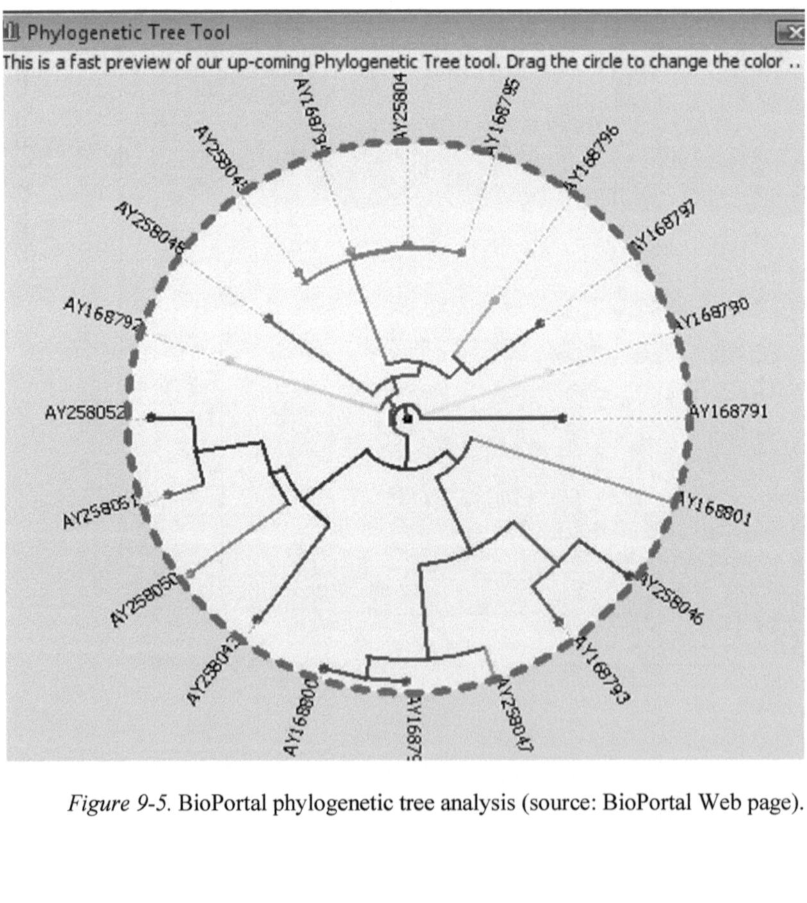

Figure 9-5. BioPortal phylogenetic tree analysis (source: BioPortal Web page).

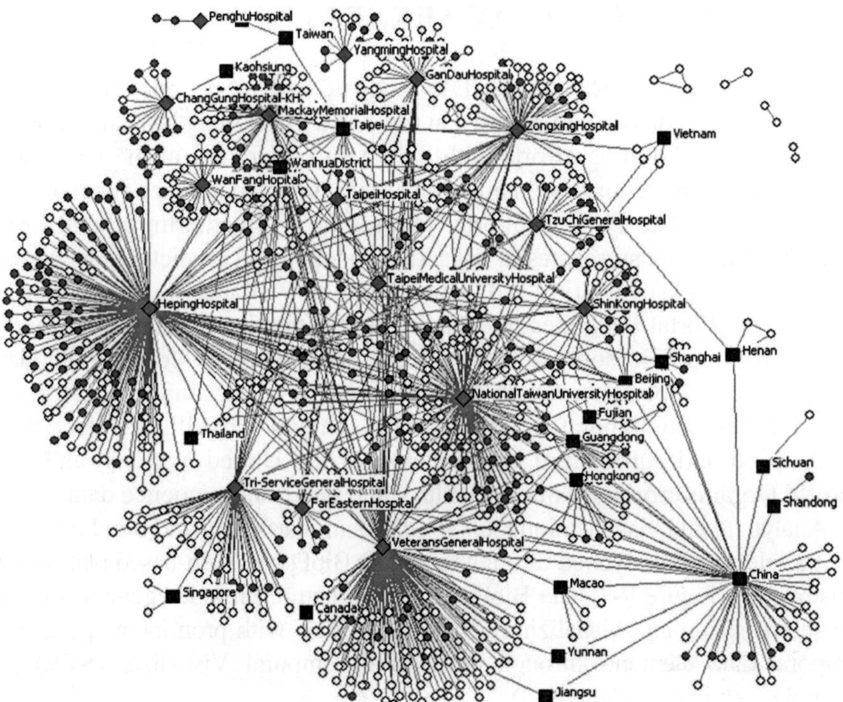

Figure 9-6. Social network analysis to analyze the SARS epidemic in Taiwan in 2003 (Chen et al., 2007).

geographical locations, which might be high risk areas such as hospitals, into social networks to examine the role of such locations in infectious disease transmission, and to identify potential bridges between locations. This helps to maintain situational awareness and target incident investigation and mitigation efforts more effectively. Social Network Analysis was also employed to analyze the SARS epidemic in Taiwan in 2003.

Data confidentiality, security, and access control are among the key research and development issues for the BioPortal project. An access control mechanism is implemented based on data confidentiality and user access privileges. For example, access privileges to the zip code and county level of individual patient records may be granted to selected public health epidemiologists. The project also developed various Memoranda of Understanding (MOUs) for data sharing among different local and state agencies.

4. CASE STUDY: FOOT-AND-MOUTH DISEASE SITUATIONAL AWARENESS

Foot-and-Mouth Disease (FMD) is considered to be one of the most contagious infectious animal diseases in the world. BioPortal plays an important role in the collaborative efforts with the FMD Laboratory at the University of California, Davis, for developing global real time surveillance for foot-and-mouth disease. The FMD BioPortal focuses on: (1) gathering global FMD data; (2) identifying surrogates of risks; (3) modeling and predicting FMD virus evolution; and (4) evaluating and testing FMD surveillance methodologies.

FMD BioPortal integrates information and data related to foot-and-mouth disease from public sources and collects proprietary or confidential data through secure specific routing structures. Major data sources include the World Reference Laboratory at Pirbright, animal surveillance data from FAO (Food and Agriculture Organization of the United Nations) and OIE (World Organisation for Animal Health), and GenBank sequence data.

Analytical and visualization tools for data summarization and trend detection can be selected and invoked through the FMD BioPortal Web-based platform as illustrated in Figure 9-7. The BioPortal infrastructure provides generic support for summarizing and visualizing FMD-related data with prominent spatial and temporal data elements through the Spatial-Temporal Visualizer (STV) (an example is shown in Figure 9-8).

A major enhancement to STV developed specifically for FMD BioPortal is the phylogenetic tree visualization that allows the incorporation of genomic information visualization in addition to the existing spatial and temporal data visualization capabilities (Figure 9-9). The phylogenetic tree visualization is used to display temporal-spatial genomic variation of FMD isolates and allows user-driven evaluation of differences in genomic variation over time and geographic location.

In addition, FMD News monitoring is an ongoing effort by the Artificial Intelligence Lab at the University of Arizona and the FMD Lab at UC Davis to collect open source FMD breaking news. A team of epidemiologists from different countries at the FMD Lab reviews more than 40 Web sites daily and sends out the selected news items in a summary format to a listserv. An automatic FMD related news collection and classification system was recently developed by the AI Lab at the University of Arizona.

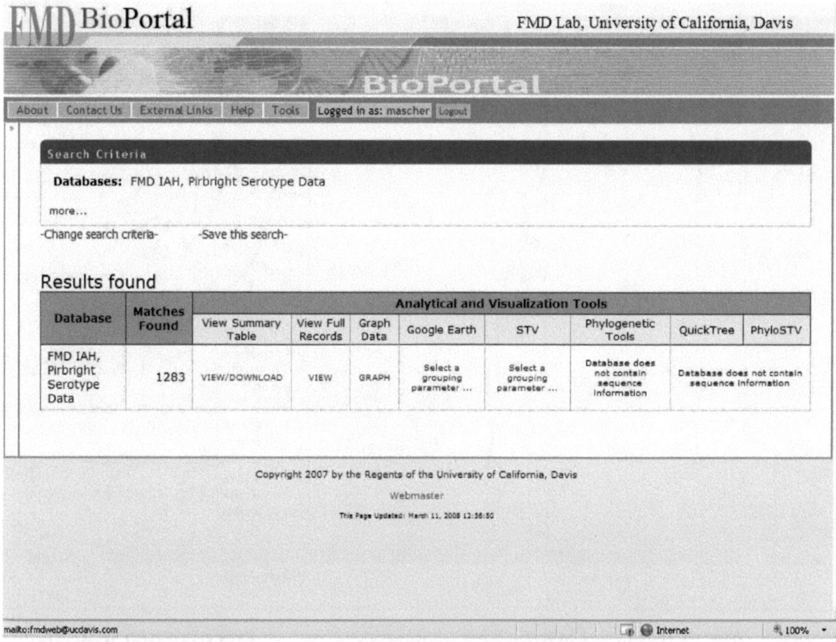

Figure 9-7. FMD BioPortal for accessing analytical and visualization tools (source: FMD BioPortal Web site).

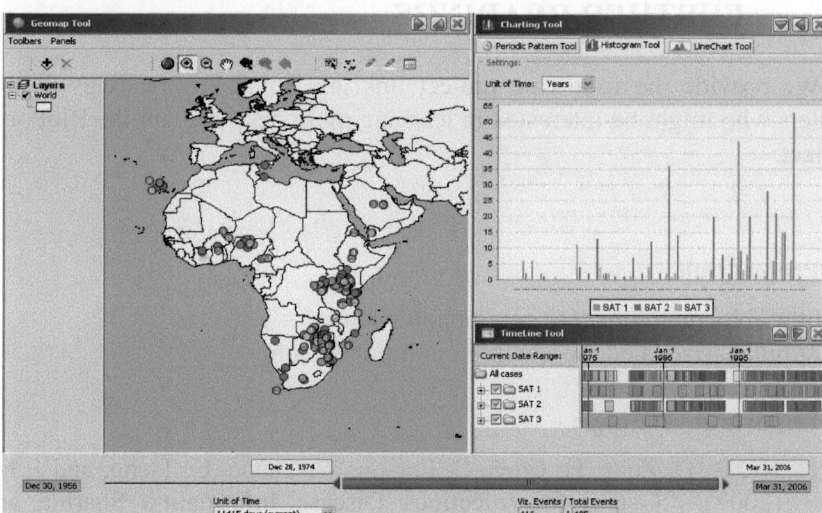

Figure 9-8. Visualization of FMD geographical distribution (source: FMD BioPortal Web site).

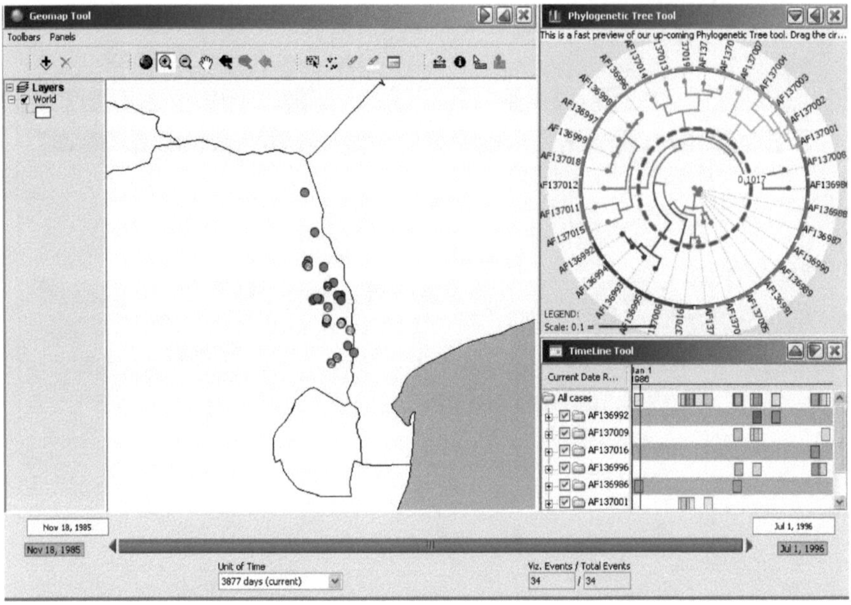

Figure 9-9. FMD phylogenetic tree visualization (source: FMD BioPortal Web site).

5. FURTHER READINGS

We provide the following project link and some key readings for the readers who might be interested in learning more details about the BioPortal project.

Project link:

http://biocomputingcorp.com/bphome.html
http://ai.arizona.edu/research/bioportal/index.htm

Important readings:

1. Hu, P., D. Zeng, H. Chen, C. Larson, W. Chang, C. Tseng, and J. Ma (2007). "System for Infectious Disease Information Sharing and Analysis: Design and Evaluation," *IEEE Transactions on Information Technology in Biomedicine*, Vol. 11, No. 4.
2. Lu, H.-M., D. Zeng, L. Trujillo, K. Komatsu, and H. Chen (2008). "Ontology-Enhanced Automatic Chief Complaint Classification for Syndromic Surveillance," *Journal of Biomedical Informatics,* Vol. 41, No. 2, pp 340–356.

3. Chang, W., D. Zeng, and H. Chen (2008). "A Stack-Based Prospective Spatio-Temporal Data Analysis Approach," *Decision Support Systems*, Vol. 45, No. 4, pp 697–713.
5. Zhang, Y.L., Y. Dang, Y.-D. Chen, H. Chen, M. Thurmond, C.-C. King, D. Zeng, C. Larson (2008). "BioPortal Infectious Disease Informatics research: disease surveillance and şituational awareness," *in proceedings of International Conference on Digital Government Research*, pp 393–394.

Chapter 10

ESSENCE

The Electronic Surveillance System for the Early Notification of Community-Based Epidemics (ESSENCE) was developed by the Johns Hopkins University Applied Physics Laboratory (JHU/APL) in collaboration with the Maryland Department of Health and Mental Hygiene, the District of Columbia Department of Health, and the Virginia Department of Health under the sponsorship of the Defense Advanced Research Projects Agency (DARPA). It is now used in the Department of Defense Global Emerging Infections System (DoD-GEIS). It is currently deployed in the National Capital Area (NCA) (Lombardo et al., 2004). The system monitors both military and civilian healthcare data daily for early outbreak detection and warning, fusing information from multiple data sources that vary in their medical specificity, spatial organization, scale, and time-series behavior (Burkom et al., 2004). ESSENCE has gone through a series of important development stages, and its most current prototype is ESSENCE IV.

Figure 10-1 shows the system architecture of ESSENCE. It collects public health status information from three major channels: clinical data, nonclinical syndromic data, and health events-related information. The accessibility of the collected information is managed by either disclosure control or sharing polices to ensure the privacy of personal healthcare information. Automated outbreak detection and alerting are supported. Situation and threat awareness and epidemiology investigation support are integrated with secured Web-based visualization and user interfaces.

H. Chen et al., *Infectious Disease Informatics: Syndromic Surveillance for Public Health and BioDefense*, Integrated Series in Information Systems 21, DOI 10.1007/978-1-4419-1278-7_10,

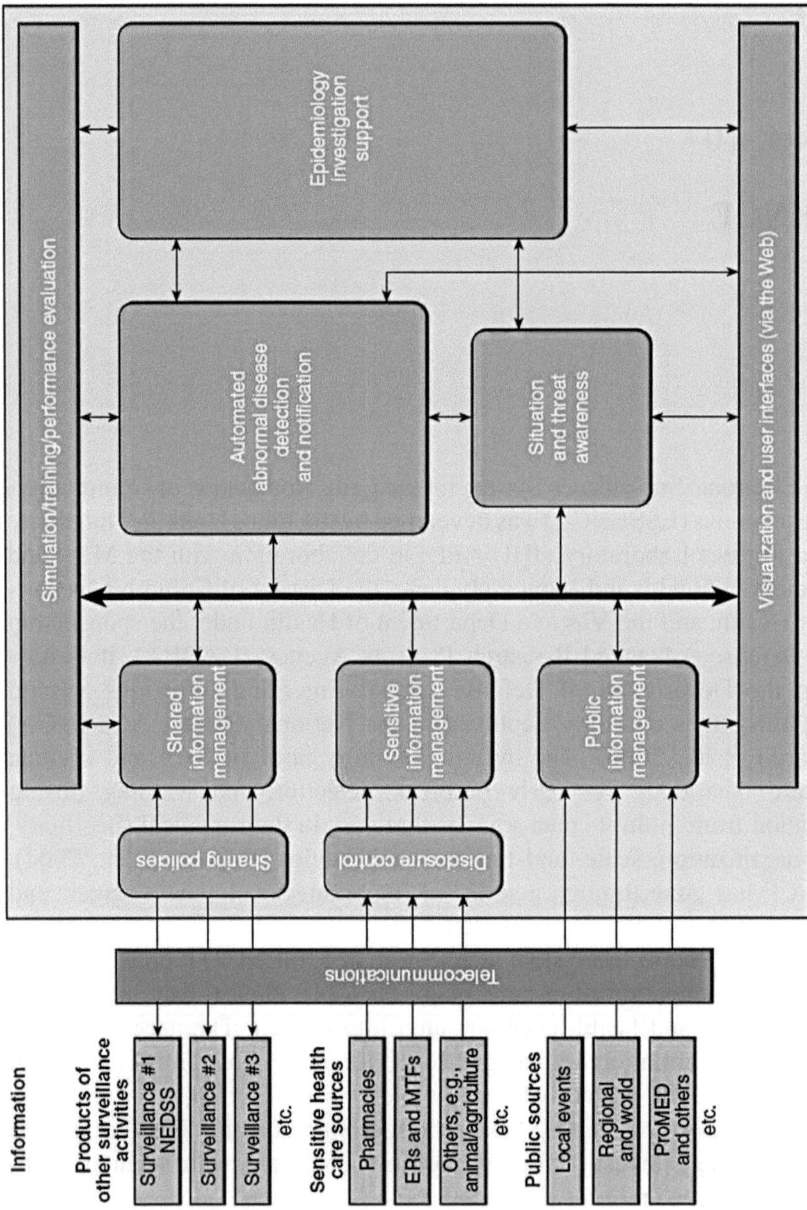

Figure 10-1. ESSENCE system architecture (Lombardo et al., 2003).

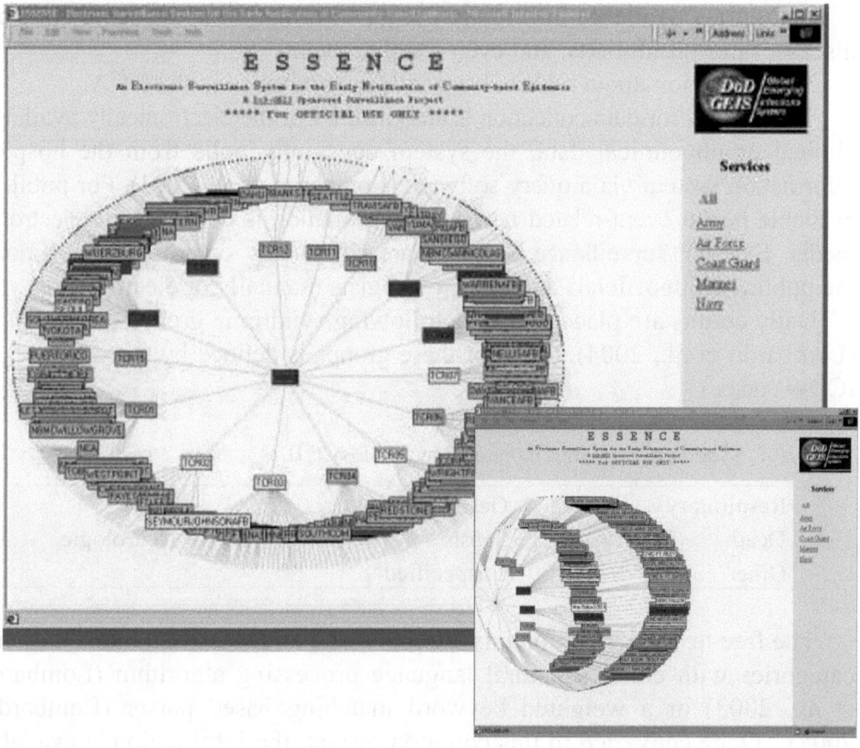

Figure 10-2. Graphs of all the reporting MTFs (icons are highlighted in one of three colors based on the degree of departure from historical data for one or more syndrome group on any given day).

Participation of military treatment facilities (MTFs) constitutes an important part of ESSENCE system. Figure 10-2 shows all the reporting MTFs (icons are highlighted in one of three colors based on the degree of departure from historical data for one or more syndrome group on any given day).

1. ESSENCE DATA COLLECTION

ESSENCE now mainly collects three types of data (Lombardo et al., 2003):

1. Chief complaint data from hospital ERs; ICD-9-CM codes, OTC sales of pharmaceuticals, nurse hotline calls; school absenteeism; and veterinary reports; 100% of the clinical visits of military and their dependents are included.

2. Publicly available information (e.g., information about local endemic disease, sales promotions, and even weather events).

3. Information about external surveillance activities in the NCA.

The process for data collection is automated. For the electronically available clinical or nonclinical data, the system constantly polls from the hospital information system via a query software (Lombardo et al., 2003). For publicly available health event-related news, the information is collected via electronic media. External surveillance activities are continually communicated among the public health officials and epidemiologists manually or electronically.

Daily counts are placed into the following syndrome groups (Table 10-1) (Lombardo et al., 2004). (Each of these groups is defined by a specific set of ICD-9 codes.)

Table 10-1. Syndrome categories monitored by ESSENCE II.

Respiratory	Gastrointestinal	Rash
Death	Sepsis	Neurologic
Other	Unspecified	

The free text chief complaints are processed and classified into syndrome categories with either a natural language processing algorithm (Lombardo et al., 2003) or a weighted keyword matching based parser (Lombardo, 2004). "Once converted to this common format, the information is available for use or for other surveillance activities. Within minutes of the query to the hospital emergency room electronic log, the system can forward counts of the syndrome groups to the participating hospital, state, and county surveillance activities. This information in most cases is available via electronic media. Likewise, the occurrence of high-profile events in the community may change detection and alerting thresholds" (Lombardo et al., 2003).

The time lag in data collection is currently a major limitation of ESSENCE. Most of the data can be received within 1–3 days after patient visits. However, improved timely reporting, optimized automated data transmission, and more frequent data uploads should decrease the data lag to one day.

2. ESSENCE DATA ANALYSIS AND SYSTEM EVALUATION

The temporal analysis methods for outbreak detection currently used in ESSENCE include an autoregressive modeling algorithm and the Exponentially Weighted Moving Average (EWMA) technique. CDC's Early Aberration Reporting System (EARS) algorithms are also included for temporal analysis as reference algorithms for assessing the performance enhancement provided by the ESSENCE algorithms (Lombardo et al., 2003). For spatial anomaly detection, the Kulldorff scan statistic as implemented in the SaTScan software is used as a primary spatial analysis tool. A modified version of scan statistic is also developed to produce approximate clusters of space-time interaction.

In ESSENCE, the outbreak detection methods take a "data-fusion" approach that includes multiple data streams. Burkom and Elbert applied the Kulldorff statistic to multiple data sources in ESSENCE by treating them as covariates while using whatever spatial information is available in each source (Burkom, 2003). A multiple univariate strategy can also be applied to the multiple data stream analysis, by treating each data stream separately with a univariate outbreak detection method. Then a consensus approach based on Bayes Belief Network (BBN) is used to combine the outputs of the multiple univariate algorithms to optimize the decision (Burkom et al., 2004). The BBN approach increases the sensitivity while controlling the false-alert rate. Table 10-2 lists the three categories of outbreak detection methods currently employed in ESSENCE.

The outbreak detection capacity with ESSENCE has been tested in a few studies. In the 2003 study (Lombardo et al., 2003), several outbreak scenarios were developed to test the performance, each scenario consisting of a series of real data streams with a simulated outbreak superimposed. The value of multiple data sources added to the detection performance is discussed by plotting the performance of the algorithms for respiratory syndrome as a function of the number of infected people and the involvement of different data sources (ER visits, absenteeism data, OTC influenza medication sales, and school absentee totals). It shows that the absenteeism data contributes to the timeliness in the detection by 2 days and require a smaller population of infected people.

In the Bio-ALIRT evaluation program, three of the ESSENCE's detection algorithms (Provider-count-adjusted MSPC, multiple univariate EWMA, and Bayes Belief Network combination) aggregating multiple data sources were tested for respiratory or gastrointestinal syndromes (Burkom et al., 2004). Sensitivity and timeliness are measured as performance assessment metrics.

Table 10-2. Analytical methods used in ESSENCE for early outbreak detection.

Temporal analysis	Spatial analysis	Spatial-temporal analysis
Autoregressive modeling	Scan statistic	Modified scan statistic
EWMA		
EARS algorithms (as reference)		

The performance results of the three methods are summarized in (Lombardo et al., 2004). In general, the provider-count-adjusted MSPC and multiple univariate EWMA algorithm reduce the median detection time by 5 days for the most constrained false-alert rate, whereas the BBN improved timeliness by 2 days. The BBN also detected an additional outbreak at the lowest specificity (Lombardo et al., 2004).

3. ESSENCE INTERFACE, INFORMATION DISSEMINATION, AND REPORTING

ESSENCE provides a map-based visualization tool that can display both raw case/event data and clusters/hotspots identified by scan statistics. The user can enter zip codes or click on an area on the map to select subsets of data of interest. The details about cases or events are presented as tables or time-series graphs. ESSENCE provides the second portal listing alerts generated as the output of the detection processes. These lists consist of color-coded flags to indicate the extent of deviations from the baseline normalcy. Upper confidence limits (UCLs) for the daily predictions are computed and used as thresholds for alerts. If an observed case count exceeds the 95% UCL but not the 99% UCL, a low-level (yellow) alert is generated. If the count exceeds the 99% UCL, a high-level (red) flag results. The user can organize the alert lists for selected data of interest. They can also sort these lists by various criteria and access data or port them to the map visualization tool to view the spatial distribution of flagged cases.

The third ESSENCE tool, the query portal, allows a user to select subsets of data and data elements from drop-down menus and view these data elements over a user-specified timeframe as graphs or tables. The fourth portal can be used to generate summary reports, which can then be exported outside of ESSENCE for further analysis. The user can select any data elements in the archive and view historic counts as well as upward or downward trends.

Information dissemination in ESSENCE is based on user roles and jurisdictions. A basic function of ESSENCE is to deliver alerts and surveillance information to the military and civilian public health authorities in the NCA. The system provides detection outputs as well as the details of underlying data streams via secure Web sites. Information is provided in many separate information layers. In ESSENCE, this data layering approach was implemented to facilitate the distribution to various user roles. "For example, a user who logs on from an emergency room may be able to see only the emergency room data from his or her jurisdiction, whereas a user recognized as a director of epidemiology would have access to all the information within his or her jurisdiction as well as the shared information from the surrounding jurisdictions in the region" (Lombardo, 2003).

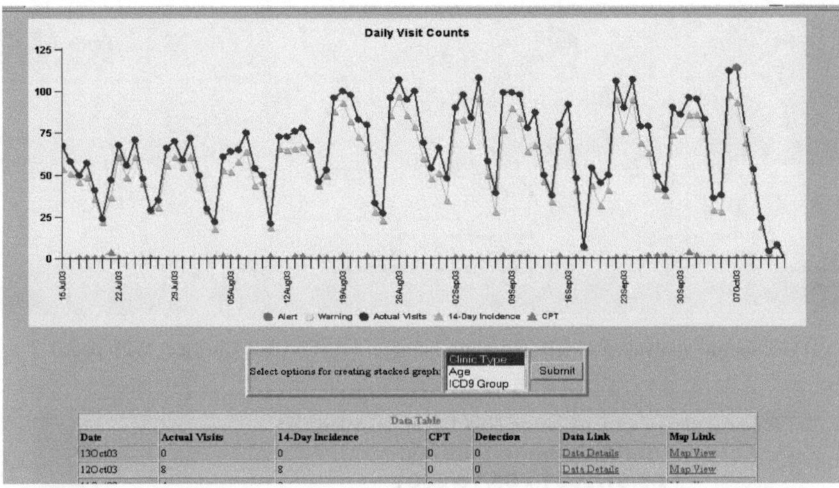

(a) Temporal analysis with time-series plot (source: Tricare presentation (2005c)).

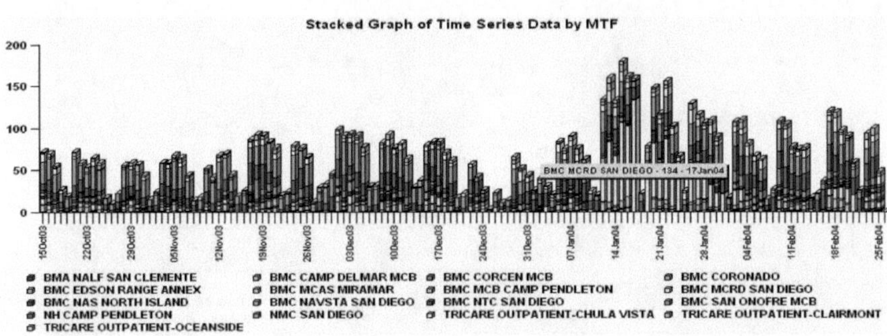

(b) Temporal analysis with stacked graph of time-series (source: Tricare presentation (2005c)).

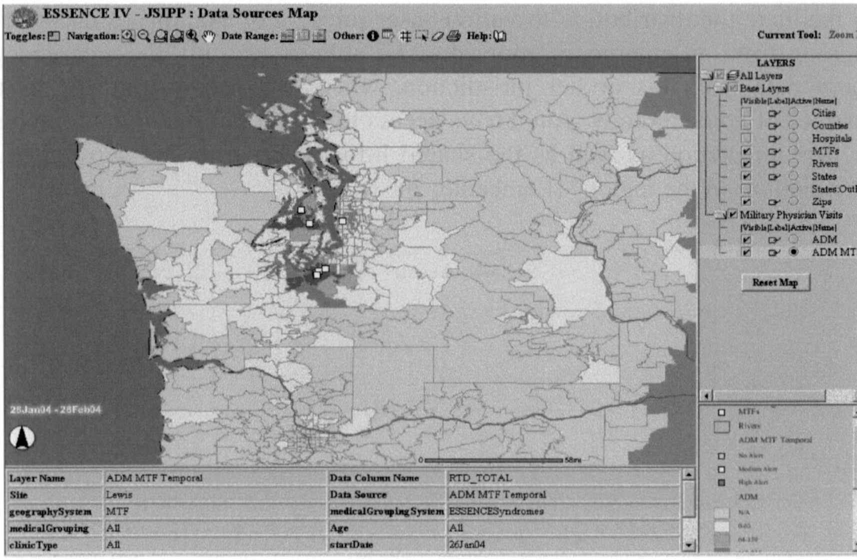

(c) Geospatial analysis and GIS mapping (source: ESSENCE IV project Web page).

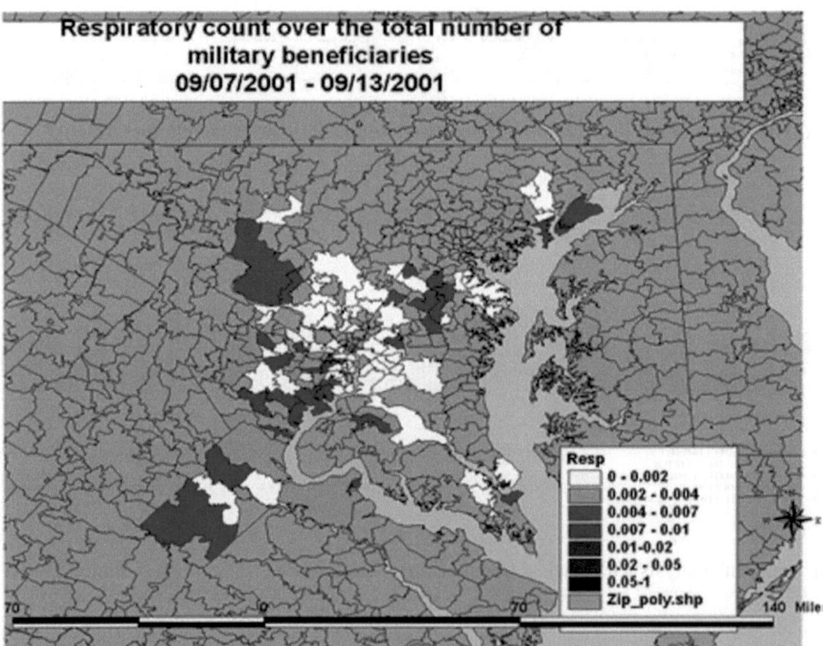

(d) GIS mapping of the National Capital Region for respiratory syndrome (source: ESSENCE IV project Web page).

Figure 10-3. Visualization of ESSENCE system.

4. FURTHER READINGS

We provide the following project link and some key readings for the readers who might be interested in learning more details about the ESSENCE system.

Project link:

http://eedweb.dhss.mo.gov/

Important readings:

1. Lombardo, J., and H. Burkom, et al. (2003). "A systems overview of the Electronic Surveillance System for the Early Notification of Community-based Epidemics (ESSENCE II)." *Journal of Urban Health: Bulletin of the New York Academy of Medicine*, **80**(2): pp 32–42.
2. Burkom, H., and E. Elbert, et al. (2004). "Role of Data Aggregation in Biosurveillance Detection Strategies with Applications from ESSENCE." MMWR (CDC) 53(Suppl): pp 67–73.
3. Lombardo, J., and H. Burkom, et al. (2004). "Electronic Surveillance System for the Early Notification of Community-Based Epidemics (ESSENCE II), Framework for Evaluating Syndromic Surveillance Systems." Syndromic surveillance: report from a national conference, 2003. MMWR 2004 53(Suppl): pp 159–165.

Chapter 11

NEW YORK CITY SYNDROMIC SURVEILLANCE SYSTEMS

The New York City (NYC) Department of Health and Mental Hygiene (DOHMH) has conducted prospective surveillance of syndromes since 1995 (Heffernan et al., 2004a). The DOHMH syndromic surveillance system consists of Emergency Department (ED)-visits-based surveillance system and a few other complementary surveillance systems for Emergency Medical Services (EMS) ambulance dispatch calls, retail pharmacy sales, and work absenteeism data. These systems started operating separately, and different analytical methods are being employed by each of them. A "drop-in" syndromic surveillance system that deployed CDC field-staff to conduct 24 hours surveillance for bioterrorism related illness was implemented following the September 11th 2001 attack (Das et al., 2003; CDC, 2002). We use Table 11-1 to summarize these systems that comprise the syndromic surveillance activities in New York City. However, in the following text, the case study will focus around the ED visits based syndromic surveillance system in NYC.

H. Chen et al., *Infectious Disease Informatics: Syndromic Surveillance for Public Health and BioDefense*, Integrated Series in Information Systems 21, DOI 10.1007/978-1-4419-1278-7_11,

Table 11-1. The syndromic surveillance systems in New York City.

Syndromic system	Analytical approaches	Analysis frequency	Data transmission
Emergency Medical Services (EMS) Ambulance Dispatch Calls (Greenko et al., 2003)	An adaptation of the excess influenza mortality cyclical (linear) regression model	Daily	Calls
Emergency Department Visits (Heffernan et al., 2004b)	Prospective temporal and spatial scan statistics	Daily	FTP or Email attachments
Retail Pharmacy Sales (cough and influenza medications, and antidiarrheal medicines)	A linear regression model similar to that used in the EMS system, controlling for season, holidays, day of the week, promotional sales, positive influenza tests, and temperature	Daily (weekdays only)	FTP
Worker absenteeism	CUSUM method with a 14-day baseline	Daily	
A "drop-in" syndromic surveillance system following the 9/11 attack (CDC, 2002)	Same techniques that had been developed for the EMS ambulance dispatch system	Daily	CDC field-staff collected the data at 15 NYC hospital ERs

1. NYC ED SYNDROMIC SURVEILLANCE SYSTEM DATA COLLECTION

By November 2003, 44 of NYC's 67 EDs participated in this system, thereby capturing 80% of all NYC ED patient visits (Heffernan et al., 2004a). Data files are transmitted to DOHMH daily, either as email attachments or through FTP. Half of the participating hospitals have already automated the transmission process. Files can be in several formats, most commonly as fixed-column or delimited ASCII text. "Data are read and translated into a standard format, concatenated into a single SAS dataset, verified for completeness and accuracy, and appended to a master archive." (Heffernan et al., 2004a, 2004b).

The chief complaints captured by the ED visit records are classified into eight exclusive syndrome categories (Table 11-2) with an SAS algorithm developed in-house. This algorithm scans the chief complaint field for character strings assigned to a syndrome. The coding algorithm is designed to capture a wide variety of common misspellings and abbreviations. If the chief complaints contain words or phrases from multiple categories, it will be coded according to the following priority-based assignment scheme: common cold > sepsis/dead on arrival > respiratory > diarrhea > fever > rash > asthma > vomiting > other visits. This scheme attempts to place each chief complaint into a single, specific syndrome. The two syndromes of particular interest for bioterrorism surveillance are the respiratory and fever syndromes in persons older than 13 years of age (Heffernan et al., 2004b).

Table 11-2. Exclusive syndrome categories of collected chief complaints in NYC ED syndromic surveillance system.

Common cold	Sepsis	Respiratory
Diarrhea	Fever	Rash
Asthma	Vomiting	

2. NYC ED SYNDROMIC SURVEILLANCE SYSTEM DATA ANALYSIS AND FIELD INVESTIGATIONS

The NYC ED syndromic surveillance system uses an adaption of Kulldorff and Mostashari's one-dimensional temporal to evaluate citywide trends in syndrome visits and spatial scan statistic (Kulldorff, 1997, 2001) to evaluate clustering in ED visits by hospital address and patient home zip code.

The temporal scan statistic is a special case of the prospective space-time scan statistic. The analysis is conducted in a prospective setting with daily runs and a variable-length window consisting of the last 1, 2, or 3 days. In particular, the ratio of syndrome visits to nonsyndrome (other) visits during the most recent 1, 2, or 3 days is compared with a 2-week baseline.

The spatial scan statistic approach requires comparing the observed to the expected number of cases in each geographic area. To control for purely spatial differences, expected counts of syndrome visits are derived from each area's history, rather than from the underlying census population. To detect rapidly emerging outbreaks, the approach takes the data from the observed cases from the last day and compares them with data from a 14-day baseline period, with a 1-day gap between the baseline and the date on which spatial clustering is being evaluated.

The surveillance signals produced by the system are first reviewed by medical epidemiologists on a daily basis. A report consisting of graphs and a brief summary is distributed by electronic mail to program staff. Further validations are conducted through field investigations. Detailed field investigations of syndromic signals are meant to (1) identify the etiology of signals; (2) determine why a given syndromic surveillance system failed to detect an outbreak captured through traditional surveillance; (3) validate the utility of syndromic surveillance for early infectious disease outbreak detection.

3. NYC ED SYNDROMIC SURVEILLANCE SYSTEM VISUALIZATION, INFORMATION DISSEMINATION, AND REPORTING

Daily analyses are reviewed with a medical epidemiologist, and a report containing detailed graphs and a brief summary is distributed by email to related program staff. If a signal investigation is performed, a more detailed report will be prepared and made available by the next day. "An external report summarizing citywide public health trends is also distributed daily to state and regional health officials, the New York City Office of Emergency Management, police departments, and fire departments. Hospital-specific, confidential reports are shared quarterly with participating emergency departments, comparing their facility to overall citywide trends" (Heffernan et al., 2004a, 2004b).

Spatial syndromic signals are followed up by reviewing the descriptive summary of the emergency department visits included in the signal. Hospital(s) contributing the largest number of excess cases are paid particular attention, by examining the specific syndromes triggering the signal and the line list of patients with their chief complaints produced, along with summary statistics for age, sex, and zip code. Syndromic signals are communicated to other hospital ED staff through phone calls to alert them of unusual disease patterns and to ask whether they have noted an increase in the frequency of syndrome visits or admission of seriously ill patients. Signals of elevated concern are further investigated by conducting field investigations including chart reviews, patient interviews, and onsite discussions with clinicians.

Some sample graphs from the presentations of DOHMH syndromic surveillance made at the National Syndromic Surveillance Conference (Mostashari, 2002) are as shown in Figures 11-1 to 11-3.

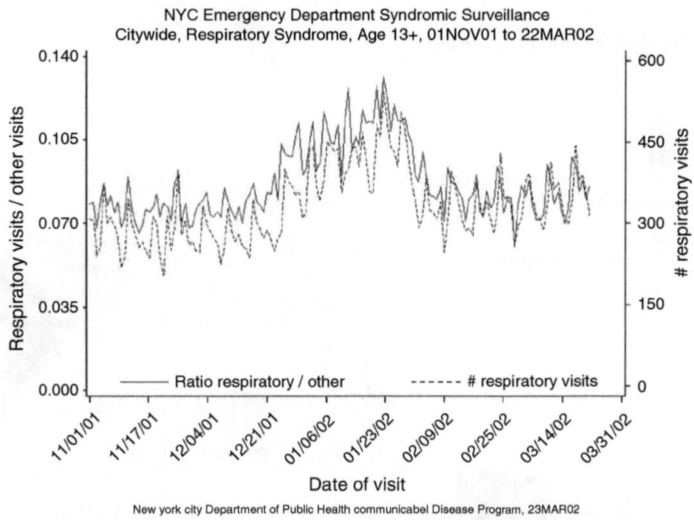

Figure 11-1. Plotting of NYC ED respiratory visits from November 2001 through March 2002 (Mostashari, 2002).

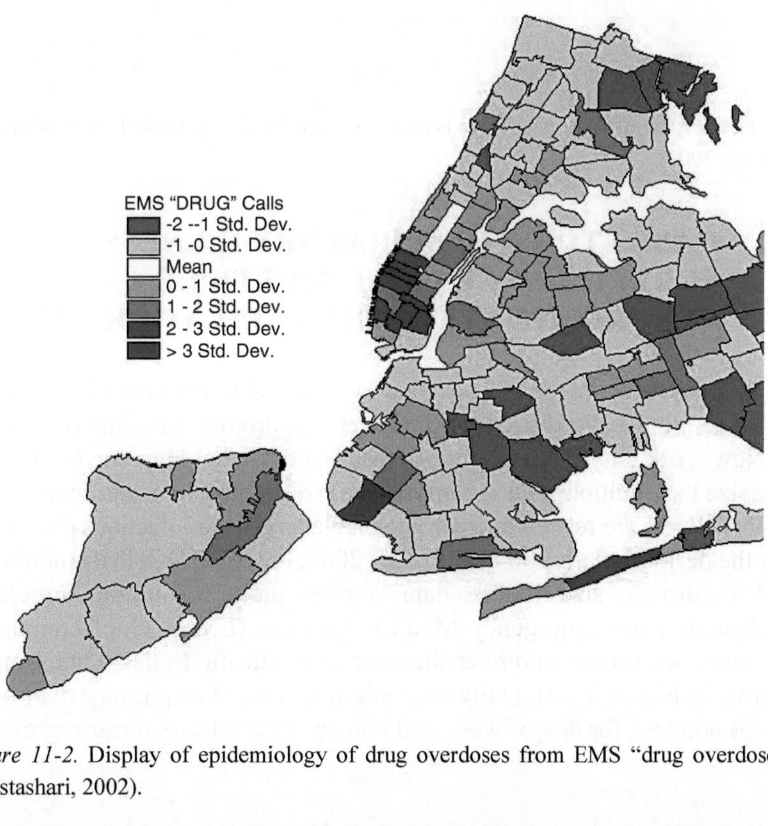

Figure 11-2. Display of epidemiology of drug overdoses from EMS "drug overdose" calls (Mostashari, 2002).

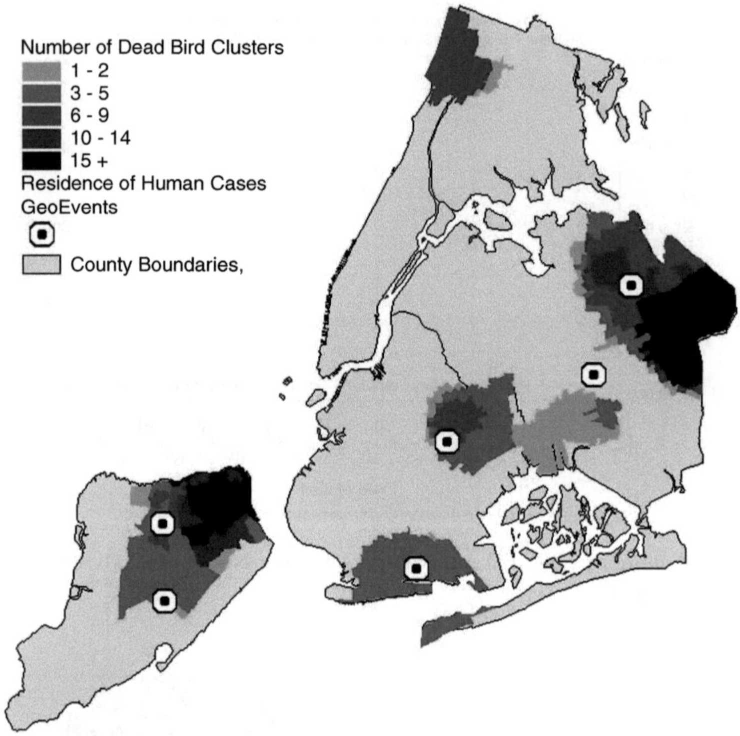

Figure 11-3. Display of West Nile Virus activities in New York City through September 2001 (Mostashari, 2002).

4. CASE STUDY: RESPIRATORY ILLNESS SURVEILLANCE USING MULTIPLE SYNDROMIC SYSTEMS IN NEW YORK CITY

Community-wide increases in respiratory illness detected through syndromic surveillance are usually difficult to interpret. Syndromic surveillance analysts at the New York City Department of Health and Mental Hygiene (DOHMH) hypothesize that multiple data streams can help distinguish whether increases in respiratory illness are related to environmental allergens or infectious diseases.

For the period June 1, 2004 to May 31, 2005, the NYC DOHMH monitored several syndromic surveillance data sources daily, including ambulance dispatch calls from Emergency Medical Services (EMS), chief complaints from emergency rooms, and over-the-counter medication sales (data samples are shown in Figure 11-4). Daily citywide ratio of ED respiratory over other visits was adjusted for day-of-week and holiday effects using linear regression.

Volume spikes in the daily adjusted ratio were identified using the EARS CUSUM C3 method with a 14-day baseline. During the study period, five sustained, citywide spikes in ED respiratory illness were observed. Figure 11-5 shows the plot of ED respiratory illness ratio over other visits adjusted day-of-week and holiday effects, with CUSUM signals marked and the corresponding areas shaded in gray.

		Call-type							
Date	**Time**	**Initial**	**Final**	**RunNo**	**Zip**	**Unit**	**DispoUnit**	**Dispo**	**Hosp**
5/5/2003	0:00:12			1	11211				
5/5/2003	0:00:05			2	10455		67C	23	
5/5/2003	0:00:21			3	11218				
5/5/2003	0:00:28			4	10458		56	43	
5/5/2003	0:00:39			5	10013			84	

Date	**Store**	**Zip**	**Dept**	**Subdept**	**Descrip**	**Promo**	**Sold**	**Stock**	**UPC**
9/1/2002	323	10006	113	001	MOTRIN CHILD COLD GRAPE 4 OZ	N		61	0300450903044
9/1/2002	323	10006	114	001	EXCEDRIN XSTR CAPS 24'S	N		7	0319810000217
9/1/2002	323	10006	115	001	DR ASPRN LITE COAT 500'S	N	0	27	0033261111116
9/1/2002	323	10006	116	002	CLARITIN 24hr REDI TAB 10ct	N	0	8	0041100060662
9/1/2002	323	10006	122	002	LUDENS BAG HNY-LEM BNS 30CT	N	1	15	0000083000591

Figure 11-4. Sample ambulance dispatch calls and over-the-counter pharmacy data.

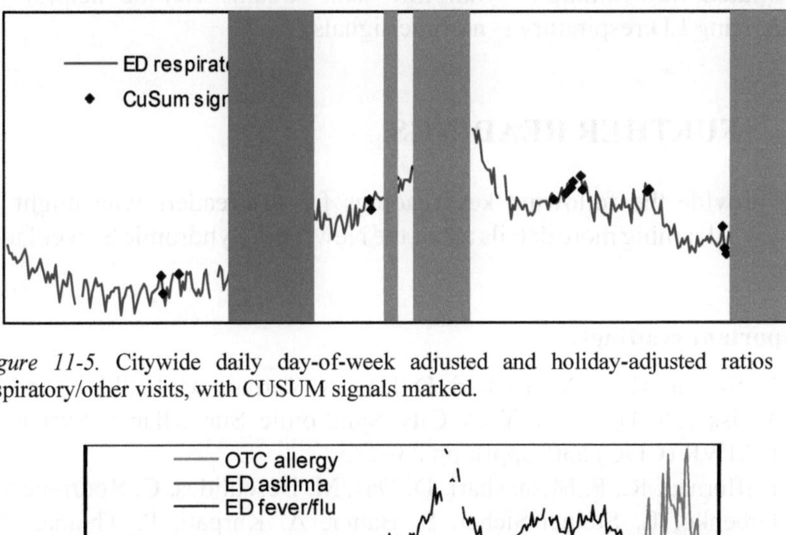

Figure 11-5. Citywide daily day-of-week adjusted and holiday-adjusted ratios of ED respiratory/other visits, with CUSUM signals marked.

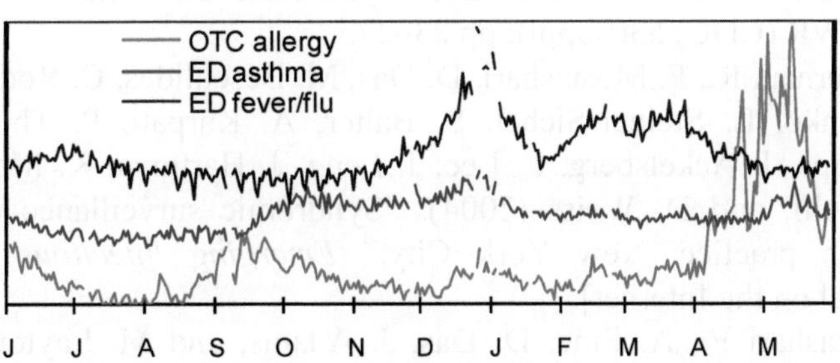

Figure 11-6. Plots of daily citywide ratios of OTC allergy over analgesics sales (gray), ED asthma over other visits (green), and ED fever-flu over other visits (blue).

To investigate whether the signals are related to influenza or allergy season, the adjusted daily citywide ratios of OTC allergy over analgesics sales (gray), ED asthma over other visits (green), and ED fever-flu over other visits (blue) were also plotted (see Figure 11-6).

Comparing two sets of plots, i.e., the adjusted ratios of ED respiratory/ other visits (Figure 11-5) and ratios of OTC, ED asthma, and ED-fever-flu (Figure 11-6), six signals of ED respiratory illness over a 15-day period in September and October were preceded by a spike in OTC allergy sales, and so were nine signals in May. These signals also coincided with increasing ED asthma visits while ED fever-flu visits remained constant. Instead, three consecutive signals in late November, 16 signals in December and 7 signals in February coincided with increasing ED fever-flu visits, while these periods showed minimal to no increases in ED asthma visits or OTC allergy sales. The signal patterns in the multiple data streams suggested that respiratory illness increases in Fall and Spring could be attributed to allergy or asthma, whereas the Winter increase in respiratory illness is more likely to be attributed to influenza (Das, 2005).

The respiratory illness syndromic surveillance practice at New York City demonstrated how multiple syndromic data streams can be helpful for characterizing ED respiratory syndrome signals.

5. FURTHER READINGS

We provide the following key readings for the readers who might be interested in learning more details about the New York Syndromic Surveillance system.

Important readings:

1. Heffernan, R., F. Mostashari, D. Das, A. Karpati, M. Kulldorf, and D. Weiss (2004). "New York City Syndromic Surveillance Systems." MMWR (CDC) 53(Suppl): pp 23–27.
2. Heffernan, R., F. Mostashari, D. Das, M. Besculides, C. Rodriguez, J. Greenko, L. Steiner-Sichel, S. Balter, A. Karpati, P. Thomas, M. Phillips, J. Ackelsberg, E. Lee, J. Leng, J. Hartman, K. Metzger, R. Rosselli, and D. Weiss (2004). "Syndromic surveillance in public health practice, New York City." *Emerging Infectious Diseases* [serial on the Internet].
3. Mostashari F., A. Fine, D. Das, J. Adams, and M. Layton (2003). "Use of ambulance dispatch data as an early warning system for community-wide influenza-like illness, New York City." *Journal of Urban Health* 80(2 Suppl 1), pp i43–i49.

4. Heffernan, R., F. Mostashari, D. Das, M. Besculides, C. Rodriguez, J. Greenko, L. Steiner-Sichel, S. Balter, A. Karpati, P. Thomas, M. Phillips, J. Ackelsberg, E. Lee, J. Leng, J. Hartman, K. Metzger, R. Rosselli, and D. Weiss (2004). "System Descriptions New York City Syndromic Surveillance Systems." *MMWR(CDC)* 53(Suppl), pp 23–27.
5. Das, D., Metzger, K., Heffernan, R., Balter, S., Weiss, D. and Mostashari, F. 2005. "Monitoring Over-The-Counter Medication Sales for Early Detection of Disease of Disease Outbreaks—New York City, "*MMWR(CDC)* 54(Suppl), pp. 41–46.

Chapter 12

EARS

The Early Aberration Reporting System (EARS) was first developed at the US CDC. Current EARS system development and research activities are supported by the National Center for Infectious Diseases (NCID) Bioterrorism Preparedness and Response Program (Hutwagner et al., 2003). EARS provides national, state, and local health departments with several alternative aberration detection methods to analyze and visualize public health surveillance data for syndromic surveillance (Figure 12-1). "As of mid 2006, approximately 90 city, county and state public health offices, in addition to some international offices, use EARS to assist in the early identification of outbreaks of disease and bioterrorism events" (CDC, 2006a; Hutwagner et al., 2003). "The National Center for Infectious Diseases (NCID) Bioterrorism Preparedness and Response Program provides technical support and research and development for EARS activities" (Hutwagner et al., 2003).

EARS has been used in practice with several outbreaks flagged. "In one instance, a state health official thought they had a shigella outbreak. After running EARS on their notifiable diseases, the outbreak was confirmed and they were able to easily identify the county involved" (Hutwagner et al., 2003). "EARS has also linked an increase in asthma cases to an increase in the ozone level that was not large enough to trigger an ozone alarm. Another site using EARS identified the beginning of the West Nile Virus season and implemented spraying for mosquitoes" (Hutwagner et al., 2003).

EARS has also been used for several large public events. These events include the 2004 G8 Summit in Georgia, the 2004 Democratic National Convention in Boston, the 2004 Republican National Convention in New York City, and the 2004 Summer Olympics in Greece. The Florida State

H. Chen et al., *Infectious Disease Informatics: Syndromic Surveillance for Public Health and BioDefense*, Integrated Series in Information Systems 21, DOI 10.1007/978-1-4419-1278-7_12,

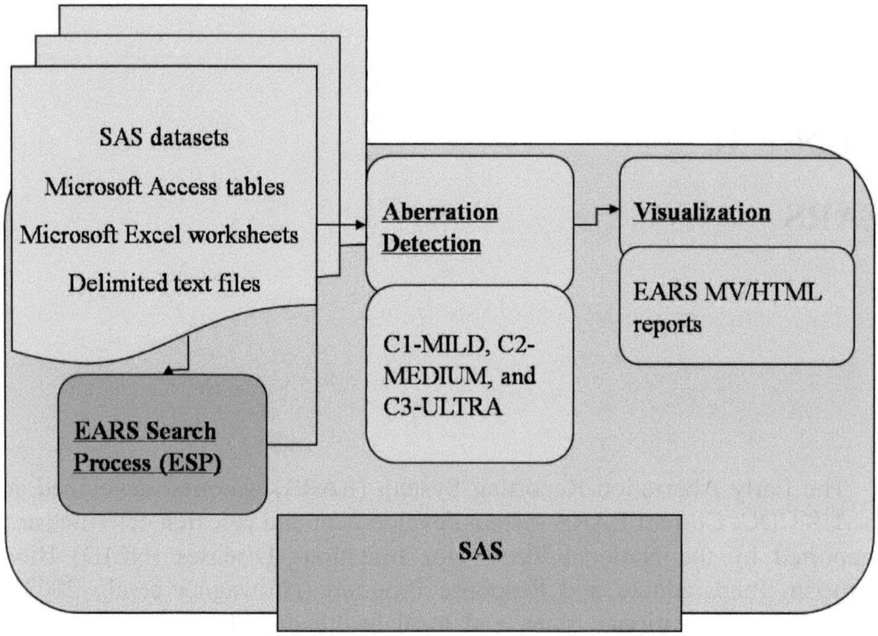

Figure 12-1. EARS SAS-based system architecture.

Department of Health used EARS following the 2004 hurricane season. EARS detected increases in animal bites and carbon monoxide during the post-hurricane monitoring period. EARS was also used for the 2005 hurricane season following Hurricanes Katrina and Rita for syndromic surveillance.

1. EARS DATA COLLECTION AND DATA PREPROCESSING

Users can feed EARS a variety of syndromic surveillance data streams for analysis. These data are chief complaints, admission codes, and discharge codes, over-the-counter drug sales, 911 emergency calls, physician office data, and school and business absenteeism. Data need to be saved as SAS datasets, Microsoft Access database tables, Microsoft Excel worksheets, or any delimited text files. EARS does not support real-time data streaming; in other words, it works in batch mode by loading the data manually.

EARS analyzes syndromic data from emergency departments based on chief complaint, admission codes and discharge codes, 911 emergency calls, physician office data, school and business absenteeism, and over the counter drug sales. EARS is also used for nationally notifiable disease information. Some EARS users, who receive their data via file transfer by a given time, have EARS set up to run as a scheduled task. Other users run EARS once a day or as needed from their laptop or desktop. In addition, users have taken the summary file that is produced and linked it back to the data for additional drill-down analysis. The majority of EARS users are able to run and review the information from several sources within 5–15 minutes a day.

In EARS, chief complaints are searched and recognized as a symptom and thus grouped into a particular syndrome category by using an internal function called EARS Search Process (ESP). ESP searches the chief complaint field for specific words that describe illnesses of interest that EARS should monitor. The syndrome categories predefined by the words are embedded within the EARS code. The syndrome definitions can be customized and expended by the users with the built-in logic equations to relate symptom names to the syndrome name.

It is also allowed to run the EARS search process (ESP) feature without running EARS. This makes it possible to build new symptoms and syndrome equations without running the entire EARS process.

2. KEY EARS ABERRATION DETECTION METHODS

EARS uses three limited baseline aberration detection methods called C1-MILD, C2-MEDIUM, and C3-ULTRA (CDC, 2006a) and two historical methods (at least 5 years historical data) – seasonally adjusted CUSUM method and historical limits method. The terms mild, medium, and ultra refer to the level of sensitivity of the three statistical methods. For example, the least sensitive statistical method is named C1-MILD since it is considered to have the lowest sensitivity. These methods were designed for public health surveillance data with varying degrees of available historical information. The seasonally adjusted CUSUM method is based on the positive 1-sided CUSUM where the count of interest is compared with the 5-year mean and the 5-year standard deviations for that period. The seasonally adjusted CUSUM was originally applied to laboratory-based *Salmonella* serotype data (Hutwagner et al., 2005). The historical limits method compares the current sum of 4 time periods to the mean of the sum of 15 totals of 4 time periods surrounding the current point of interest over 5 years (Hutwagner et al., 2005).

The length of the baseline comparison period for C1, C2, and C3 methods is one week. This time window allows the algorithms to account for possible fluctuations in the expected case count attributable to any particular day of the week. "In addition, the baseline period is always selected from the previous week or a recent week relative to the current value; therefore, if the syndrome of interest is seasonal, the baseline period most often represents values selected from the same season" (Hutwagner, 2005b).

"The selection of the baseline period relative to the current value is different for the C1-MILD method relative to the other two methods. For the C2-MEDIUM and C3-ULTRA methods, the baseline period is further back in time relative to the baseline period for the C1-MILD method. The baseline period for C1-MILD is obtained from the previous 7 days in closest proximity to the current value, (day[t-7] through day[t-1])" (Hutwagner, 2005b).

Figure 12-2 summarizes the evaluation results of performances of algorithm C1, C2, C3, and NBC 7-day, NBC 14-day and NBC 28-day in terms of sensitivity vs. false alarm rate. They are all CUSUM - based methods. The

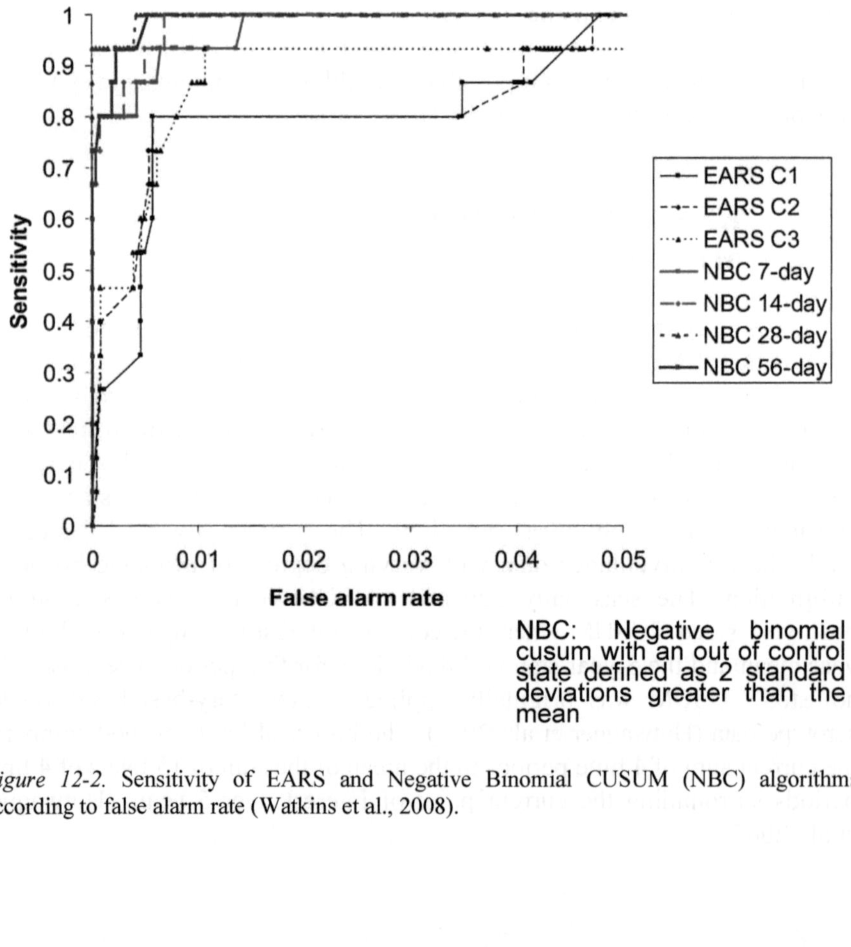

Figure 12-2. Sensitivity of EARS and Negative Binomial CUSUM (NBC) algorithms according to false alarm rate (Watkins et al., 2008).

class of Negative Binomial CUSUM (NBC) algorithms are CUSUM algorithm variations that are with an out of control state defined as 2 standard deviations greater than the mean. The evaluation is based on the detection of outbreaks of Ross River Virus disease in Western Australia. As shown in Figure 12-2, NBC algorithms show significantly higher sensitivity when compared with the EARS C1, C2, and C3 algorithms, particularly at low false alarm rates. It suggests that the NBC algorithms have a greater level of agreement with epidemiological opinion than the EARS algorithms with respect to the existence of outbreaks of Ross River Virus disease. However, the performance of individual EARS and NBC algorithms were not significantly different when timeliness was also incorporated into the analyses (Watkins et al., 2008).

3. EARS VISUALIZATION, INFORMATION DISSEMINATION, AND REPORTING

EARS generates time-series events occurrence plots for a period of time that is specified by the user. The plots are flagged with red marks according to the output of the C1-MILD, C2-MEDIUM, and C3-ULTRA methods. By clicking on the red marks, EARS can bring the users the original data that produced the flagged aberration. Figure 12-3 is a sample EARS 30-day graph report.

The EARS program presents its analysis in a complete HTML Web site containing tables and graphs linked through a homepage. Viewing EARS output requires only a Web browser. This output can be viewed simultaneously by several different public health officials at different locations (Hutwagner et al., 2003).

The EARS MV Report is the latest reporting tool introduced in EARS version 4. This tool allows the user to quickly view all the data for each syndrome on one page. The user can of course examine data tables in detail to view graphs, maps and the original data associated with any flagged output.

As depicted in Figure 12-4, the EARS MV Report window has two panels. The left panel, labeled "MV Report Contents," shows the contents of the entire report. The right panel shows the selected output. In the example below, the table output is shown in the right panel. The user can easily use the "Back" button on the contents panel to sift through previous output selections (CDC, 2006a).

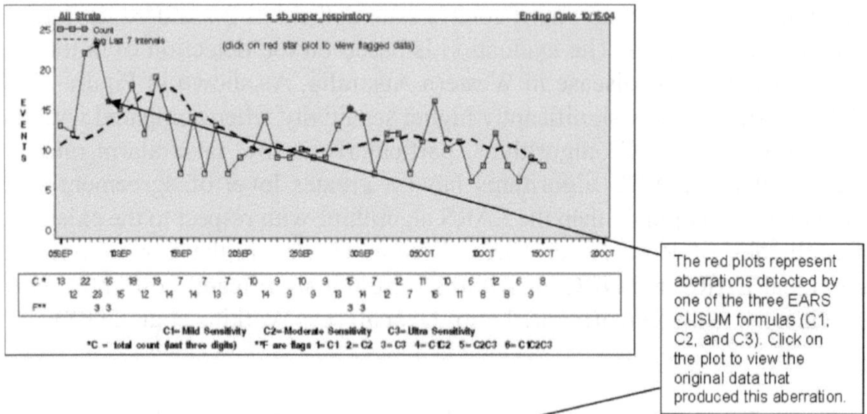

date=09/08/2004

hospclin	MEDREC	AGE	SEX	RACE	ETHNIC	chief_complaint
Hospital A	MA1016322	0	F	H	1	DIFFICULTY BREATHING
Hospital A	MA316322	29	F	B	2	SOB
Hospital A	MA416322	2	F	W	2	RESPIRATORY DISTRESS

Figure 12-3. Sample EARS 30-day graph report (source: CDC EARS Web site).

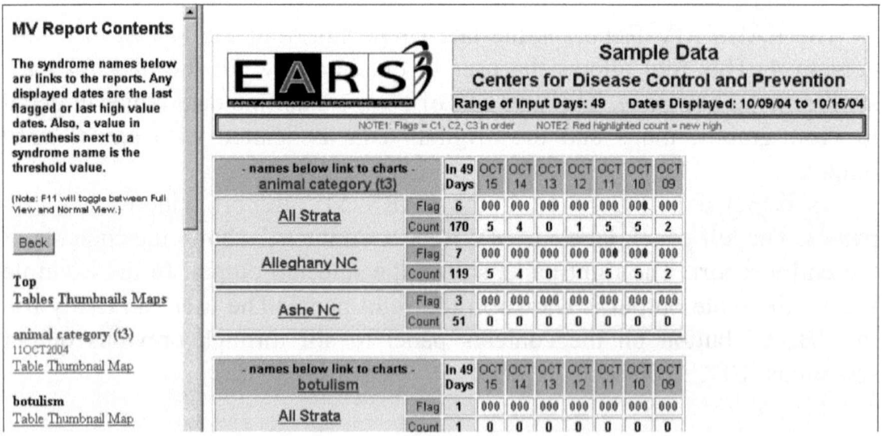

- names below link to charts - animal category (t3)		In 49 Days	OCT 15	OCT 14	OCT 13	OCT 12	OCT 11	OCT 10	OCT 09
All Strata	Flag	6	000	000	000	000	000	000	000
	Count	170	5	4	0	1	5	5	2
Alleghany NC	Flag	7	000	000	000	000	000	000	000
	Count	119	5	4	0	1	5	5	2
Ashe NC	Flag	3	000	000	000	000	000	000	000
	Count	51	0	0	0	0	0	0	0

- names below link to charts - botulism		In 49 Days	OCT 15	OCT 14	OCT 13	OCT 12	OCT 11	OCT 10	OCT 09
All Strata	Flag	1	000	000	000	000	000	000	000
	Count	1	0	0	0	0	0	0	0

Figure 12-4. EARS MV report (source: CDC EARS Web site).

4. CASE STUDY: POSTHURRICANE PUBLIC HEALTH SURVEILLANCE WITH EARS

In response to Hurricane Katrina, CDC and the Louisiana Department of Health and Hospitals (LDHH) implemented active public health surveillance in September, 2005, to monitor for injuries and illnesses at functioning hospitals and other acute-care facilities in the greater New Orleans area. At the same time, LDHH and Office of Public Health (LAOPH) recognized the need for communicable disease surveillance in the evacuation centers (ECs). Starting from August 2005, approximately 50,000 persons began moving into ECs throughout the state of Louisiana. In Figure 12-5, the number of persons under EC surveillance is plotted by date.

For EC surveillance, initially, communicable disease data were entered into a database and then analyzed by comparing daily results with a 3-day moving average. Beginning September 14, data were analyzed using EARS statistical software. CUSUM scores were computed for each syndromic category. An elevated CUSUM score suggests a potential outbreak. Elevated CUSUM scores and suspicious cases and clusters identified were investigated by telephone. Those cases that could not be reconciled by telephone were referred to LAOPH for investigation. During the period September 15 to October 26, review of individual EC surveillance forms led to 86 follow-up investigations by

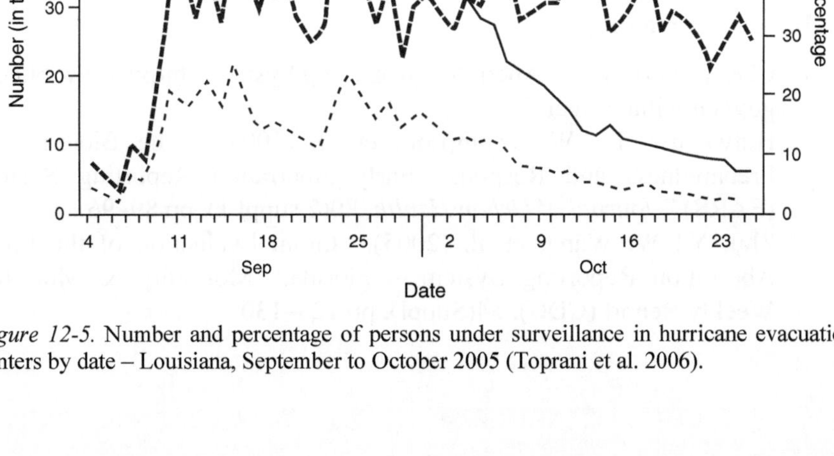

Figure 12-5. Number and percentage of persons under surveillance in hurricane evacuation centers by date – Louisiana, September to October 2005 (Toprani et al. 2006).

telephone; of these, 67 (74%) led to further investigation by LAOPH. "The EARS syndromic surveillance system produced 194 CUSUM scores that warranted telephone investigation; 46 (15%) were referred for follow-up by LAOPH. Of 56 investigations referred to LAOPH after implementation of EARS, 42 (75%) were identified by both an elevated CUSUM score and epidemiologist review of surveillance forms, 10 (18%) were identified by epidemiologist review only, and 4 (7%) were identified by an elevated CUSUM score only" (Toprani et al., 2006).

An active surveillance system was also implemented in hospital EDs and acute-care facilities starting in September 2005, to respond to this major disaster. The initial implementation was based on paper forms. Because intensive labor forces were required to maintain the paper-based system, an ED-based electronic syndromic surveillance system was implemented on October 17, 2005. Six participating EDs in the New Orleans area consented to transmit ED data electronically (e.g., patient demographics and chief complaint) every 24 hours to LDHH, where data were analyzed using EARS. This experience suggests that electronic ED-based syndromic surveillance is a more sustainable method to continue long-term surveillance for injury and illness after the initial response phase of a major disaster.

5. FURTHER READINGS

We provide the following project link and some key readings for the readers who might be interested in learning more details about the EARS system.

Project link:

http://www.bt.cdc.gov/surveillance/ears/

Important readings:

1. CDC (2006). "Early Aberration Reporting System." http://www.bt.cdc.gov/surveillance/ears/.
2. Hutwagner, L., W. Thompson, et al. (2003). "The Bioterrorism Preparedness and Response Early Aberration Reporting System (EARS)." *Journal of Urban Health*, 80(2 suppl 1), pp 89–96.
3. Zhu, Y., W. Wang, et al. (2005). "Initial Evaluation of the Early Aberration Reporting System – Florida." Morbidity & Mortality Weekly Report (CDC), 54(Suppl), pp 123–130.

4. CDC (2006). "Injury and Illness Surveillance in Hospitals and Acute-Care Facilities After Hurricanes Katrina and Rita, New Orleans Area, Louisiana, September 25–October 15, 2005." Morbidity & Mortality Weekly Report (CDC).
5. CDC (2006). "Surveillance in Hurricane Evacuation Centers – Louisiana, September–October 2005." Morbidity & Mortality Weekly Report (CDC), 55(02) pp 32–35.

Chapter 13

ARGUS

Project Argus creates and implements a biological event detection and tracking capability that provides early warning alerts on a global scale. Argus currently manages between 2,200 and 3,300 active, socially disruptive biological event case files with update report threading for approximately 175 countries and over 130 disease entities. It posits a sophisticated scaling of outbreak severity based not only on disease metrics but also on sociological and governmental reactions in the face of mild to severe epidemics (Chute, 2008).

The system relies on Internet technologies as "harvesting engines" to capture information relevant to the definitional criteria for biological-outbreak severity metrics. Official disease reports from WHO or unofficial international health status reports from ProMED are collected as indicators of possible biological events. The association of media activities and the biological events are shown in Figure 13-1. Figure 13-2 depicts the Argus system's biological event detection and tracking process.

H. Chen et al., *Infectious Disease Informatics: Syndromic Surveillance for Public Health and BioDefense*, Integrated Series in Information Systems 21, DOI 10.1007/978-1-4419-1278-7_13,

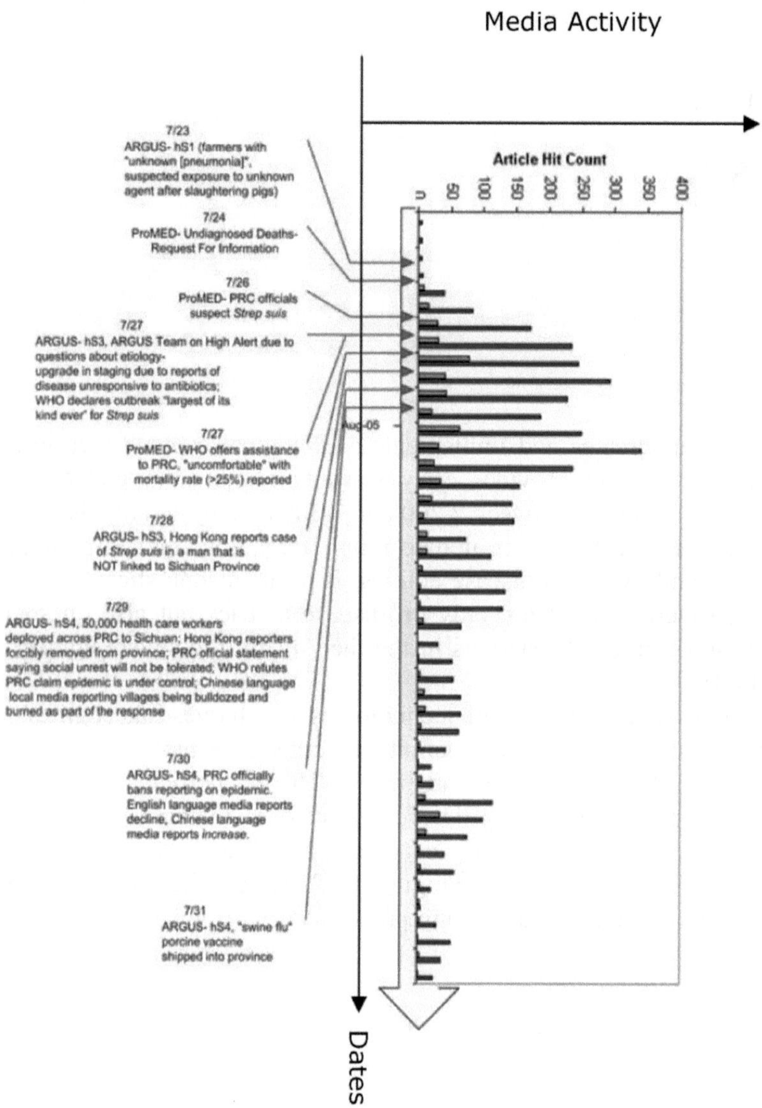

Figure 13-1. Media activities vs. time evolution of Argus monitored events (source: http://www.syndromic.org/conference/2007).

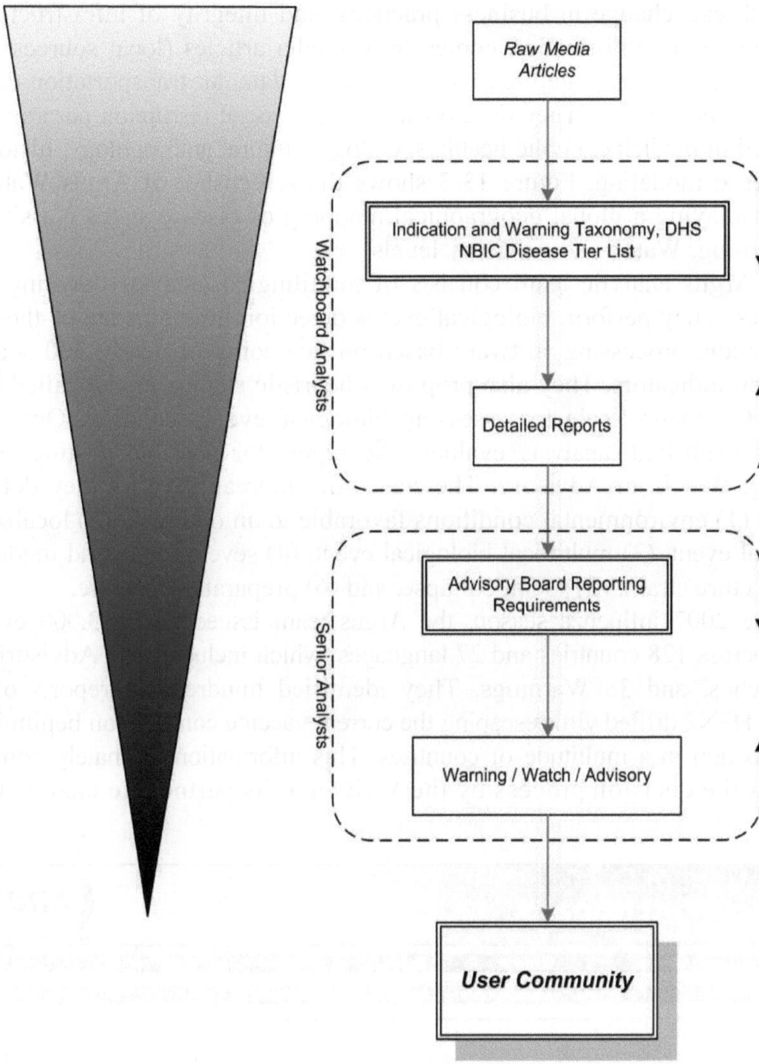

Figure 13-2. Argus biological event detection process (source: http://www.syndromic.org/conference/2007).

The major role of Argus is to monitor social disruption that is possibly caused by epidemics. Social disruption is a deviation from a routine daily activity that can be tracked and used in lieu of direct reporting of disease. Epidemiologists search through the open-source information for signs of epidemics-caused social disruption through unusual disease reports, and a number of indirect markers including demand for specialized medical services, local perception of threat, official acknowledgement of threat, official action against threat, change in business practices, and integrity of infrastructure. The open-source information comes from media articles (local sources are key) on Internet sites, satellite imagery, weather data, air transportation data, and animal health data. They developed over 200 social disruption parameters developed in medicine, public health, sociology, cultural anthropology, history, and disease modeling. Figure 13-3 shows the screenshot of Argus Watchboard displaying a global geographical mapping of disease status classified into Warning, Watch and Advisory levels.

The Argus analytic team consists of multilingual analysts covering 34 languages. They perform biological events detection through state-of-the-art online media processing software based on taxonomy of nearly 200 social disruption indicators. They also propose a heuristic staging model called the Wilson–Collmann Scale for assessing biological event evolution. Once an event is identified, analysts evaluate the report for possible posting as a Warning, Watch, or Advisory. The stages of outbreak severity they define include: (1) environmental conditions favorable to an outbreak, (2) localized biological event, (3) multifocal biological event, (4) severe social and medical infrastructure strain, (5) social collapse, and (6) preparatory posture.

In the 2007 influenza season, the Argus team issued nearly 3,000 event reports across 128 countries and 27 languages, which included 181 Advisories, 58 Watches, and 38 Warnings. They identified hundreds of reports of a possible H3N2 drifted virus escaping the current vaccine compilation beginning 8 months ago in a multitude of countries. This information ultimately contributed to the decision process by the WHO and its partners to change the

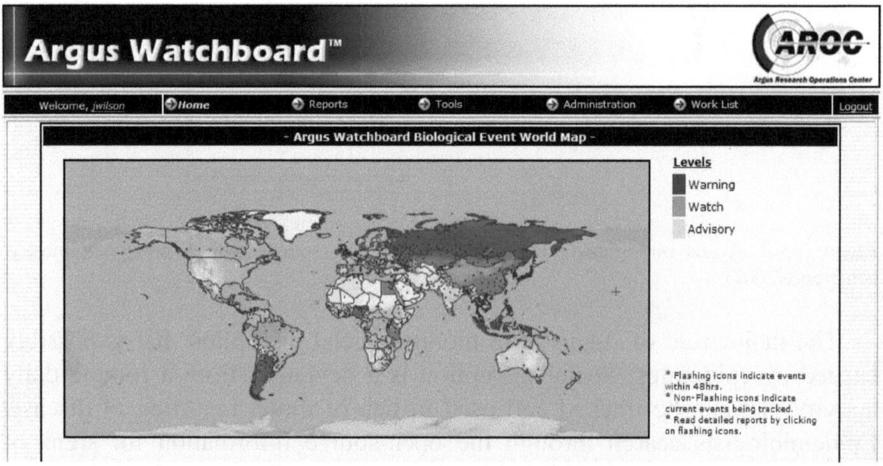

Figure 13-3. Argus Watchboard (source: http://www.syndromic.org/conference/2007).

-Biological Event Country Reports-

Country	Title	Date
NIGERIA	Measles	6/20/2007
MONGOLIA	Pox Disease; Suspicious Biological, Chemical Research	6/18/2007
ARGENTINA	Respiratory Disease, Bird Die-Off	6/22/2007
RUSSIA	Equine Influenza, Undiagnosed Disease, Alleged Intentional Poisoning	6/22/2007
INDONESIA	H5N1 Avian Influenza	6/23/2007
EGYPT	**H5N1 Avian Influenza**	**6/24/2007**
CHINA	Suspected Vaccine Failure	6/22/2007
CHILE	Respiratory Disease	6/19/2007
TANZANIA	Rift Valley Fever	6/19/2007
ECUADOR	Suspected Vaccine-Associated Illness	6/21/2007
CZECH REPUBLIC	H5N1 Avian Influenza	6/21/2007
RWANDA	Bird Die-Off	6/21/2007
BAHAMAS, THE	Bird Die-Off	6/21/2007
PANAMA	Undiagnosed Disease (Human, Bull); Bird Die-Off	6/21/2007
NEW ZEALAND	Respiratory Illness	6/22/2007
SENEGAL	Unexplained Deaths (Human)	6/18/2007
HONG KONG	H5N1 Avian Influenza	6/17/2007
BANGLADESH	H5N1 Avian Influenza	6/18/2007
ALGERIA	Undiagnosed Disease (Camels)	6/20/2007

Figure 13-4. Biological event reporting at country level (source http://www.syndromic.org/conference/2007).

southern hemisphere influenza vaccine to include an updated H3N2 strain (Wilson, 2007).

The Argus event report (Figure 13-4) highlights recent biological events with geographical locations and date, classified and color-coded as Warning, Watch, and Advisory.

We provide the following key readings for the readers who might be interested in learning more details about the ARGUS system.

Important Readings:

1. Wilson, James M. V. (2007). "Argus: A Global Detection and Tracking System for Biological Events." *Advances in Disease Surveillance* 4(21).
2. Chute, C. G. (2008). "Biosurveillance, Classification, and Semantic Health Technologies." *Journal of the American Medical Informatics Association* 15(2), pp 172–173.

Chapter 14

HEALTHMAP

HealthMap is a freely accessible, automated real-time system that monitors, organizes, integrates, filters, visualizes, and disseminates online information about emerging diseases. The goal of HealthMap is to deliver real-time intelligence on a broad range of emerging infectious diseases for a diverse audience, from public health officials to international travelers.

HealthMap.org Web site has been operational since September 2006 (Figure 14-1). US Health and Human Services and the US Department of Defense among other national or international organizations have used their data stream for surveillance activities. HealthMap currently receives approximately 15,000 unique visitors per month from around the world.

Figure 14-2 shows the system architecture of the HealthMap application, which consists of the following components: (1) data acquisition, (2) information characterization, (3) signal interpretation, and (4) dissemination and alerting.

The system acquires multistream data automatically every hour from a variety of electronic sources: online news wires, Really Simple Syndication (RSS) feeds, ProMED mailing lists, and EuroSurveillance and WHO alerts. The text data are automatically categorized into groups by disease types and locations with text mining techniques. The system now handles information in English, Spanish, and French (Brownstein et al., 2008a). HealthMap currently processes 133.5 disease alerts per day on average (95% Confidence Interval: 124.1–142.8), with approximately 50% categorized as Breaking News (65.3 reports/day). With a 30-day default window, the system may display over 800 Breaking News alerts on a given day (Freifeld et al., 2008).

H. Chen et al., *Infectious Disease Informatics: Syndromic Surveillance for Public Health and BioDefense*, Integrated Series in Information Systems 21, DOI 10.1007/978-1-4419-1278-7_14,

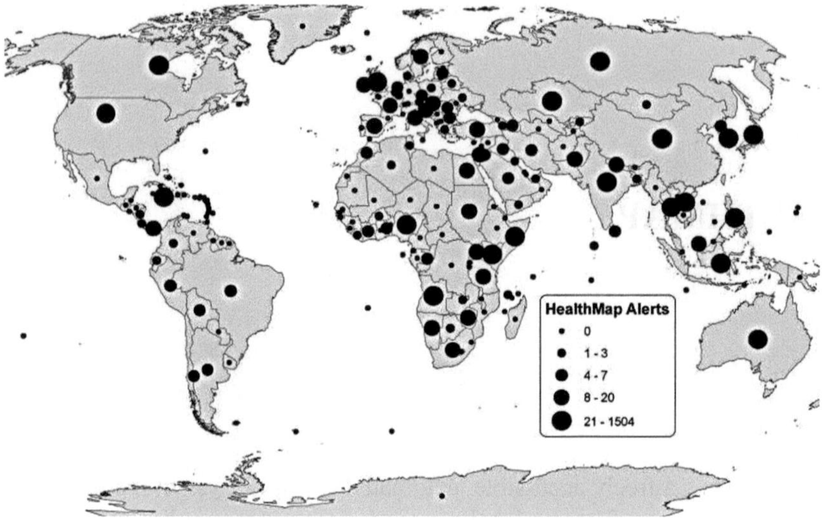

Figure 14-1. HealthMap geographic coverage, October 1, 2006 to February 16, 2007 (Freifeld et al. 2008).

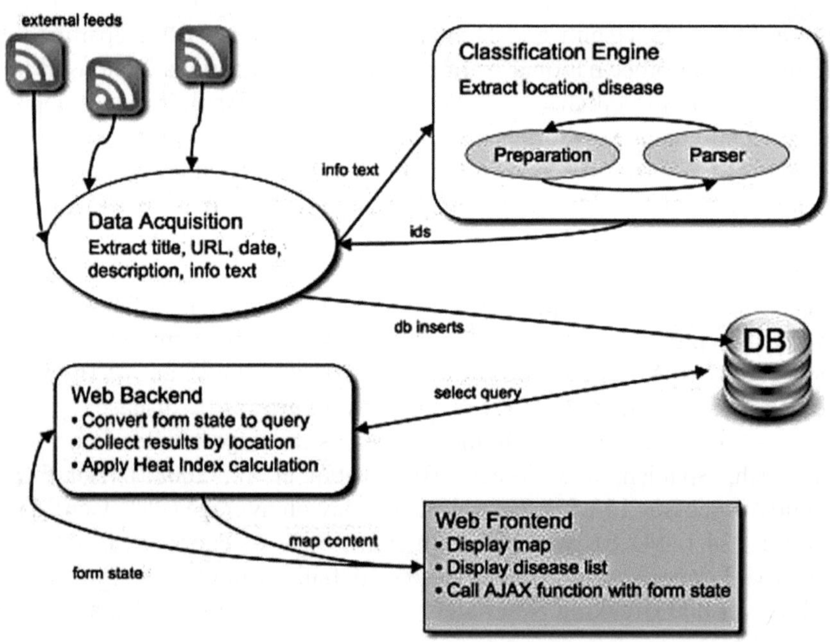

Figure 14-2. Framework for Internet-based surveillance (Freifeld et al. 2008).

HealthMap aggregates the disease reports by source, disease, and geographic location. This information characterization is performed using natural language interpretation and automated text mining and parsing techniques. The characterized information is then overlaid on an interactive map (supported by Google Maps), which allows for user access to the original report. On the left-hand panel, the HealthMap page allows improved information filtering by feeds sources, disease, and countries.

Figure 14-3. HealthMap page showing the latest information on H1N1 Flu as of May 27th, 2009 (lower-left corner: bringing up the related news at a particular location as zooming out). (source: Healthmap Web page).

In April 2009, a new strain of influenza known as swine flu (H1N1 flu) was first detected in the US and soon led to an outbreak in Mexico. It is now present in over two dozen countries around the globe including Canada, Japan and the UK. HealthMap began aggregating and filtering real-time information on the novel flu virus on April 1, weeks before the news emerged in English-language resources. HealthMap tracked early reports from the Mexican press on a "mysterious" influenza-like illness occurring in the town of La Gloria in the state of Veracruz that reportedly infected 60% of the 3,000 residents and killed 2 people.

Figure 14-3 shows a global alert map of the H1N1 disease during its 2009 outbreak as of the end of May 2009. Zooming to a specific region and clicking on a balloon bring up a list of disease related news articles at that region.

HealthMap represents a successful practice of mining the Internet for public health surveillance purposes to support and enhance the traditional public health infrastructure. It demonstrates that news reports in particular can be a valuable resource for information as inherently the media has the ability to saturate towns, cities, and communities where public health officials may or may not be present to report on potential disease outbreaks.

We provide the following project link and some key readings for the readers who might be interested in learning more details about the HealthMap Project.

Project link:

http://www.healthmap.org

Important readings:

1. Freifeld, C. C., et al., "HealthMap: Global Infectious Disease Monitoring through Automated Classification and Visualization of Internet Media Reports." *Journal of the American Medical Informatics Association* 2008. 15(2): pp 150–157.
2. Chute, C. G., "Biosurveillance, Classification, and Semantic Health Technologies." *Journal of the American Medical Informatics Association* 2008. 15(2): pp 172–173.
3. Brownstein, J. S., C. C. Freifeld, B. Y. Reis, and K. D. Mandl, "Surveillance Sans Frontières: Internet-Based Emerging Infectious Disease Intelligence and the HealthMap Project," *PLoS Medicine* Vol. 5, No. 7. (1 July 2008), e151.

Chapter 15

CHALLENGES AND FUTURE DIRECTIONS

We conclude this monograph by discussing key challenges facing syndromic surveillance research and summarizing future directions.

1. CHALLENGES FOR SYNDROMIC SURVEILLANCE RESEARCH

Although syndromic surveillance has gained wide acceptance as a response to disease outbreaks and bioterrorism attacks, many research challenges remain.

First, there are circumstances in which syndromic surveillance may not be effective or necessary. The potential benefit of syndromic surveillance as to the timeliness of detection could not be realized if there were hundreds or thousands of people infected simultaneously. In extreme cases, modern biological weapons could easily lead to mass infection via airborne or waterborne agents. In another scenario, syndromic surveillance could be rendered ineffective if the cases involved only a few people (e.g., the anthrax outbreak in 2001) and thus would not trigger any alarms and could go undetected (2005b). In this situation, one single positive diagnosis of a spore of anthrax could be sufficient to confirm the event.

Second, disease data tend to be noisy and incomplete. Although reporting of most notifiable diseases through the chain of public health agencies is required by law, the hospitals, laboratories, and clinicians participate largely on a voluntary basis. Patients making ER visits may not be representative of the population in the neighboring community; the participating hospitals and laboratories are not necessarily good random samples from which reliable statistical inference can be successfully made. This reinforces the need for careful evaluation of data sources and collection procedures.

H. Chen et al., *Infectious Disease Informatics: Syndromic Surveillance for Public Health and BioDefense*, Integrated Series in Information Systems 21, DOI 10.1007/978-1-4419-1278-7_15,

Third, many public health practitioners are unfamiliar with advanced surveillance analytics. Model selection, interpretation, and fine-tuning all require proper training. One approach that can potentially reduce the learning curve is to provide a carefully-engineered interactive visualization environment for the user to experiment with analysis methods, explore the analysis results, and validate hypotheses in an intuitive and visually informative environment.

Fourth, many false alarms are being generated by syndromic surveillance systems daily or weekly, as it is difficult to distinguish natural data variations from real outbreaks. Human reviews and follow-up investigations are necessary for signaled outbreaks, which are costly in time and labor. A typical investigation requires a group of epidemiologists, public health officials, healthcare providers, and their support staff to go through a multistep procedure for alert review and event evaluation.

Fifth, there is a critical need to develop computational and mathematical methods to facilitate response planning and related policy- and decision-making. Such methods should rely on an understanding of specific disease spreading patterns. They can be used to evaluate alternative policies and interventions and provide guidelines for scenario development, risk assessment, and trend prediction (Roberts, 2002).

2. SUMMARY AND FUTURE DIRECTIONS

- Existing systems differ significantly in scope and purpose (e.g., geographical cover-age, types of data and diseases monitored). For instance, a majority of systems surveyed focus on biodefense and detecting bioterrorism attacks; while other systems target at outbreak detection for specific diseases such as influenza (Hyman and LaForce, 2004).
- The absence of standard vocabularies and messaging protocols leads to interoperability problems among syndromic surveillance systems and underlying data sources. HL7 standards and XML-based messaging protocols represent a potential solution for addressing these problems.
- Each syndromic surveillance system implements a set of outbreak detection algorithms. There is an urgent need for a better understanding of the strengths and limitations of various detection techniques and their applicability. Also, implemented algorithms could be potentially reused across systems as sharable resources.
- System evaluation and comparison are confounded by a number of practical issues. Systematic, field-based, objective comparative studies among systems are critically needed.

With regard to promising future research directions in syndromic surveillance, we see a number of opportunities for informatics studies on a wide range of topics. We list some of the potentially fruitful areas of studies below. (a) Data visualization techniques, especially interactive visual data exploration techniques, need to be further developed to meet the specific analysis needs of syndromic surveillance. (b) Outbreak detection algorithms need to be improved in terms of sensitivity, specificity, and timeliness. In particular, how to deal with incomplete data records, how to perform privacy-conscious data mining, and how to leverage multiple data streams are all interesting research questions. Furthermore, thorough evaluation of outbreak detection algorithms using synthetic or real data is critically needed. (c) System interoperability research and event management models are worth studying. (d) In the context of bioterrorism preparation, research on predicting and responding to bio-attacks is critically needed. Work reported in (Harmon, 2003) points to an interesting direction in this area of study: by examining the preceding events based on historical data of terrorism attacks, the culminating event can be predicted to occur within a certain time window. (e) This survey is focused on human diseases. Agricultural bio-attacks and certain animal diseases (e.g., mad cow, foot-and-mouth, and avian flu) are gaining increasing attention in biosurveillance practice. For example, the US Department of Agriculture and the US Geological Survey (USGS), through its National Wildlife Health Center and other partners, administer and manage databases for wildlife diseases (e.g., http://www.usda.gov/). How to detect and respond to agricultural bioattacks and disease events poses interesting technical challenges (e.g., the importance of environmental data such as air, water, or weather). Developing cross-species syndromic surveillance approaches and cross-fertilizing methods from human and animal syndromic surveillance research hold interesting potentials.

In closing, we briefly discuss the expanding scope of syndromic surveillance systems. Although syndromic surveillance systems have been developed and deployed in many state public health departments, there is a critical need to create a cross-jurisdictional data sharing infrastructure to maximize the potential benefit and practical impact of syndromic surveillance. In a broader context, public health surveillance should be a truly global effort for pandemic diseases such as SARS. There is a need to address issues concerning global data sharing (including multilingual information processing) and development of models that work internationally. International politics, global commerce interests, and cultural and regional considerations are some of the issues that need to be considered in global syndromic surveillance.

REFERENCES

2003a. “New York City Uses GIS for Surveillance of Bioterrorism and Disease.” Retrieved May, 2008, from http://www.esri.com/news/arcnews/fall03articles/new-york-city.html

2003b. “An Overview of PHINMS.” Retrieved July 9, 2006, from http://www.nyc.gov/html/doh/downloads/pdf/acco/2004/acco-rfp-fund-20041122-PHINMS.pdf

2003c. “Public Health GIS News and Information.” Retrieved July 01, 2006, from http://www.cdc.gov/nchs/data/gis/cdcgis53.pdf

2003d. “Public Health Research Laboratories.” Retrieved Jan 06, 2006, from http://www.phrl.org

2004a. “Emergint Data Collection and Transformation System (DCTS).” Retrieved March 23, 2006, from http://www.emergint.com/jsp/datasheet.pdf

2004b. “Health Alert Network (HAN), Minnesota Department of Health.” Retrieved June 15, 2006, from www.health.state.mn.us/han/lopubhlth/2004AboutHan.pdf

2005a. “G8 Gleneagles 2005 Statement on Counter-Terrorism.” Retrieved July 31, 2006, from http://www.privacyinternational.org/article.shtml?cmd%5B347%5D=x-347-260977

2005b. “Indiana: Syndromic Surveillance.” Retrieved July 27, 2006, from http://www.drug-rehabs.org/content.php?cid=1504&state=Indiana

2005c. “MTF Participation in Homeland Security and Defense: Use of Essence for Detection and Tracking of Infectious Disease Outbreaks.” 2005 Tricare Conference. Available at: http://www.tricare.mil/conferences/2005/ppt/019Jpavlin.ppt

2006a. “Arizona Spring Biosurveillance Workshop.” Retrieved April 01, 2006, from http://ai.arizona.edu/BIO2006/

2006b. “Biodefend™.” Retrieved March 01, 2006, from http://www.bt.usf.edu.

2006c. “Clusterseer Software.” Retrieved Feb 18, 2006, from http://www.terraseer.com

2006d. “Disease Event Tracking and Epidemiologic Collection Tool.” Retrieved June 13, 2006, from http://www.ncdetect.org/

2006e. “Early Event Detection & Syndromic Surveillance.” Retrieved June 23, 2006, from http://www.firstwatch.net/

2006f. “Hospital Electronic Syndromic Surveillance in Missori.” Retrieved April 21, 2006, from http://www.dhss.mo.gov/HESS/

2006g. “Michigan Disease Surveillance System Syndromic Surveillance Project.” Retrieved April 23, 2006, from http://www.michigan.gov/mdch

2006h. “North Dakota Department of Health Syndromic Surveillance Program.” Retrieved May 12, 2006, from http://www.health.state.nd.us/ disease/ Surveillance/syndromicsurveillance.htm

2006i. “Redbat Features & Benefits.” Retrieved May 23, 2006, from http://www.icpa.net/redbat-features.html

2006j. “Satscan Software.” Retrieved Jan 18, 2006, from http://www.satscan.org

2006k. “State Electronic Notifiable Disease Surveillance System.” Retrieved June 03, 2006, from http://health.state.ga.us/epi/sendss.asp

2006l. “STC Syndromic Surveillance Product.” Retrieved May 24, 2006, from http://www.stchome.com/

2006m. “Syndromic Surveillance System in Miami-Dade County.” Retrieved June 14, 2006, from http://www.dadehealth.org/discontrol/DISCONTROLflucontainment.asp

2008. "About the International Classification of Diseases, Tenth Revision, Clinical Modification (ICD-10-CM)." http://www.cdc.gov/nchs/about/otheract/icd9/abticd10.htm.

Aamodt, G., Samuelsen, S.O., and Skrondal, A. 2006. "A Simulation Study of Three Methods for Detecting Disease Clusters," *International Journal of Health Geographics* (5:15).

Abrams, A.M., and Kleinman, K.P. 2007. "A Satscan™ Macro Accessory for Cartography (SMAC) Package Implemented with SAS® Software," *International Journal of Health Geographics* (6:6).

Babin, S., Burkom, H., Holtry, R., Tabernero, N., Davies-Cole, J., Stokes, L., and Lee, D. 2007. "An Exploration of New Uses of Traditional Data within an Ecological Study: Air Quality Effects on Pediatric Asthma Exacerbation Analysis," *Advances in Disease Surveillance* (2), p. 141.

Barry, R., and Kailar, R. 2005. "On Securing the Public Health Information Network Messaging System." Retrieved July 9, 2006, from http://middleware.Internet2.edu/pki05/proceedings/kailar-phinms.pdf

Bath, P.A. 2004. "Data Mining in Health and Medical Information," *Annual Review of Information Science and Technology (ARIST)* (38), pp. 331–369.

Beeler, G. 1998. "Hl7 Version 3 – An Object-Oriented Methodology for Collaborative Standards Development," *International Journal of Medical Informatics* (48), pp. 151–161.

Begier, E.M., Sockwell, D., Branch, L.M., Davies-Cole, J.O., Jones, L.H., Edwards, L., Casani, J.A., and Blythe, D. 2003. "The National Capitol Region's Emergency Department Syndromic Surveillance System: Do Chief Complaint and Discharge Diagnosis Yield Different Results?" *Emerg Infect Dis [serial on the Internet]* (9:3).

Benoit, G. 2002. "Data Mining," *Annual Review of Information Science and Technology (ARIST)* (36), pp. 265–310.

Besculides, M., Heffernan, R., Mostashari, F., and Weiss, D. 2004. "Evaluation of School Absenteeism Data for Early Outbreak Detection - New York City, 2001–2002," *MMWR (CDC)* (53(Suppl)), p. 230.

BioSense. 2008. "Biosense Technical Overview of Data Collection, Analysis, and Reporting." BioSense project. Available at http://www.cdc.gov/BioSense/files/BioSense_Techn_Overview_102908_webpage.pdf.

Boscoe, F.P., McLaughlin, C., Schymurab, M.J., and Kielb, C.L. 2003. "Visualization of the Spatial Scan Statistic Using Nested Circles," *Health & Place* (9), pp. 273–277.

Bouhaddov, O., Lincaln, M.J., Moulden, S.H., Frankson, F.J., erandall, G., Hughes, C., Singley, R., Insely, M. and Graham, G. 2006. "A Simple Strategy for Implementing Standard Reference Terminologies in a Distributed Healthcare" Delivery system with Minimal Input to Exiting Applications, *AMIA Annual Symposium Proceedings*, PP. 76–80.

Box, G.E.P., Jenkins, G.M., and Reinsel, G.C. 1994. *Time Series Analysis: Forecasting & Control*. Prentice Hall.

Bradley, C.A., Rolka, H., Walker, D., and Loonsk, J. 2005. "BioSense: Implementation of a National Early Event Detection and Situational Awareness System," *MMWR (CDC)* (54(Suppl)), pp. 11–20.

Bravata, D., McDonald, K., Smith, W., Rydzak, C., Szeto, H., Buckeridge, D., Haberland, C., and Owens, D. 2004. "Systematic Review: Surveillance Systems for Early Detection of Bioterrorism-Related Diseases," *Ann Intern Med* (140), pp. 910–922.

Bravata, D.M., McDonald, K., Owens, D.K., Buckeridge, D., Haberland, C., and Rydzak, C. 2002. "Bioterrorism Preparedness and Response: Use of Information Technologies and Decision Support Systems," *Evidence Report/Technology Assessment No* (59).

Brillman, J.C., Burr, T., Forslund, D., Joyce, E., Picard, R., and Umland, E. 2005. "Modeling Emergency Department Visit Patterns for Infectious Disease Complaints: Results and Application to Disease Surveillance," *BMC Medical Informatics and Decision Making* (5:4).

Brookmeyer, R., and Stroup, D. 2004. *Monitoring the Health of Populations: Statistical Surveillance in Public Health.* New York: Oxford University Press.

Brownstein, J., Freifeld, C., Reis, B., and Mandl, K. 2008a. "Surveillance Sans Frontières: Internet-Based Emerging Infectious Disease Intelligence and the Healthmap Project.," *PLoS Medicine* (5:7), pp. 1019–1024.

Buckeridge, D., Burkom, H., Campbell, M., Hogan, W., and Moore, A. 2005a. "Algorithms for Rapid Outbreak Detection: A Research Synthesis," *Journal of Biomedical Informatics* (38), pp. 99–113.

Buckeridge, D., Burkom, H., Moore, A., Pavlin, J., Cutchis, P., and Hogan, W. 2004. "Evaluation of Syndromic Surveillance Systems: Development of an Epidemic Simulation Model," *MMWR (CDC)* (53(Suppl.)), pp. 137–143.

Buckeridge, D., Graham, J., O'Connor, J., Choy, M.K., Tu, S.W., and Musen, M. 2002. "Knowledge-Based Bioterrorism Surveillance," *American Medical Informatics Association Symposium*, San Antonio, TX.

Buckeridge, D., Musen, M., Switzer, P., and Crubezy, M. 2003. "An Analytic Framework for Space–Time Aberrancy Detection in Public Health Surveillance Data," *AMIA Symposium* pp. 120–124.

Buckeridge, D., Switzer, P., Owens, D., Siegrist, D., Pavlin, J., and Musen, M. 2005b. "An Evaluation Model for Syndromic Surveillance: Assessing the Performance of a Temporal Algorithm," *MMWR (CDC)* (54(Suppl)), pp. 109–115.

Buehler, J., Berkelman, R., Hartley, D., and Peters, C. 2003. "Syndromic Surveillance and Bioterrorism-Related Epidemics," *Emerging Infectious Diseases 2003* (9:1), pp. 197–204.

Buehler, J., Hopkins, R., Overhage, J., Sosin, D., and Tong, V. 2004. "Framework for Evaluating Public Health Surveillance Systems for Early Detection of Outbreaks: Recommendations from the Cdc Working Group," *MMWR (CDC)* (53(RR-5)), pp. 1–13.

Burkom, H. 2003. "Biosurveillance Applying Scan Statistics with Multiple Disparate Data Sources," *Journal Urban Health 2003* (80:2 (Suppl)), pp. 57–65.

Burkom, H., Elbert, E., Feldman, A., and Lin, J. 2004. "Role of Data Aggregation in Biosurveillance Detection Strategies with Applications from Essence," *MMWR (CDC)* (53(Suppl)), pp. 67–73.

Burkom, H., and Murphy, S. 2007. "Data Classification for Selection of Temporal Alerting Methods for Biosurveillance." BioSurvellance workshop 2007.

Carley, K., Fridsma, D., Casman, E., Altman, N., Chang, J., Kaminsky, B., Nave, D., and Yahja, A. 2003. "Biowar: Scalable Multi-Agent Social and Epidemiological Simulation of Bioterrorism Events."

Cassa, C., Iancu, K., Olson, K., and Mandl, K. 2005. "A Software Tool for Creating Simulated Outbreaks to Benchmark Surveillance Systems," *BMC Medical Informatics and Decision Making* (5:22).

CDC. 2001. "Publication of Updated Guidelines for Evaluating Public Health Surveillance Systems," *Journal of the American Medical Association (JAMA)* (286:12), p. 1446.

CDC. 2002. "Syndromic Surveillance for Bioterrorism Following the Attacks on the World Trade Center–New York City, 2001," *MMWR* (51), pp. 13–15.

CDC. 2003. "Syndrome Definitions for Diseases Associated with Critical Bioterrorism-Associated Agents," *Atlanta, GA: US Department of Health and Human Services, CDC.*

CDC. 2004. "National Electronic Disease Surveillance System: The Surveillance and Monitoring Component of the Public Health Information Network," *Atlanta, GA: US Department of Health and Human Services.*

CDC. 2006a. "Early Aberration Reporting System." Retrieved Feb 15, 2006, from http://www.bt.cdc.gov/surveillance/ears/

CDC. 2006b. "Epidemic Information Exchange." Retrieved May 20, 2006, from http://www.cdc.gov/mmwr/epix/epix.html

CDC. 2006c. "Public Health Information Network (PHIN)."

CDC. 2007. "BioSense Real-Time Hospital Data User Guide, Application Version 2.08." Atlanta, GA: US Department of Health and Human Services, CDC; 2007. Available at http://www.cdc.gov/biosense/files/cdc_biosense_biosense_hospital_data_user_guide_v2.11.doc.

CDC. 2003. "HIPAA Privacy Rule and Public Health: Guidance from CDC and the US Department of Health and Human Services," *MMWR* (52(Suppl)), pp. 1–20.

Chang, W., Zeng, D., and Chen, H. 2005. "Prospective Spatio-Temporal Data Analysis for Security Informatics," In proceedings of the 8th IEEE International Conference on Intelligent Transportation Systems, Vienna, Austria.

Chang, W., Zeng, D., and Chen, H. 2008. "A Spatio-Temporal Data Analysis Approach Based on Prospective Support Vector Clustering," *Decision Support Systems* (45:4), pp. 697–713.

Chapman, W.W., Christensen, L., Wagner, M.M., Haug, P., Ivanov, O., Dowling, J., and Olszewski, R. 2005. "Classifying Free-Text Triage Chief Complaints into Syndromic Categories with Natural Language Processing," *Artificial Intelligence in Medicine* (33:1), pp. 31–40.

Chapman, W.W., Cooper, G.F., Hanbury, P., Chapman, B.E., Harrison, L.H., and Wagner, M.M. 2003. "Creating a Text Classifier to Detect Radiology Reports Describing Mediastinal Findings Associated with Inhalational Anthrax and Other Disorders," *Journal of the American Medical Informatics Association* (10:5), pp. 494–503.

Chen, C. 1999. "Information Visualization and Virtual Enuironments," *Berlin: Springer-Verlag.*

Chen, H., and Xu, J. 2006. "Intelligence and Security Informatics," *Annual Review of Information Science and Technology (ARIST)* (40), pp. 229–299.

Chen, Y., Tseng, C., King, C.C., Wu, T., and Chen, H. 2007. "Incorporating Geographical Contacts into Social Network Analysis for Contact Tracing in Epidemiology: A Study on Taiwan Sars Data," *Intelligence and Security Informatics: Biosurveillance, Proceedings of the Second Workshop, BioSurveillance 2007*, New Brunswick, NJ: Lecture Notes in Computer Science (LNCS 4506), Springer-Verlag.

Chin, J.P., Diehl, V.A., and Norman, K.L. 1988. "Development of an Instrument Measuring User Satisfaction of the Human-Computer Interface," *ACM CHI* Washington, DC, pp. 213–218.

Cho, J., Kim, J., Yoo, I., Ahn, M., Wang, S., Hur, T., Park, I., and Jeong, E. 2003. "Syndromic Surveillance Based on the Emergency Department in Korea," *Journal of Urban Health: Bulletin of the New York Academy of Medicine* (80:2), p. 124.

Chretien, J.-P., Burkom, H.S., Sedyaningsih, E.R., Larasati, R.P., Lescano, A.G., Mundaca, C.C., Blazes, D.L., Munayco, C.V., Coberly, J.S., Ashar, R.J., and Lewis, S.H. 2008. "Syndromic Surveillance: Adapting Innovations to Developing Settings," *PLoS Med* (5:3), pp. 0367–0372.

Chute, C.G. 2008. "Biosurveillance, Classification, and Semantic Health Technologies," *Journal of the American Medical Informatics Association* (15:2), pp 172–173.

Clothier, H.J., Fielding, J.E., and Kelly, H.A. 2006. "An Evaluation of the Australian Sentinel Practice Research Network (ASPREN) Surveillance for Influenza-Like Illness." Retrieved May 11, 2006, from http://www.health.gov.au/Internet/wcms/publishing.nsf/content/cda-cdi2903a.htm#data

Cooper, G.F., Dash, D.H., Levander, J.D., Wong, W.K., Hogan, W.R., and Wagner, M.M. 2004. "Bayesian Biosurveillance of Disease Outbreaks," *Twentieth Conference on Uncertainty in Artificial Intelligence*, Banff, Alberta, Canada, pp. 94–103.

Costa, M.A., Kulldorff, M., Kleinman, K., Yih, W.K., Platt, R., Brand, R., and Hsu, J. 2007. "Comparing the Utility of Ambulatory Care and Emergency Room Data for Disease Outbreak Detection," *Advances in Disease Surveillance* (4).

Costagliola, D., Flahault, A., Galinec, D., Garnerin, P., Menares, J., and Valleron, A. 1981. "A Routine Tool for Detection and Assessment of Epidemics of Influenza-Like Syndromes in France," *American Journal of Public Health* (81:1), pp. 97–99.

Cronin, B. 2005. "Intelligence, Terrorism National Security," *Annual Review of Information Science and Technology (ARIST)* (39), pp. 395–432.

Crubézy, M., O'Connor, Pincus, Z., and Musen, M.A. 2005. "Ontology-Centered Syndromic Surveillance for Bioterrorism," *IEEE Intelligent Systems* (20:5), pp. 26–35.

Daniel, J.B., Heisey-Grove, D., Gadam, P., Yih, W., Mandl, K., DeMaria, A.J., and Platt, R. 2005. "Connecting Health Departments and Providers: Syndromic Surveillance's Last Mile," *MMWR (CDC)* (54(Suppl)), pp. 147–151.

Das, D., Weiss, D., and Mostashari, F. 2003. "Enhanced Drop-in Syndromic Surveillance in New York City Following September 11, 2001," *J Urban Health* (80:1(suppl)), pp. 176–188.

Dembek, Z., Carley, K., and Hadler, J. 2005. "Guidelines for Constructing a Statewide Hospital Syndromic Surveillance Network," *MMWR (CDC)* (54(Suppl)), pp. 21–26.

Dembek, Z., Carley, K., Siniscalchi, A., and Hadler, J. 2004. "Hospital Admissions Syndromic Surveillance – Connecticut, September 2001–November 2003," *MMWR (CDC)* (53(Suppl)), pp. 50–52.

DIMACS. 2006. "DIMACS Working Group on Biosurveillance Data Monitoring and Information Exchange." Retrieved April 01, 2006, from http://dimacs.rutgers.edu/Workshops/Surveillance/

Doroshenko, A., Cooper, D., Smith, G., Gerard, E., Chinemana, F., Verlander, N., and Nicoll, A. 2005. "Evaluation of Syndromic Surveillance Based on National Health Service Direct Derived Data – England and Wales," *MMWR* (54(Suppl)), pp. 117–122.

Drociuk, D., Gibson, J., and Hodge, J.J. 2004. "Health Information Privacy and Syndromic Surveillance Systems," *MMWR (CDC)* (53(Suppl)), pp. 221–225.

Duchin, J., Karras, B., Trigg, L., Bliss, D., Vo, D., Ciliberti, J.S.L., Rietberg, K., and Lober, W. 2001. "Syndromic Surveillance for Bioterrorism Using Computerized Discharge Diagnosis Databases," *Proc AMIA Symp*, p. 897.

Duczmal, L., and Buckeridge, D. 2005. "Using Modified Spatial Scan Statistic to Improve Detection of Disease Outbreak When Exposure Occurs in Workplace – Viginia," *MMWR (CDC)* (54(Suppl)), p. 187.

Edge, V., Pollari, F., and Lim, G. 2004. "Syndromic Surveillance of Gastrointestinal Illness Using Pharmacy Over-The-Counter Sales: A Retrospective Report of Waterborne Outbreaks in Saskatchewan and Ontario," *Canada Journal of Public Health* (95), pp. 446–450.

Edge, V.L., Lim, G.H., Aramini, J.J., Sockett, P., and Pollari, F.L. 2003. "Development of an Alternative Surveillance Alert Program (ASAP): Syndromic Surveillance of Gastrointestinal Illness Using Pharmacy Over-The-Counter Sales," *Journal of Urban Health: Bulletin of the New York Academy of Medicine* (80:2), p. i138.

Emergisoft. 2006. "Emergisoft's ED Sydromic Surveillance Solutions," Retrieved June 12, 2006, from http://www.emergisoft.com/productinfo/syndromic_surveillance/

Espino, J.U., and Wagner, M.M. 2001. "The Accuracy of ICD-9 Coded Chief Complaints for Detection of Acute Respiratory Illness," *Proc AMIA Symp*, pp. 164–168.

Espino, J.U., Wagner, M.M., Szczepaniak, C., Tsui, F.-C., Su, H., Olszewski, R., Liu, Z., Chapman, W.W., Zeng, X., Ma, L., Lu, Z., and Dara, J. 2004. "Removing a Barrier to Computer-Based Outbreak and Disease Surveillance-the Rods Open Source Project," *MMWR (CDC)* (53(Suppl)), pp. 34–41.

ESRI. "West Nile Virus Disease Monitoring." http://www.esri.com/news/arcuser/0701/wnvirus.html.

EWORS. 2006. "Early Warning Outbreak Recognition System (EWORS)." Retrieved April 12, 2006, from http://www.namru2.med.navy.mil/ewors.htm

Eysenbach, G. 2006. "Infodemiology: Tracking Flu-Related Searches on the Web for Syndromic Surveillance," *AMIA Annu Symp Proc*, pp. 244–248.

Ford, D., Kaufman, J.H., Thomas, J., Eiron, I., and Hammer, M. 2005. "Spatiotemporal Epidemiological Modeler – a Tool for Spatiotemporal Modeling of Infectious Agents across the United States." Retrieved Oct 10, 2006, from http://www.alphaworks.ibm.com/tech/stem

Freifeld, C.C., Mandl, K.D., Reis, B.Y., and Brownstein, J.S. 2008. "Healthmap: Global Infectious Disease Monitoring through Automated Classification and Visualization of Internet Media Reports," *Journal of the American Medical Informatics Association* (15:2), pp. 150–157.

Fung, K.W., Hole, W.T., and Srinivasan, S. 2006. "Who Is Using the UMLS and How – Insights from the UMLS User Annual Reports," *AMIA Annual Symposium Proceedings*, pp. 274–278.

German, R.R. 2000. "Sensitivity and Predictive Value Positive Measurements for Public Health Surveillance Systems," *Epidemiology* (11:6), pp. 720–727.

Gesteland, P.H., Wagner, M.M., Chapman, W.W., Espino, J.U., Tsui, F.-C., Gardner, R.M., Rolfs, R.T., Dato, V.M., James, B.C., and Haug, P.J. 2002. "Rapid Deployment of an

Electronic Disease Surveillance System in the State of Utah for the 2002 Olympic Winter Games," *Proceedings of AMIA Symposium 2002*, pp. 285–289.

Ginsberg, M., Johnson, J., Tokars, J., Martin, C., English, R., Rainisch, G., Lei, W., Hicks, P., Burkholder, J., Miller, M., Crosby, K., Akaka, K., and Sugerman, A.S.D. 2008. "Monitoring Health Effects of Wildfires Using the BioSense System – San Diego County, California, October 2007," *MMWR(CDC)* (57:27), pp. 741–747.

Goldenberg, A., Shmueli, G., Caruana, R.A., and Fienberg, S.E. 2002. "Early Statistical Detection of Anthrax Outbreaks by Tracking Over-The-Counter Medication Sales," *Proceedings of the National Academy of Sciences USA* (99:8), pp. 5237–5240.

Goplin, J., Feist, M., and Miller, T. 2007. "Variation of Chief Complaint-Based Respiratory Symptom Data in One Hospital's Nurse Advice Call Center and Emergency Department," *Advances in Disease Surveillance* (2), p. 105.

Goss, L., Carrico, R., Hall, C., and Humbaugh, K. 2003. "A Day at the Races: Communitywide Syndromic Surveillance During the 2002 Kentucky Derby Festival," *Journal of Urban Health: Bulletin of the New York Academy of Medicine* (80:2), p. i124.

Greenko, J., Mostashari, F., Fine, A., and Layton, M. 2003. "Clinical Evaluation of the Emergency Medica Services (EMS) Ambulance Dispatch-Based Syndromic Surveillance System, New York City," *Journal of Urban Health: Bulletin of the New York Academy of Medicine* (80:2), pp. i50–i56.

Grigoryan, V.V., Wagner, M.M., Waller, K., Wallstrom, G.L., and Hogan, W.R. 2005. "The Effect of Spatial Granularity of Data on Reference Dates for Influenza Outbreaks," in: *RODS Laboratory Technical Report, 2005*.

Halasz, S., Brown, P., Goodall, C., Cochrane, D.G., and Allegra`, J.R. 2006. "The N-gram CC Classifier: A Novel Method of Automatically Creating CC Classifiers Based on ICD-9 Groupings," *Advances in Disease Surveillance 2006* (1:30).

Halkidi, M., Batistakis, Y., and Vazirgiannis, M. 2002. "Cluster Validity Methods: Part I" *SIGMOD Rec.* (31:2), pp 40–45.

Hamby, T. 2006. "New Jersey Experience and Protocol Development." Biosurveillance Information Exchange Working Group.

Heffernan, R., Mostashari, F., Das, D., Besculides, M., Rodriguez, C., Greenko, J., Steiner-Sichel, L., Balter, S., Karpati, A., Thomas, P., Phillips, M., Ackelsberg, J., Lee, E., Leng, J., Hartman, J., Metzger, K., Rosselli, R., and Weiss, D. 2004. "New York City Syndromic Surveillance Systems," *MMWR (CDC)* (53(Suppl)), pp. 23–27.

Heffernan, R., Mostashari, F., Das, D., Karpati, A., Kulldorff, M., and Weiss, D. 2004. "Syndromic Surveillance in Public Health Practice, New York City," *Emerg Infect Dis [serial on the Internet]*.

HL7. 2006. "Health Level 7." Retrieved June 30, 2006, from http://www.HL7.org

Hogan, W.R., Tsui, F.-C., Ivanov, O., Gesteland, P.H., Grannis, S., Overhage, M., Robinson, J.M., and Wagner, M.M. 2003. "Detection of Pediatric Respiratory and Diarrheal Outbreaks from Sales of Over-The-Counter Electrolyte Products," *Journal of American Medical Informatics Association* (10:6), pp. 555–562.

Hogan, W.R., Wagner, M.M., and Tsui, F.-C. 2002. "Experience with Message Format and Code Set Standards for Early Warning Public Health Surveillance Systems," *AMIA poster*.

Hooda, J., Dogdu, E., and Sunderraman, R. 2004. "Health Level-7 Compliant Clinical Patient Records System," *2004 ACM Symposium on Applied Computing*, Nicosia, Cyprus: New York: ACM Press, pp. 259–263.

Hope, K., Merritt, T., Eastwood, K., Main, K., Durrheim, D., Muscatello, D., Todd, K., and Zheng, W. 2008. "The Public Health Value of Emergency Department Syndromic Surveillance Following a Natural Disaster," *Commun Dis Intell* (32:1), pp. 92–94.

Hu, P.J.-H., Zeng, D., Chen, H., Larson, C.A., Chang, W., and Tseng, C. 2005. "Evaluating an Infectious Disease Information Sharing and Analysis System," *IEEE International Conference on Intelligence and Security Informatics (ISI-2005)*, Atlanta, Georgia: Springer Lecture Notes in Computer Science, pp. 412–417.

Hunscher, D., Boyd, A., Green, L.A., and Clauw, D.J. 2006. "Representing Natural-Language Case Report Form Terminology Using Health Level 7 Common Document Architecture, LOINC, and SNOMED-CT: Lessons Learned," *AMIA Annual Symposium Proceedings*, p. 961.

Hurt-Mullen, K., and Coberly, J. 2005. "Syndromic Surveillance on the Epidemiologist's Desktop: Making Sense of Much Data," *MMWR (CDC)* (54(Suppl)), pp. 141–147.

Hutwagner, L., Browne, T., Seeman, G.M., and Fleischauer, A.T. 2005a. "Comparing Aberration Detection Methods with Simulated Data," *Emerg Infect Dis [serial on the Internet]* (11), pp. 314–316.

Hutwagner, L., Thompson, W., Seeman, G.M., and Treadwell, T. 2003. "The Bioterrorism Preparedness and Response Early Aberration Reporting System (EARS)," *Journal of Urban Health* (80(2 suppl 1)), pp. 89–96.

Hutwagner, L., Thompson, W., Seeman, G.M., and Treadwell, T. 2005b. "A Simulation Model for Assessing Aberration Detection Methods Used in Public Health Surveillance for Systems with Limited Baselines," *Statistics in Medicine* (24), pp. 543–550.

Ivanov, O., Gesteland, P.H., Hogan, W., Mundorff, M.B., and Wagner, M.M. 2003. "Detection of Pediatric Respiratory and Gastrointestinal Outbreaks from Free-Text Chief Complaints," *AMIA Annual Symposium Proceedings*, pp. 318–322.

Ivanov, O., Wagner, M.M., Chapman, W.W., and Olszewski, R.T. 2002. "Accuracy of Three Classifiers of Acute Gastrointestinal Syndrome for Syndromic Surveillance," *AMIA Symp*, pp. 345–349.

Jackson, M.L., Baer, A., Painter, I., and Duchin, J. 2007. "A Simulation Study Comparing Aberration Detection Algorithms for Syndromic Surveillance," *BMC Medical Informatics and Decision Making* (7:6).

Jeremy, U., Espino, M., Wagner, C., Szczepaniak, F-C., Tsui, H., Su, R., Olszewski, Z., Liu, W., Chapman, X., Zeng, L., Ma, Z., Lu, and Dara, J. 2004. "Removing a Barrier to Computer-Based Outbreak and Disease Surveillance – the RODS Open Source Project," *MMWR (CDC)* (53(Suppl)), pp. 34–41.

Johnson, J.M. 2006. "To Ignore or Not to Ignore?" – Follow-up to Statistically Significant Signals." Biosurveillance Information Exchange Working Group.

Johnson, J.M., Hicks, L., McClean, C., and Ginsberg, M. 2005. "Leveraging Syndromic Surveillance During the San Diego Wildfires, 2003," *MMWR (CDC)* (54(Suppl)), p. 190.

Karras, B.T. 2005. "Syndromic Surveillance Information Collection – King County (SSIC-KC) for Bioterrorism Detection." Retrieved July 10, 2006, from http://www.phig.washington.edu/projectform_show.php?id=6

Kaufman, Z., Cohen, E., Peled-Leviatan, T., Lavi, C., Aharonowitz, G., Dichtiar, R., Bromberg, M., Havkin, O., Shalev, Y., Marom, R., Shalev, V., Shemer, J., and Green, M. 2005. "Using Data on an Influenza B Outbreak to Evaluate a Syndromic Surveillance System – Israel, June 2004 [Abstract]," *MMWR (CDC)* (54(Suppl)), p. 191.

Kleinman, K., Lazarus, R., and Platt, R. 2004. "A Generalized Linear Mixed Models Approach for Detecting Incident Cluster/Signals of Disease in Small Areas, with an Application to Biological Terrorism (with Invited Commentary)," *American Journal of Epidemiology* (159), pp. 217–224.

Kleinman, K., and Abrams, A. 2006. "Assessing Surveillance Using Sensitivity, Specificity and Timeliness," *Statistical Methods in Medical Research* (15:5), pp. 445–464.

Kleinman, K., Abrams, A., Kulldorff, M., and Platt, R. 2005a. "A Model-Adjusted Spacetime Scan Statistic with an Application to Syndromic Surveillance," *Epidemiology and Infection* (119), pp. 409–419.

Kleinman, K., Abrams, A., Mandl, K., and Platt, R. 2005b. "Simulation for Assessing Statistical Methods of Biologic Terrorism Surveillance," *MMWR (CDC)* (54(Suppl)), pp. 103–110.

Kleinman, K., Lazarus, R., and Platt, R. 2004. "A Generalized Linear Mixed Models Approach for Detecting Incident Cluster/Signals of Disease in Small Areas, with an Application to Biological Terrorism (with Invited Commentary)," *American Journal of Epidemiology* (159), pp. 217–224.

Kotok, A. 2003. "EBXML Case Study: Centers for Disease Control and Prevention, Public Health Information Network Messaging System (PHINMS)." Retrieved Aug 11, 2006, from http://www.ebxml.org/case_studies/documents/casestudy_cdc_phinms.pdf

Kulldorff, M. 1997. "A Spatial Scan Statistic," *Communications in Statistics: Theory and Methods* (26), pp. 1481–1496.

Kulldorff, M. 1999. "Spatial Scan Statistics: Models, Calculations, and Applications," *Scan Statistics and Applications*, J.B. Glaz (ed.). Birkhauser, Boston: pp. 303–322.

Kulldorff, M. 2001. "Prospective Time Periodic Geographical Disease Surveillance Using a Scan Statistic," *Journal of the Royal Statistical Society* (Series A:164), pp. 61–72.

Kulldorff, M., Fang, Z., and Walsh, S. 2003. "A Tree-Based Scan Statistic for Database Disease Surveillance," *Biometrics* (9), pp. 641–646.

Kulldorff, M., Mostashari, F., Duczmal, L., Yih, K., Kleinman, K., and Platt, R. 2005. "Multivariate Spatial Scan Statistics for Disease Surveillance."

Lawson, A. B., and Kleinman, K. 2005. *Spatial & Syndromic Surveillance for Public Health*. New York: Wiley.

Lazarus, R., Kleinman, K., Dashevsky, I., Adams, C., Kludt, P., DeMaria, A.J., and Platt, R. 2002. "Use of Automated Ambulatory-Care Encounter Records for Detection of Acute Illness Clusters, Including Potential Bioterrorism Events," *Emerg Infect Dis [serial online]* (Available at: http://www.cdc.gov/ncidod/EID/vol8no8/02-0239.htm).

Lazarus, R., Kleinman, K., Dashevsky, I., DeMaria, A., and Platt, R. 2001. "Using Automated Medical Records for Rapid Identification of Illness Syndromes (Syndromic Surveillance): The Example of Lower Respiratory Infection," *BMC Public Health* (1:9).

Le, S.Y., and Carrat, F. 1999. "Monitoring Epidemiologic Surveillance Data Using Hidden Markov Models," *Statistics in Medicine* (18), pp. 3463–3478.

Leroy, G., and Chen, H. 2001. "Meeting Medical Terminology Needs – the Ontology-Enhanced Medical Concept Mapper," *IEEE Transactions on Information Technology in Biomedicine* (5), pp. 261–270.

Levine, N. 2002. "Crimestat III: A Spatial Statistics Program for the Analysis of Crime Incident Locations," *Washington, DC, The National Institute of Justice*.

Li, H., Faruque, F., Williams, W., and Finley, R. 2006. "Real-Time Syndromic Surveillance." Retrieved May, 2008, from http://www.esri.com/news/arcuser/0206/geostat1of2.html

Li, Y., Yu, L., Xu, P., Lee, J., Wong, T., Ooi, P., and Sleigh, A. 2004. "Predicting Super Spreading Events during the 2003 Severe Acute Respiratory Syndrome Epidemics in Hong Kong and Singapore," *American Journal of Epidemiology* (160), pp. 719–728.

Lober, W.B., Karras, B.T., and Wagner, M.M. 2002. "Roundtable on Bioterrorism Detection: Information System-Based Surveillance," *Journal of American Medical Informatics Association* (9), pp. 105–115.

Lober, W.B., Trigg, L.J., Karras, B.T., Bliss, D., Ciliberti, J., Stewart, L., and Duchin, J.S. 2003. "Syndromic Surveillance Using Automated Collection of Computerized Discharge Diagnoses," *Journal of Urban Health: Bulletin of the New York Academy of Medicine* (80:2), pp. 97–106.

Lombardo, J., Burkom, H., Elbert, E., Magruder, S.F., Lewis, S.H., Loschen, W., Sari, J., Sniegoski, C., Wojcik, R., and Pavlin, J. 2003. "A Systems Overview of the Electronic Surveillance System for the Early Notification of Community-Based Epidemics (ESSENCE II)," *Journal of Urban Health: Bulletin of the New York Academy of Medicine* (80:2), pp. 32–42.

Lombardo, J., Burkom, H., and Pavlin, J. 2004. "Electronic Surveillance System for the Early Notification of Community-Based Epidemics (ESSENCE II), Framework for Evaluating Syndromic Surveillance Systems," *Syndromic surveillance: report from a national conference, 2003. MMWR 2004* (53(Suppl)), pp. 159–165.

Lu, H.-M., King, C.-C., Wu, T.S., Shin, F.-Y., Hsiao, J.-Y., Zeng, D., and Chen, H. 2007a. " Chinese Chief Complaint Classification for Syndromic Surveillance," in: *Intelligence and Security Informatics: BioSurveillance,* D. Zeng, Gotham, I., Komatsu, K., Lynch, C., Thurmond, M., Madigan, D., Lober, B., Kvach, J., and Chen, H (ed.). New Brunswick, NJ: Springer Lecture Notes in Computer Science, No. 4506.

Lu, H.-M., Zeng, D., Trujillo, L., Komatsu, K., and Chen, H. 2008. "Ontology-Enhanced Automatic Chief Complaint Classification for Syndromic Surveillance," *Journal of Biomedical Informatics* (41:2), pp. 340–356.

Ma, H., Rolka, H., Mandl, K., Buckeridge, D., Fleischauer, A., and Pavlin, J. 2005. "Implementation of Laboratory Order Data in Biosense Early Event Detection and Situation Awareness System," *MMWR (CDC)* (54(Suppl)), pp. 27–30.

Ma, J., Zeng, D., and Chen, H. 2006. "Spatial-Temporal Cross-Correlation Analysis: A New Measure and a Case Study in Infectious Disease Informatics," *ISI 2006*, San Diego, CA: Springer Lecture Notes in Computer Science, pp. 542–547.

MacEachren, A., Brewer, C., and Pickle, L. 1998. "Visualizing Georeferenced Data: Representing Reliability of Health Statistics," *Environment and Planning A* (30:9), pp. 1547–1561.

Madign, D. 2005. "Bayesian Data Mining for Health Surveillance," *Spatial & Syndromic Surveillance for Public Health,* A.B. Lawson and K. Kleinman (eds.). New York: Wiley.

Magruder, S.F. 2003. "Evaluation of Over-The-Counter Pharmaceutical Sales as a Possible Early Warning Indicator of Human Disease," *Johns Hopkins APL Technical Digest* (24:4).

Mandl, K.D., Overhage, J.M., Wagner, M.M., Lober, W.B., Sebastiani, P., Mostashari, F., Pavlin, J.A., Gesteland, P.H., Treadwell, T., Koski, E., Hutwagner, L., Buckeridge, D.L., Aller, R.D., and Grannis, S. 2004. "Implementing Syndromic Surveillance: A Practical Guide Informed by the Early Experience," *Journal of American Medical Informatics Association* (11:2), pp. 141–150.

Matlab. "Matlab Mapping Toolbox." http://www.mathworks.com/.

Meynard, J.-B., Chaudet, H., Texier, G., Ardillon, V., Ravachol, F., Deparis, X., Jefferson, H., Dussart, P., Morvan, J., and Boutin, J.-P. 2008. "Value of Syndromic Surveillance within the Armed Forces for Early Warning During a Dengue Fever Outbreak in French Guiana in 2006," *BMC Medical Informatics and Decision Making* (8:29).

Miller, S., Fallon, K., and Anderson, L. 2003. "New Hampshire Emergency Department Syndromic Surveillance System " *Journal Journal of Urban Health* (80(Suppl)), p. 118.

Moore, A., and Lee, M.S. 1998. "Cached Sufficient Statistics for Efficient Machine Learning with Large Datasets," *Journal of Artificial Intelligence Research* (8), pp. 67–91.

Moore, A.W., Cooper, G., Tsui, F.-C., and Wagner, M.M. 2002. "Summary of Biosurveillance-Relevant Statistical and Data Mining Techniques," *RODS Laboratory Technical Report*.

Mostashari, F. 2002. "Lessons Learned from the National Syndromic Surveillance Conference. Presentation at the 2002 National Syndromic Surveillance Conference, New York." from http://dimacs.rutgers.edu/Workshops/AdverseEvent/slides/Mostashari.ppt

Mostashari, F., and Hartman, J. 2003. "Syndromic Surveillance: A Local Perspective," *Journal of Urban Health: Bulletin of the New York Academy of Medicine* (80:2).

Mostashari, F., Olson, D., and Paladini, M. 2008. "Distributed Surveillance Taskforce for Real-Time Influenza Burden Tracking and Evaluation-Distribute". http://www.syndromic.org/projects/Distribute_041108.ppt.

Muscatello, D., Churches, T., Kaldor, J., Zheng, W., Chiu, C., and Correll, P. 2005. "An Automated, Broad-Based, near Realtime Public Health Surveillance System Using Presentations to Hospital Emergency Departments in New South Wales, Australia," *BMC Public Health* (5), pp. 141–152.

Naumova, E.N., O'Neil, E., and MacNeill, I. 2005. "INFERNO: A System for Early Outbreak Detection and Signature Forecasting," *MMWR (CDC)* (54(Suppl)), pp. 77–83.

NBII. 2006. "Highly Pathogenic Avian Influenza Early Detection Data System." Retrieved June 14, 2006, from http://wildlifedisease.nbii.gov/

Neill, D., Moore, A., and Cooper, G. 2005. "A Bayesian Spatial Scan Statistic," *Neural Information Processing Systems* (18).

Nekomoto, T.S., Riggins, W.S., and Franklin, M. 2003. "Pilot Results: Syndromic Surveillance Utilizing Catalis Health Point-of-Care Technology in a Rural Texas Outpatient Clinic." Retrieved June 23, 2006, from www.thecatalis.com/syndromic/SyndromicSurveillanceusingCatalis.pdf

Neubauer, A. 1997. "The EWMA Control Chart: Properties and Comparison with Other Quality-Control Procedures by Computer Simulation," *Clinical Chemistry* (43:4), pp. 594–601.

Ohkusa, Y., Shigematsu, M., Taniguchi, K., and Okabe, N. 2005a. "Experimental Surveillance Using Data on Sales of Over-The-Counter Medications – Japan, November 2003 – April 2004," *MMWR (CDC)* (54(Suppl)), pp. 47–52.

Ohkusa, Y., Sugawara, T., Hiroaki, S., Kawaguchi, Y., Taniguchi, K., and Okabe, N. 2005b. "Experimental Three Syndromic Surveillances in Japan: OTC, Outpatient Visits and Ambulance Transfer [Poster]," *2005 syndromic surveillance conference* Seattle, WA.

Olson, D.R., Heffernan, R.T., Paladini, M., Konty K., Weiss, D., and Mostashari, F. 2007. "Monitoring the Impact of Influenza by Age: Emergency Department Fever and Respiratory Complaint Surveillance in New York City. *PLoS Med. Aug.* 4(8), pp.e 247.

Olszewski, R.T. 2003. "Bayesian Classification of Triage Diagnoses for the Early Detection of Epidemics," *16th Int FLAIRS Conference*, pp. 412–416.

Pan, E. 2004. "The Value of Healthcare Information Exchange and Interoperability, Center for Information Technology Leadership, Boston."

Pavlin, J.A. 2003. "Investigation of Disease Outbreaks Detected by Syndromic Surveillance Systems," *Journal of Urban Health: Bulletin of the New York Academy of Medicine* (80:2), pp. 107–114.

Pelat, C., Boëlle, P.-Y., Cowling, B.J., Carrat, F., Flahault, A., Ansart, S., and Valleron, A.-J. 2007. "Online Detection and Quantification of Epidemics," *BMC Medical Informatics and Decision Making* (7:29).

Pinner, R., Rebmann, C., Schuchat, A., and Hughes, J. 2003. "Disease Surveillance and the Academic, Clinical, and Public Health Communities," *Emerging Infectious Diseases* (9), pp. 781–787.

Platt, R., Bocchino, C., Caldwell, B., Harmon, R., Kleinman, K., Lazarus, R., Nelson, A.F., Nordin, J.D., and Ritzwoller, D.P. 2003. "Syndromic Surveillance Using Minimum Transfer of Identifiable Data: The Example of the National Bioterrorism Syndromic Surveillance Demonstration Program," *Journal of Urban Health: Bulletin of the New York Academy of Medicine* (80:2).

Quenel, P., Dab, W., Hannoun, C., and Cohen, J. 1994. "Sensitivity, Specificity and Predictive Values of Health Service Based Indicators for the Surveillance of Influenza-A Epidemics," *International Journal of Epidemiology* (23), pp. 849–855.

Racer, C.F. 2007. "Bird Flu: The Media and Syndromic Surveillance Cynthia," *Advances in Disease Surveillance* (4).

Rath, T.M., Carreras, M., and Sebastiani, P. 2003. "Automated Detection of Influenza Epidemics with Hidden Markov Models," *Lecture Notes in Computer Science* Berlin: Springer, pp. 521–532.

Reingold, A. 2003. "If Syndromic Surveillance is the Answer, What is the Question?," *Biosecurity and Bioterrorism: Biodefense Strategy, Practice, and Science* (1), pp. 1–5.

Reis, B., and Mandl, K. 2003. "Time Series Modeling for Syndromic Surveillance," *BMC Medical Informatics and Decision Making* (3:2).

Reis, B., and Mandl, K. 2004. "Syndromic Surveillance: The Effects of Syndrome Grouping on Model Accuracy and Outbreak Detection," *Annals of Emergency Medicine* (44:3), pp. 235–241.

Reis, B., Pagano, M., and Mandl, K. 2003. "Using Temporal Context to Improve Biosurveillance," *Proceedings of the National Academy of Sciences USA* (100:4), pp. 1961–1965.

Reis, B.Y., Kohane, I.S., and Mandl, K.D. 2007. "An Epidemiological Network Model for Disease Outbreak Detection," *PLoS Medicine* (4:6), pp. 1019–1031.

Rhodes, B., and Kailar, R. 2005. "On Securing the Public Health Information Network Messaging System." Retrieved July 9, 2006, from http://middleware.Internet2.edu/pki05/proceedings/kailar-phinms.pdf

Ritter, T. 2002. "Leaders: Lightweight Epidemiology Advanced Detection and Emergency Response System," *SPIE*, pp. 110–120.

Roberts, F.S. 2002. "Challenges for Discrete Mathematics and Theoretical Computer Science in the Defense against Bioterrorism," DIMACS.

Rogerson, P.A. 1997. "Surveillance Systems for Monitoring the Development of Spatial Patterns," *Statistics in Medicine* (16:18), pp. 2081–2093.

Rogerson, P.A. 2005. "Spatial Surveillance and Cumulative Sum Methods," *Spatial & Syndromic Surveillance for Public Health,* K.K. Andrew B Lawson (ed.). New York: Wiley, pp. 95–113.

Romaguera, R.A., German, R.R., and Klaucke, D.N. 2000. "Evaluating Public Health Surveillance," *Principles and Practice of Public Health Surveillance, 2nd Ed,* S.M. Teutsch and R.E. Churchill (eds.). New York: Oxford University Press.

Serfling, R.E. 1963. "Methods for Current Statistical Analysis of Excess Pneumonia Influenza Deaths," *Public Health Reports* (78), pp. 494–506.

Shahar, Y., and Musen, M. 1996. "Knowledge-Based Temporal Abstraction in Clinical Domains," *Artificial Intelligence in Medicine* (8), pp. 267–298.

Shmueli, G., and Fienberg, S.E. 2006. "Current and Potential Statistical Methods for Monitoring Multiple Data Streams for Bio-Surveillance," *Statistical Methods in Counter-Terrorism: Game Theory, Modeling, Syndromic Surveillance, and Biometric Authentication*, A. Wilson, G. Wilson and D.H. Olwell (eds.). Berlin: Springer.

Shneiderman, B. 1996. "The Eyes Have It: A Task by Data Type Taxonomy for Information Visualization," *IEEE Workshop on Visual Languages*, pp. 336–343.

Shneiderman, B. 1998. *Designing the User Interface: Strategies for Effective Human-Computer Interaction, 3rd Ed.* Reading, MA: Addison-Wesley.

Siegrist, D. 1999. "The Threat of Biological Attack: Why Concern Now?" *Emerging Infectious Diseases* (5), pp. 505–508.

Siegrist, D., McClellan, G., Campbell, M., Foster, V., Burkom, H., Hogan, W., Cheng, K., Pavlin, J., and Kress, A. 2004. "Evaluation of Algorithms for Outbreak Detection Using Clinical Data from Five US Cities." Technical Report, Darpa Bio-Alirt Program.

Siegrist, D., and Pavlin, J. 2004. "Bio-Alirt Biosurveillance Detection Algorithm Evaluation," *MMWR (CDC)* (53(Suppl)), pp. 152–158.

Sniegoski, C.A. 2004. "Automated Syndromic Classifi Cation of Chief Complaint Records," *Johns Hopkins Apl Technical Digest* (25:1), pp. 68–75.

Sokolow, L.Z., Grady, N., Rolka, H., Walker, D., McMurray, P., English-Bullard, R., and Loonsk, J. 2005. "Deciphering Data Anomalies in Biosense," *MMWR (CDC)* (54(Suppl)), pp. 133–140.

Sonesson, C., and Bock, D. 2003. "A Review and Discussion of Prospective Statistical Surveillance in Public Health," *Journal of the Royal Statistical Society Series A* (166:1), pp. 5–21.

Suzuki, S., Ohyama, T., Taniguchi, K., Kimura, M., Kobayashi, J., Okabe, N., Sano, T., Kuwasaki, T., and Nakatani, H. 2003. "Web-Based Japanese Syndromic Surveillance for

Fifa World Cup 2002," *Journal of Urban Health: Bulletin of the New York Academy of Medicine* (80:2), p. i123.

Takahashi, K., Kulldorff, M., Tango, T., and Yih, K. 2008. "A Flexibly Shaped Space-Time Scan Statistic for Disease Outbreak Detection and Monitoring," *International Journal of Health Geographics* (7:14).

TerraSeer. "Spacestat." http://www.terraseer.com/products/spacestat.html.

Thomas, D., Arouh, S., Carley, K., Kraiman, J., and Davis, J. 2005. "Automated Anomaly Detection Processor for Biologic Terrorism Early Detection – Hampton, Virginia," *MMWR (CDC)* (54(Suppl)), p. 203.

Thomas, M., and Mead, C. 2005. "The Architecture of Sharing – an HL7 Version 3 Framework Offers Semantically Interoperable Healthcare Information," in: *Healthcare Informatics*.

Thurmond, M. 2006. "Global Foot-and-Mouth Disease Modeling and Surveillance." Arizona Biosurveillnace Workshop.

Thurmond, M., Perez, A., Tseng, C., Chen, H., and Zeng, D. 2007. "Global Foot-and-Mouth Disease Surveillance Using Bioportal," *Intelligence and Security Informatics: Biosurveillance,* D. Zeng, I. Gotham, K. Komatsu, C. Lynch, M. Thurmond, D. Madigan, B. Lober, J. Kvach and H. Chen (eds.). Springer Lecture Notes in Computer Science.

Toprani, P. and Sergienko, E. 2006. "Surveillance in Hurricane Evacuation, Centers-Louisiana, September-October 2005," *MMWR(CDC)* 55(02), PP. 32–35.

Travers, D., Barnett, C., Ising, A., and Waller, A. 2006. "Timeliness of Emergency Department Diagnoses for Syndromic Surveillance," *AMIA Annual Symposium Proceedings*, pp. 769–773.

Travers, D.A., and Haas, S.W. 2004. "Evaluation of Emergency Medical Text Processor, a System for Cleaning Chief Complaint Textual Data," *Academic Emergency Medicine* (11), pp. 1170–1176.

Tsui, F.-C., Espino, J.U., Dato, V.M., Gesteland, P.H., Hutman, J., and Wagner, M.M. 2003. "Technical Description of Rods: A Real-Time Public Health Surveillance System," *Journal of American Medical Informatics Association 2003* (10), pp. 399–408.

Tsui, F.-C., Espino, J.U., and Wagner, M.M. 2005. "The Timeliness, Reliability, and Cost of Real-Time and Batch Chief Complaint Data."

Tsui, F.-C., Wagner, M.M., Dato, V.M., and Chang, C.C.H. 2001. "Value of ICD-9-Coded Chief Complaints for Detection of Epidemics," *Symposium of Journal of American Medical Informatics Association.*

Uhde, K.B., Farrell, C., Geddie, Y., Leon, M., and Cattani, J. 2005. "Early Detection of Outbreaks Using the Biodefend™ Syndromic Surveillance System – Florida, May 2002 – July 2004 " *MMWR (CDC)* (54(Suppl)), p. 204.

Umland, E., Brillman, J., Koster, F., Joyce, E., Forslund, D., Picard, R., Burr, T., Sewell, C., Castle, S., and Bersell, K. 2003. "Fielding the Bio-Surveillance Analysis, Feedback, Evaluation and Response (B-Safer) System," *BTR* Albuquerque, NM, pp. 185–190.

USDA. 2006. "An Early Detection System for Highly Pathogenic H5N1 Avian Influenza in Wild Migratory Birds, U.S. Interagency Strategic Plan." Retrieved July 13, 2006, from http://www.usda.gov/documents/wildbirdstrategicplanpdf.pdf

Vergu, E., Grais, R.F., Sarter, H., Fagot, J.-P., Lambert, B., Valleron, A.-J., and Flahault, A. 2006. "Medication Sales and Syndromic Surveillance, France," *Emerging Infectious Diseases [serial on the Internet]* (12:3), pp. 416–421.

Wagner, M.M., Espino, J., Tsui, F.C., Gesteland, P., Chapman, W.W., Ivanov, O., Moore, A., Wong, W., Dowling, J., and Hutman, J. 2004a. "Syndrome and Outbreak Detection Using Chief-Complaint Data – Experience of the Real-Time Outbreak and Disease Surveillance Project," *MMWR (CDC)* (53(Suppl)), pp. 28–32.

Wagner, M.M., Moore, A.W., and Aryel, R. 2006. *Handbook of Biosurveillanec*. Elsevier.

Wagner, M.M., Robinson, J.M.l., Tsui, F.-C., Espino, J.U., and Hogan, W.R. 2003. "Design of a National Retail Data Monitor for Public Health Surveillance," *Journal of the American Medical Informatics Association* (10:5), pp. 409–418.

Wagner, M.M., Tsui, F.-C., Espino, J., Hogan, W., Hutman, J., Hersh, J., Neill, D., Moore, A., Parks, G., Lewis, C., and Aller, R. 2004b. "National Retail Data Monitor for Public Health Surveillance," *MMWR (CDC)* (53(Suppl)), pp. 40–42.

Wagner, M.M., Tsui, F.-C., Espino, J.U., Dato, V.M., Sittig, D.F., Caruana, R.A., McGinnis, L.F., Deerfield, D.W., Druzdzel, M.J., and Fridsma, D.B. 2001. "The Emerging Science of Very Early Detection of Disease Outbreaks," *J Public Health Management Practice* (7:6), pp. 51–59.

Wallstrom, G.L., Wagner, M., and Hogan, W. 2005. "High-Fidelity Injection Detectability Experiments: A Tool for Evaluating Syndromic Surveillance Systems," *MMWR (CDC)* (54:Suppl), pp 85–91.

Watkins, R.E., Eagleson, S., Beckett, S., Garner, G., Veenendaal, B., Wright, G., and Plant, A.J. 2005. "Using GIS to Create Synthetic Disease Outbreaks," *BMC Medical Informatics and Decision Making* (7:4).

Watkins, R.E., Eagleson, S., Veenendaal, B., Wright, G., and Plant, A.J. 2008. "Applying Cusum-Based Methods for the Detection of Outbreaks of Ross River Virus Disease in Western Australia," *BMC Medical Informatics and Decision Making* (8:37).

Watzlaf, V.J.M., Garvin, J.H., Moeini, S., and Anania-Firouzan, P. 2007. "The Effectiveness of ICD-10-CM in Capturing Public Health Diseases," *Perspectives in Health Information Management* (4:6).

Wong, W.-K., Moore, A.W., Cooper, G.F., and Wagner, M.M. 2005. "What's Strange About Recent Events (WSARE): An Algorithm for the Early Detection of Disease Outbreaks," *Journal of Machine Learning Research* (6) pp. 1961–1998.

Wong, W.K., Moore, A., Cooper, G., and Wagner, M. 2003. "WSARE: What's Strange About Recent Events? " *Journal of Urban Health* (80:(2 Suppl. 1)), pp. 66–75.

Wong, W.K., Moore, A., Cooper, G.F., and Wagner, M. 2002. "Rule-Based Anomaly Pattern Detection for Detecting Disease Outbreaks," *AAAI-02*, Edmonton, Alberta pp. 217–223.

Wurtz, R. 2004. "White Paper: ELR, LOINC, SNOMED, and Limitations in Public Health ".

Yan, P., Chen, H., and Zeng, D. 2008. "Syndromic Surveillance Systems: Public Health and Biodefence," *Annual Review of Information Science and Technology* (42).

Yan, P., Zeng, D., and Chen, H. 2006. "A Review of Public Health Syndromic Surveillance Systems," *ISI 2006,* S.M.e. al. (ed.), San Diego, CA, USA: Springer, pp. 249–260.

Yeh, A.B., Huang, L., and Wu, Y.-f. 2004. "A Likelihood-Ratio-Based Ewma Control Chart for Monitoring Variability of Multivariate Normal Processes," *IIE Transactions* (36:9), pp. 865–879.

Yeh, A.B., Lin, D.K.J., Zhou, H., and Venkataramani, C. 2003. "A Multivariate Exponentially Weighted Moving Average Control Chart for Monitoring Process Variability," *Journal of Applied Statistics* (30:5), pp. 507–536.

Yih, W., Caldwell, B., and Harmon, R. 2004. "The National Bioterrorism Syndromic Surveillance Demonstration Program," *MMWR (CDC)* (53(Suppl)), pp. 43–46.

Yih, W.K., Abrams, A., Danila, R., Green, K., Kleinman, K., Kulldorff, M., Miller, B., Nordin, J., and Platt, R. 2005. "Ambulatory-Care Diagnoses as Potential Indicators of Outbreaks of Gastrointestinal Illness – Minnesota," *MMWR (CDC)* (54(Suppl)), pp. 157–162.

Zelicoff, A. 2002. "The Rapid Syndrome Validation Project (RSVP) ™ Users' Manual and Description."

Zelicoff, A., Brillman, J., and Forslund, D. 2001. "The Rapid Syndrome Validation Project (RSVP)," *AMIA Symposium*, pp. 771–775.

Zeng, D., Chang, W., and Chen, H. 2004a. "A Comparative Study of Spatio-Temporal Hotspot Analysis Techniques in Security Informatics," *7th IEEE Transactions on Intelligent Transportation Systems*, Washington, DC, pp. 106–111.

Zeng, D., Chen, H., Tseng, C., Chang, W., Eidson, M., Gotham, I., and Lynch, C. 2005a. "Bioportal: A Case Study in Infectious Disease Informatics." *JCDL*, Denver, CA, USA, p. 418.

Zeng, D., Chen, H., Tseng, C., Larson, C.A., Eidson, M., Gotham, I., Lynch, C., and Ascher, M. 2005b. "Bioportal: An Integrated Infectious Disease Information Sharing and Analysis Environment," *DG.O 2005*, Atlanta, Georgia, USA, pp. 235–236.

Zeng, D., Chen, H., Tseng, L., Larson, C.A., Eidson, M., Gotham, I., Lynch, C., and Ascher, M. 2004b. "West Nile Virus and Botulism Portal: A Case Study in Infectious Disease Informatics," *Intelligence and Security Informatics (ISI-2004)*, Springer Lecture Notes in Computer Science, pp. 28–41.

Zhang, G., O'Connell, E., Leguen, F., Bustamante, M., Rodriguez, D., and Borroto-Ponce, R. 2007. "Use of Epidemiological Knowledge to Create Syndromic Surveillance Reports," *Advances in Disease Surveillance* (4), p. 211.

Zhang, J., Tsui, F., Wagner, M., and Hogan, W. 2003. "Detection of Outbreaks from Time Series Data Using Wavelet Transform," *AMIA Symp*, pp. 748–752.

Zhong, S., Xue, Y., Ca, C., Cao, W., Li, X., Guo, J., and Fang, L. 2005. "The Application of Space-Time Analysis Tools of GIS in Spatial Epidemiology: A Case Study of Hepatitis B in China Using GIS," *Geoscience and Remote Sensing Symposium, 2005* (3:25–29), pp. 1612–1615.

Zhu, B., and Chen, H. 2005. "Information Visualization," *Annual Review of Information Science and Technology (ARIST)* (39), pp. 139–177.

Zhu, Y., Wang, W., Atrubin, D., and Wu, Y. 2005. "Initial Evaluation of the Early Aberration Reporting System – Florida," *MMWR (CDC)* (54(Suppl)), pp. 123–130.

SUBJECT INDEXES

MIX
Papier aus verantwortungsvollen Quellen
Paper from responsible sources
FSC® C105338

If you have any concerns about our products,
you can contact us on
ProductSafety@springernature.com

In case Publisher is established outside the EU,
the EU authorized representative is:
Springer Nature Customer Service Center GmbH
Europaplatz 3, 69115 Heidelberg, Germany

Printed by Libri Plureos GmbH
in Hamburg, Germany